Get the eBook FREE!

(PDF, ePub, Kindle, and liveBook all included)

We believe that once you buy a book from us, you should be able to read it in any format we have available. To get electronic versions of this book at no additional cost to you, purchase and then register this book at the Manning website.

Go to https://www.manning.com/freebook and follow the instructions to complete your pBook registration.

That's it!
Thanks from Manning!

Platform Engineering on Kubernetes

MAURICIO SALATINO

MANNING
SHELTER ISLAND

Manning Publications Co.
20 Baldwin Road
PO Box 761
Shelter Island, NY 11964

Development editor:	Ian Hough
Technical development editor:	Raphael Villela
Review editor:	Dunja Nikitović
Production editor:	Aleksandar Dragosavljević
Copy editor:	Katie Petito
Technical proofreader:	Werner Dijkerman
Typesetter:	Tamara Švelić Sabljić
Cover designer:	Marija Tudor

ISBN 9781617299322
Printed and bound by CPI Group (UK) Ltd, Croydon, CR0 4YY

First and foremost, this book is dedicated to my wife and family, who helped and supported me throughout writing this book. Without their help and support, this would have been impossible.

This book is dedicated to all cloud-native practitioners, communities, and organizations that are invested in using open-source and cloud-native projects to design, build and deliver better software for their customers.

contents

foreword

The cloud native landscape has matured to a point where we can finally start building practical solutions. A plethora of projects have emerged, each with a unique focus on solving a portion of the grander vision. We now find ourselves struggling to cobble together these disparate projects into an end-to-end product. How can we manage the inherent complexity that this litany of tools brings and construct a complete solution?

Platform Engineering on Kubernetes by Mauricio Salatino offers a comprehensive answer to this question in the form of platform engineering. The discipline of platform engineering is positioned to make cloud-native development accessible to application developers through highly productive and reliable delivery of their software to production environments. I consider platform engineering to be the crucial modern discipline that will tame complexity and deliver the tantalizing promises made long ago when Kubernetes first made cloud-native technology available for the masses.

This book provides much needed insight into how modern platforms can be architected to effectively integrate the most useful cloud-native technologies from the ecosystem and solve real problems for the application developer customers of your platform. It efficiently provides practical guidance, learned through hands-on exercises and examples, to instill real skills for building a meaningful platform solution. The valuable information contained within these pages will enable platform teams to build a self-service developer platform as their product, allowing developers to deliver their applications to production with greater speed and reliability than they've ever seen before.

I've personally met a wealth of amazing individuals within the cloud-native ecosystem from my time as a co-creator, maintainer, and steering committee member on two separate projects in the Cloud Native Computing Foundation. From my experience, Mauricio is uniquely positioned to author this beneficial book that walks you through integrating all of these projects into a complete platform, as he has consistently been an integrator within the ecosystem himself by bringing together people, communities, and technology on numerous occasions. Mauricio has demonstrated an uncanny ability to identify shared interests across project visions, to bring the right people together, and find common ground that unifies the efforts into a cohesive approach. He has shown a consistent dedication to his rare gift of finding paths that make us better together through our collaboration and synergy rather than competition or duplication.

In the same way that Mauricio brings together people and technology, he has brought together many projects into a valuable whole within these pages. I expect that lessons learned within this book will be some of the most rewarding steps you take in realizing your platform engineering vision. Please enjoy the journey!

—JARED WATTS
FOUNDING ENGINEER, UPBOUND

preface

I started working on this book more than two years ago. After working for the cloud-native communities for more than four years, I've learned many lessons I'd like to share with teams to speed up their Kubernetes adoption journey. Because I contributed to several open-source projects (most included in this book), creating a table of content for a book idea wasn't that difficult. On the other hand, writing a book about a forever-changing ecosystem proved challenging. But as you will find out when reading this book, platform engineering is all about managing the complexities of constantly evolving projects and requirements from different teams that need the right tools to do their job.

This book has allowed me to meet and work with the best people in the industry from different backgrounds and communities who share my passions: open source, cloud native, and knowledge sharing. I've toured the world, presenting at conferences in the cloud-native space, always gathering feedback from community members, developers, and teams struggling to keep up with the amazing amount of open-source projects created daily. I hope this book helps you and your team to evaluate, integrate, and build platforms on top of Kubernetes.

acknowledgments

I would like to give special thanks to everyone who contributed to the examples provided in this book (both the original repository at https://github.com/salaboy/from-monolith-to-k8s/ and the new one at https://github.com/salaboy/platforms-on-k8s/). This book was written for and by the community of the projects mentioned.

Special thanks to my brother Ezequiel Salatino (https://salatino.me/), who designed and built the frontend applications so readers can experience a website instead of a bunch of REST endpoints. I will be forever grateful to Matheus Cruz and Asare Nkansah, who helped me build big chunks of the examples without expecting anything in return. Finally, thank you to my friend Thomas Vitale for sharing thorough reviews of multiple editions of the drafts; all your comments made the content of this book more accurate and focused.

I couldn't have done this book without all the support provided by the Manning team. I want to thank development editor, Ian Hough, for the countless hours spent on the manuscript. Acquisitions editor, Michael Stephens, for strongly believing in the book idea since day one, Raphael Villela as technical editor for all the technical advice provided, and Werner Dijkerman as technical proofer for his comments and ensuring that all of the code is in good working order.

To all the reviewers: Alain Lompo, Alexander Schwartz, Andres Sacco, Carlos Panato, Clifford Thurber, Conor Redmond, Ernesto Cárdenas Cangahuala, Evan Anderson, Giuseppe Catalano, Gregory A. Lussier, Harinath Mallepally, John Guthrie, Jonathan Blair, Kent Spillner, Lucian Torje, Michael Bright, Mladen Knezic, Philippe Van Bergen, Prashant Dwivedi, Richard Meinsen, Roman Levchenko, Roman Zhuzha, Sachin Rastogi, Simeon Leyzerzon,

Simone Sguazza, Stanley Anozie, Theo Despoudis, Vidhya Vinay, Vivek Krishnan, Werner Dijkerman, William Jamir, Zoheb Ainapore, your suggestions helped make this a better book.

Project-specific thanks:

- *Argo Project* (https://argoproj.github.io/)—I want to thank Dan Garfield from Codefresh for his continuous support of the book and his contributions to the OpenGitOps (https://opengitops.dev/) initiative.
- *Crossplane* (https://crossplane.io)—I want to thank Jared Watts for his constant willingness to help and push things forward. Also, I want to thank Viktor Farcic and Stefan Schimanski for always supporting the Crossplane community. The Crossplane community has taught me many valuable lessons that shaped my career.
- *Dagger* (https://dagger.io)—I want to thank Marcos Nils and Julian Cruciani for their help with the Dagger examples and their willingness to improve things when time can be saved for developers.
- *Dapr* (https://dapr.io)—Big thanks and appreciation to both Yaron Schneider and Mark Fussel for their constant support to get this book out of the door and to the entire Diagrid (https://diagrid.io)—team, who is building amazing products on top of Dapr.
- *Keptn* (https://keptn.sh)—Big thanks to Giovanni Liva and Andreas Grabner for their speedy response and the amazing work that they have done in the Keptn and OpenFeature communities.
- *Knative* (https://knative.dev)—The entire Knative community is awesome, but special thanks to Lance Ball, who led the Knative Functions working group to build something amazing.
- *Kratix* (https://kratix.io)—Special thanks to Abby Bangser for sharing her platform insights and reviewing key chapters in the book. All your comments and remarks made this book way more valuable.
- *OpenFeature* (https://openfeature.dev)—I wanted to thank James Milligan for his help in getting the OpenFeature and `flagd` examples working.
- *Tekton* (https://tekton.dev)—Big thanks to Andrea Fritolli for his amazing work on the Tekton community and for always answering my Slack messages.
- *Vcluster* (https://vcluster.com)—Both Ishan Khare and Fabian Kramm had been instrumental to the work that I've done for this book. Their willingness to get things working had gone above and beyond. Big thanks for creating and maintaining the `vcluster`, Devspace (https://www.devspace.sh/), and DevPod (https://devpod.sh/) projects.

about this book

Platform Engineering on Kubernetes was written to help teams going through a Kubernetes adoption journey. The book uses a developer-centric approach to cover building, packaging, and deploying cloud-native applications to Kubernetes clusters, but it doesn't stop there. Once you and your teams understand how to use Kubernetes for your applications, you face new challenges related to managing Kubernetes extensions, multi-tenancy, and multi-cluster setups.

Platforms on top of Kubernetes need to integrate a wide range of tools to enable specialized teams to perform their daily tasks while at the same time preventing them from learning how all these tools work. Platform teams are in charge of learning, curating, and integrating tools to make the life of development teams, data scientists, operations teams, testing teams, product teams, and everyone involved with the software delivery process of your organization easier.

Most of the content is focused around Kubernetes and built to be agnostic of the technology stack used for application-specific features. If you are getting started with Kubernetes or you are a cloud-native practitioner, this book can help you to understand how multiple projects can be combined to build team-specific experiences and reduce the cognitive load involved in their day-to-day jobs, no matter the programming language you and your teams are using.

How this book is organized: a roadmap

This book is organized into nine chapters, and it uses the concept of a "walking skeleton" to build a platform to support the teams in building a Conference application. The flow of the book goes as follows:

Chapter 1 introduces what platforms are, why you need one, and how the platforms we will cover in this book compare to what cloud providers offer. This chapter introduces the business use case for the Conference application that further chapters will explore.

Chapter 2 evaluates the challenges of building cloud native and distributed applications that run on Kubernetes. This chapter encourages the reader to deploy the Conference application and explore its design by changing its configuration and testing different scenarios. By looking at the challenges teams will face when deploying and running applications on top of Kubernetes and providing a playground to experiment by using the walking skeleton, the book aims to enable readers with enough experience to tackle bigger challenges.

Chapter 3 focuses on all the extra steps needed to build, package, and distribute artifacts to run our applications in different cloud providers. This chapter introduces the concept of service pipeline and explores two different but complementary projects: Tekton and Dagger.

Once our artifacts are ready to be deployed, chapter 4 is centered around the concept of the environment pipeline. By defining our environment pipelines and by using a GitOps approach, teams can manage the configuration of multiple environments using a declarative approach. This chapter explores Argo CD as a tool to configure and manage your environments.

Applications can't work on their own. Most applications require infrastructural components such as databases, message brokers, and identity providers, among others, to work. Chapter 5 covers a Kubernetes-native approach to provision application infrastructure components across cloud providers using a project called Crossplane.

Once we have taken care of building, packaging, and deploying our applications and other components that our applications need to run, chapter 6 proposes the reader build a platform on top of Kubernetes using all that we have learned so far but focusing only on a simple use case: creating development environments.

Platforms are not only about creating environments, managing clusters, and deploying applications. Platforms should provide customized workflows for teams to be productive. Chapter 7 focuses on enabling development teams with application-level APIs that platform teams can decide how to wire to available resources. This chapter evaluates tools like Dapr and OpenFeature to enable teams with more than clusters and a place to run their applications.

While enabling developers to be more efficient will improve software delivery times, if new releases are blocked and not deployed in front of customers, all the effort will be wasted. Chapter 8 focuses on showing techniques, more precisely release strategies, that can be used to experiment with new releases before fully committing to them. This chapter evaluates Knative Serving and Argo Rollouts to implement different release strategies that your teams can use to experiment with new features in a controlled way.

Because platforms are software, we need to measure how effective we are when evolving them. Chapter 9 evaluates two approaches to tap into the tools we are using to build our platform and calculate key metrics that allow the platform engineering team to evaluate their platform initiatives. This chapter looks into CloudEvents, CDEvents, and the Keptn Lifecycle Toolkit as options to gather events, store them, and aggregate them to calculate meaningful metrics.

By the end of the book, the reader ends up with a clear picture and hands-on experience of how platforms are built on top of Kubernetes, what the priorities of the platform engineering teams are, and why learning and keeping up to date with the cloud-native space is so important to be successful.

About the code

This book contains many examples of source code both in numbered listings and in line with normal text. In both cases, source code is formatted in a `fixed -width font like this` to separate it from ordinary text. Sometimes code is also **`in bold`** to highlight code that has changed from previous steps in the chapter, such as when a new feature adds to an existing line of code.

In many cases, the original source code has been reformatted; we've added line breaks and reworked indentation to accommodate the available page space in the book. In rare cases, even this was not enough, and listings include line-continuation markers (➥). Additionally, comments in the source code have often been removed from the listings when the code is described in the text. Code annotations accompany many of the listings, highlighting important concepts.

You can get executable snippets of code from the liveBook (online) version of this book at https://livebook.manning.com/book/platform-engineering -on-kubernetes. The complete code for the examples in the book is available for download from the Manning website at https://www.manning.com/books/ platform-engineering-on-kubernetes.

Each chapter links to step-by-step tutorials where readers are encouraged to get their hands dirty with the tools and projects running in their environments. You can find all the source code and step-by-step tutorials on the following GitHub repository at https://github.com/salaboy/platforms-on-k8s/.

liveBook discussion forum

Purchase of *Platform Engineering on Kubernetes* includes free access to liveBook, Manning's online reading platform. Using liveBook's exclusive discussion features, you can attach comments to the book globally or to specific sections or paragraphs. It's a snap to make notes for yourself, ask and answer technical questions, and receive help from the author and other users. To access the forum, go to https://livebook.manning.com/book/platform-engineering-on-kubernetes/discussion. You can also learn more about Manning's forums and the rules of conduct at https://livebook.manning.com/discussion.

Manning's commitment to our readers is to provide a venue where a meaningful dialogue between individual readers and between readers and the author can take place. It is not a commitment to any specific amount of participation on the part of the author, whose contribution to the forum remains voluntary (and unpaid). We suggest you try asking the author some challenging questions lest his interest stray! The forum and the archives of previous discussions will be accessible from the publisher's website as long as the book is in print.

about the author

MAURICIO SALATINO works for Diagrid (https://diagrid.io) as an Open Source Software Engineer. He is currently a Dapr OSS Contributor and Knative Steering Committee member. Before working at Diagrid, Mauricio spent the last 10 years building tools for Cloud-Native developers at companies such as Red Hat and VMware. When he is not writing tools for developers or contributing to Open Source projects in the Cloud Native space, he teaches about Kubernetes and Cloud-Native via his Blog https://salaboy.com and/or LearnK8s (https://learnk8s.io).

about the cover illustration

The figure on the cover of *Platform Engineering on Kubernetes* is "Femme des Isles d'Argentiere et de Milo," or "A Woman from the Isles of Argentiera and Milos," taken from a collection by Jacques Grasset de Saint-Sauveur, published in 1788. Each illustration is finely drawn and colored by hand.

In those days, it was easy to identify where people lived and what their trade or station in life was just by their dress. Manning celebrates the inventiveness and initiative of the computer business with book covers based on the rich diversity of regional culture centuries ago, brought back to life by pictures from collections such as this one.

(The rise of) platforms on top of Kubernetes

This chapter covers

- Understanding platforms and why we need them
- Building a platform on top of Kubernetes
- Introducing a "walking skeleton" application

Platform engineering is not a new term in the tech industry. But it is quite new in the cloud-native space and the context of Kubernetes. We were not using the term in the cloud-native communities when I started writing this book back in 2020. However, by the time of writing this book (2023), platform engineering had become the new hot topic in cloud-native and Kubernetes communities. This book aims to go on a journey to explore what platforms are and why you would use Kubernetes, and more specifically, the Kubernetes APIs at the core, to build a platform and enable your internal teams to deliver software more efficiently.

To understand why platform engineering became a trend in the industry, you first need to understand the cloud native and Kubernetes ecosystems. Because this book assumes that you are already familiar with Kubernetes, containers, and cloud-native applications, we will focus on describing the challenges you will face when architecting, building, and running these applications on top of Kubernetes and cloud

1

providers. We will take a developer-focused approach, meaning that most of the topics covered are tackled in a way that relates to developers' day-to-day tasks and how a myriad of tools and frameworks in the cloud-native space will affect them.

The ultimate goal for every software development team is to deliver new features and bug/security fixes to their customers. New features and more stable applications translate directly to competitive business advantages and happy customers. To deliver more software efficiently, development teams must have access to the tools they need to do their work. The main objective of the platform and platform engineering teams is to enable developers to deliver software more efficiently. This requires a different technological approach and a cultural shift towards treating development teams as internal customers of the platforms we will be building.

We will use a simple application (composed of multiple services) as an example throughout the chapters to build a platform that supports the teams building, releasing, and managing this application by using all open source tools in the cloud-native space.

1.1   *What is a platform, and why do I need one?*

Platforms are a collection of services that help companies get their software running in front of their customers (internal or external). Platforms aim to be a one-stop shop for teams to have all the tools that they need to be productive and continuously deliver business value—with the rise in popularity and with the growing demand to improve development cycles, platforms that once used to provide us only with computing resources had leveled up the stack to provide more and more services.

Platforms are not new, and neither are cloud platforms. Cloud providers like AWS, Google, Microsoft, Alibaba, and IBM have provided us platforms for years. These cloud providers offer teams many tools to build, run, and monitor their business-critical applications using a pay-as-you-go model. From a business agility perspective, these platforms offered by cloud providers have fundamentally shifted the expectations for teams consuming their services. This allows companies and teams to start fast and create applications that can scale globally without a significant initial investment. If no one uses the applications they are building, their bills will not be large at the end of the month. On the other side of the spectrum, if you are successful and your applications are popular, you must get ready for a large bill at the end of the month. The more resources (storage, network traffic, services, etc.) you use, the more you pay. Another aspect to consider is that if you rely on the tools provided by your cloud provider, it is harder to move away from them as your entire organization gets used to that cloud provider's tools, workflows, and services. It becomes a painful experience to plan and migrate applications across different providers.

In the following sections, we will cover the current state of cloud platforms and what kind of platforms we will discuss in this book. Lately, as always happens in our industry, terms that can be useful to describe very concrete tools and practices tend to be abused by marketing teams and become buzzwords. We must set the context for the rest of the book to avoid confusion.

1.1.1 Cloud services and domain-specific needs

We can organize cloud services into different layers, something that we need to do to understand where the industry is today and where it is heading. The following diagram shows a set of categories of the services provided by cloud providers, starting from low-level infrastructure services, such as provisioning hardware on demand to high-level application services, where developers can interact with machine-learning models without worrying where these models are running. Figure 1.1 shows these layers, starting at the bottom with low-level computing resources and going up the stack with application-level and industry-specific services.

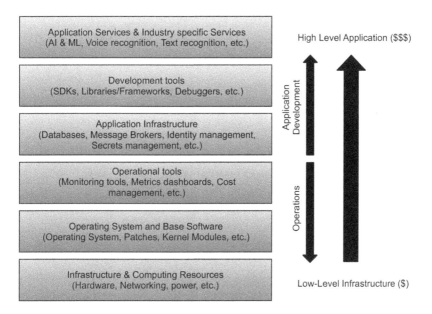

Figure 1.1   Cloud provider's services categories

The higher the category, the more you will need to pay for the service, because these services usually take care of all the underlying layers and operational costs for you. For example, suppose you provision a new highly available PostgreSQL database in a managed service offered by a cloud provider. Figure 1.2 shows an example of a relational database such as PostgreSQL.

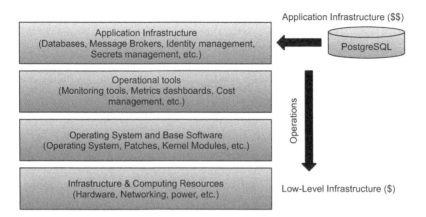

Figure 1.2   Provisioning a PostgreSQL database instance in the cloud

In that case, the service cost includes the cost and management of the database software needed, the operating system where the database runs, and the hardware needed to run it. Because you might want to monitor and get metrics on how the database performs when your application is under heavy load, the cloud provider also wires up all the monitoring tools available for the service. Then it is up to you to do the math: is it worth paying a cloud provider to make all these decisions for us, or can you build an internal team with enough knowledge to run and operate all these software and hardware on-premises? Sometimes, money is not a problem; you must deal with company or industry policies and regulations. In such cases, can you run your workloads and host your data in a cloud provider?

1.1.2   *Your job as an organization*

Keeping up to date with all the provided services, libraries, frameworks, and tools is a full-time job. Operating and maintaining the wide range of software and hardware that companies need to run their applications requires you to have the right teams in place, and at the end of the day, if you are not a large and mature organization in terms of your software delivery practices, or if you are not getting any competitive advantage by managing your own hardware/software stack, adopting a cloud provider is usually the right way to go.

It is still the job of each company and developer to look at the available services and choose what they will use and how they will mix and match these services to build new features. It is common to find cloud architects (experts on a specific cloud provider, or on-premises experts) in each organization defining how and which services will be used to build core applications. It is also common to engage with the cloud provider's consulting services to get advice and guidance on specific use cases and best practices.

Cloud providers might suggest tools and workflows to create applications. Still, each organization needs to go through a learning curve and mature its practices around applying these tools to solve its specific challenges. Staffing cloud provider experts is always a good idea, because they bring knowledge from previous experiences, saving time for less-experienced teams.

In this book, we will focus on organization-specific platforms, not generic cloud platforms that you can buy off the shelf, like those offered by cloud providers. We also want to focus on platforms that can work on-premises on our organization's hardware. This is important for more regulated industries that cannot run on public clouds. This forces us to have a broader view of tools, standards, and workflows that can be applied outside the realm of a cloud provider. Consuming services from more than one cloud provider is also becoming increasingly popular. This can result from working for a company that acquired or became acquired by another company using a different provider, ending up in a situation where multiple providers must coexist, and there should be a shared strategy for both. In other situations, in more regulated industries, organizations are forced to run workloads on different providers (including on-prem workloads) to guarantee resiliency in situations where an entire cloud provider can go down.

The kind of platforms we will be looking at extends the layers of customer behavior mentioned before to include company-specific services, company-specific standards, and developer experiences that allow the organization's development teams to build complex systems for the organization and their customers. Figure 1.3 shows how, no matter whether we are consuming cloud services, third-party services, or internal services, organizations must mix and match these services by building layers on top that are focused on solving business-specific challenges.

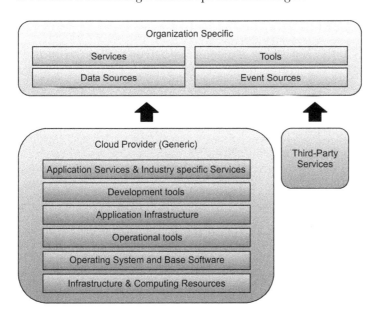

Figure 1.3 Organization-specific layers

These extra layers are, most of the time, "glue" between existing services, data, and event sources combined to solve particular challenges the business faces or to implement new features for their customers. It is common to rely on third-party service providers for more business-specific tools, for example, industry-specific or generic CRM (Customer Relationship Management) systems, such as Salesforce.

For the customers, the platform, the cloud provider, and where the services are running are entirely irrelevant. Internally, for development teams, the platform acts as an enabler for development teams to do their work. Platforms are not static, and their main objective is to help the organization improve and excel at continuously delivering high-quality software to its customers.

No matter the industry where your company operates and whether you choose to use a cloud provider, your company's combinations of tools and workflows to deliver new features to its customers can be described as your platform. Technically, platforms are all about system integrations, best practices, and composable services that we can combine to build more complex systems. This book will look at standard practices, tools, and behaviors that make platforms successful and how you can build your cloud-native platforms, whether running on one or more cloud providers or on-premises.

We will use cloud providers as a reference to compare the services and tools they provide and learn how we can achieve similar results in a multi-cloud provider and on-premises way by using open-source tools. But before looking into concrete tools, it is essential to understand what kind of experiences we can get from cloud providers.

1.1.3   *Working with cloud platforms*

One common denominator between all cloud providers is that they provide services using an API-first approach. This means that to access any of their services, an API will be available to the users to request and interact with this service. These APIs expose all the service functionality, such as which resources can be created, with which configuration parameters, where (in which region of the world) we want the resource to run, etc. Another important aspect of these APIs is that they require a team to own these API definitions; this means that a team will be in charge of identifying how these APIs are going to be used and how they are going to evolve and have clear definitions of what these APIs are not responsible for.

Each cloud provider can be analyzed by looking at their APIs, because there will usually be one API for each offered service. It is common to see services in the beta or alpha stage only offered through the APIs for early users to experiment, test, and provide feedback before the service is officially announced. While the structure, format, and style tend to be similar for all the services provided by a cloud provider, there are no standards across cloud providers to define how these services should be exposed and which features they need to support.

Manually crafting complex requests against the cloud provider services, APIs is complex and error prone. It is a common practice by cloud providers to simplify the developer's life by providing SDKs (software development kits) that consume the services

APIs implemented in different programming languages. This means developers can programmatically connect and use a cloud provider's services by including a dependency (library, the cloud provider SDK) for their applications. While this is handy, it introduces some strong dependencies between the application's code and the cloud provider, sometimes requiring us to release our application code to upgrade these dependencies.

In the same way that with APIs, with SDKs, there are no standards, and each SDK heavily depends on the programming language ecosystem's best practices and tools. There are cases where the SDKs don't play nice with frameworks or tools that are popular in the programming language that you are using. Examples where SDKs/Clients can go wrong, include database drivers that don't align with the version provided by the cloud provider or languages and ecosystems that the Cloud Provider does not yet support. In such cases, going directly to the API is possible but hard and usually discouraged, because your teams will maintain all the code required to connect to the cloud provider services.

Cloud providers also provide CLIs (command-line interfaces), tools for operations teams and some developers' workflows. CLIs are binaries you can download, install, and use from your operating system terminal. CLIs interact directly with the cloud providers' APIs but don't require you to know how to create a new application to interact with the services as with SDKs. CLIs are particularly useful for continuous integration and automation pipelines, where resources might need to be created on demand, for example, to run our integration tests.

Figure 1.4 shows applications and automation such as CI/CD pipelines and integration tests consuming the same APIs but using different tools designed by the cloud provider to simplify these scenarios. The figure also shows the Dashboard component, usually running inside the cloud provider, which provides visual access to all the services and resources being created.

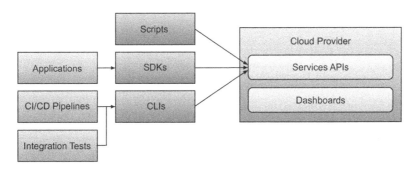

Figure 1.4   Cloud providers' SDKs, CLIs, and Dashboard clients

Finally, due to the number of services provided and the interconnections between the services, cloud providers offer dashboards and user interfaces to access and interact with all the offered services. These dashboards also offer reporting, billing, and other functions that are hard to visualize using the CLIs or directly via the APIs. By using these dashboards, users can access most of the standard features provided by the services and real-time access to see what is being created inside the cloud provider.

As mentioned, dashboards, CLIs, and SDKs require your teams to learn about many cloud provider-specific flows, tools, and nomenclature. Because of the number of services provided by each cloud provider, it is no wonder why finding experts that can cover more than a single provider is challenging.

Because this is a Kubernetes-focused book, I wanted to show the experience provided by a cloud provider to create a Kubernetes cluster, which demonstrates the dashboard, CLI, and API exposed by the Google Cloud Platform. Some cloud providers provide a better experience than others, but overall, you should be able to achieve the same with all the major ones.

1.1.4 GCP dashboard, CLIs, and APIs

Look at the Google Kubernetes Engine dashboard in figure 1.5 to create new Kubernetes clusters. As soon as you click Create a New Cluster, you are presented with a form asking you to fill in a few required fields, such as the name of the cluster.

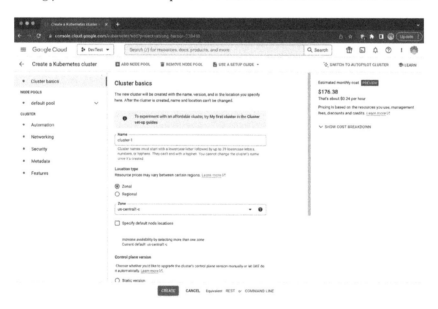

Figure 1.5 Google Kubernetes Engine creation form

Cloud providers do a fantastic job at having sensible defaults to avoid asking you to fill in 200 parameters before creating the needed resource. Once you have filled in all the required fields, the form offers a quick way to start the provisioning process by just clicking the Create button down the bottom. It is pretty interesting to see that, in this case, the Google Cloud Platform offers you an estimated cost per hour of the resource that you have configured. This highlights the difference between providing features for technical teams and providing a full service, covering the needs of technical teams and clarifying how these decisions can affect the business as a whole. You can start tweaking parameters to see how this cost changes (usually, it goes up).

Figure 1.6   Create via a dashboard, REST, or using a Command Line Interface (CLI) tool

As shown in figure 1.6, right beside the Create button, you can see the REST option. The cloud provider here helps you by crafting the REST request to their APIs needed to create the resource you can configure using the forms. This is quite handy if you don't want to spend hours looking at their API documents to find the shape of the payload and properties needed to create the request; see figure 1.7.

Figure 1.7   Create via Kubernetes cluster using a REST request

Finally, the CLI command option, using the cloud provider CLI, in this case, `gcloud`, is once again crafted to contain all the parameters the CLI command needs based on what you have configured in the form, as shown in figure 1.8.

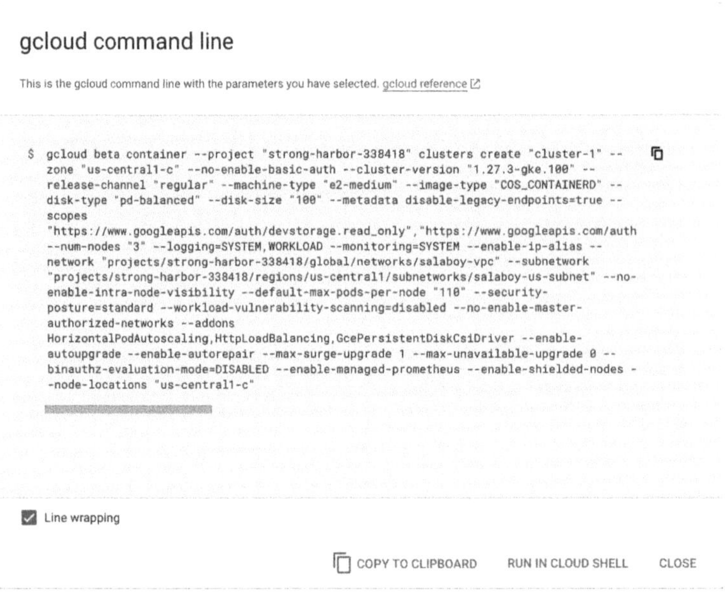

gcloud command line

This is the gcloud command line with the parameters you have selected. gcloud reference ⧉

```
$  gcloud beta container --project "strong-harbor-338418" clusters create "cluster-1" --      ⧉
   zone "us-central1-c" --no-enable-basic-auth --cluster-version "1.27.3-gke.100" --
   release-channel "regular" --machine-type "e2-medium" --image-type "COS_CONTAINERD" --
   disk-type "pd-balanced" --disk-size "100" --metadata disable-legacy-endpoints=true --
   scopes
   "https://www.googleapis.com/auth/devstorage.read_only","https://www.googleapis.com/auth
   --num-nodes "3" --logging=SYSTEM,WORKLOAD --monitoring=SYSTEM --enable-ip-alias --
   network "projects/strong-harbor-338418/global/networks/salaboy-vpc" --subnetwork
   "projects/strong-harbor-338418/regions/us-central1/subnetworks/salaboy-us-subnet" --no-
   enable-intra-node-visibility --default-max-pods-per-node "110" --security-
   posture=standard --workload-vulnerability-scanning=disabled --no-enable-master-
   authorized-networks --addons
   HorizontalPodAutoscaling,HttpLoadBalancing,GcePersistentDiskCsiDriver --enable-
   autoupgrade --enable-autorepair --max-surge-upgrade 1 --max-unavailable-upgrade 0 --
   binauthz-evaluation-mode=DISABLED --enable-managed-prometheus --enable-shielded-nodes -
   -node-locations "us-central1-c"
```

☑ Line wrapping

                                    ⧉ COPY TO CLIPBOARD   RUN IN CLOUD SHELL   CLOSE

Figure 1.8   Create via Kubernetes cluster using the `gcloud` **CLI**

Notice the horizontal scroll in figure 1.8; this command can become extremely complex. The Google Cloud Platform's user experience team has done a wonderful job simplifying how teams can set all these parameters by relying on sensible defaults. There are no differences between these approaches regarding the expected behavior, but you need to consider that when you use the cloud provider's dashboard, your account credentials are being used from your current session. If you are crafting a request or using the CLI from outside the cloud provider's network, you must first authenticate with the cloud provider before issuing the request or executing the command to create the resource(s). It is essential to notice that these interactions will differ from cloud provider to cloud provider. You cannot expect the commands to be similar in AWS or Azure, the dashboard interactions, or how the security mechanism works to authenticate the CLIs or REST requests.

1.1.5   *Why do cloud providers work?*

While one can argue that dashboards, CLIs, APIs, and SDKs are the primary artifacts we will consume from cloud providers, but the big question is: how will we combine these tools to deliver software? Suppose you analyze why organizations worldwide trust AWS, Google Cloud Platform, and Microsoft Azure. You will likely find that by adopting an API-first approach and offering dashboards, CLIs, SDKs, and a myriad of services, these platforms provide teams with three main features that define platforms today (figure 1.9):

- *APIs (contracts):* No matter which tools you use, the platform must expose a set of APIs enabling teams to consume or provision the resources needed to do their work. These APIs are the responsibility of the platform engineering teams to maintain and evolve
- *Golden paths to production:* The platform codifies and automates workflows required by teams to get their changes into production environments where live customers/users can access them.
- *Visibility:* At all times, by looking at the cloud provider dashboard, the organization can monitor which resources are being used, how much each service costs, deal with incidents, and have a complete picture of how the organization delivers software.

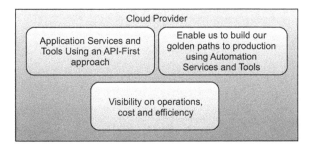

Figure 1.9   Cloud provider platforms' advantages

These key features are provided using a competitive pay-as-you-go model that heavily relies on demand (traffic), at a global scale (not for all services), allowing the organization to externalize all the operation and infrastructure costs.

While cloud providers are going higher and higher up the stack (providing high-level services, not just provisioning hardware and application infrastructure such as databases), your teams still need to learn and glue these services together to solve their business challenges.

This is where Kubernetes and the CNCF landscape (Cloud-Native Computing Foundation, https://www.cncf.io/) become key areas to explore for learning how to build platforms that are cloud-provider agnostic and allow us to pick and choose from a big pool of vibrant projects. Let's move on to that next.

1.2   *Platforms built on top of Kubernetes*

We have briefly discussed what platforms are and how cloud providers are driving the way forward to define what these platforms can do for organizations and development teams in charge of delivering software. But how does this map to Kubernetes? Isn't Kubernetes a platform?

Kubernetes was designed to be a declarative system for our cloud-native applications. Kubernetes defines a set of building blocks that allows us to run and deploy our workloads. Nowadays, every major cloud provider offers Kubernetes-managed services, which enables us with a standardized way of packaging (containers) and deploying workloads across cloud providers. Because Kubernetes comes with its tools and ecosystem (the CNCF landscape, https://landscape.cncf.io/), you can create cloud-agnostic workflows to build, run, and monitor your applications. But learning Kubernetes is just the starting point, because the building blocks provided by Kubernetes are very low level and designed to be composed to build tools and systems that solve more concrete scenarios. Combining these low-level building blocks provided by Kubernetes to build more complex tools to solve more specific challenges is a natural evolutionary step.

While Kubernetes provides us with APIs (the Kubernetes APIs), a CLI (kubectl), and a dashboard (Kubernetes Dashboard, https://kubernetes.io/docs/tasks/access -application-cluster/web-ui-dashboard/), Kubernetes is not a platform. Kubernetes is a meta-platform or a platform to build platforms, because it provides all the building blocks you need to build concrete platforms that will solve domain-specific challenges.

Figure 1.10 shows how Kubernetes tools and components map to what we have discussed about platforms and cloud providers.

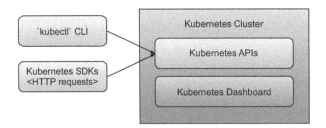

Figure 1.10   Kubernetes offer us a CLI, SDKs and dashboards, is it a platform?

Kubernetes can be extended, and that's why this book will look into specific projects using the Kubernetes APIs, tools, or internal mechanisms to solve generic challenges like continuous integration, continuous delivery, provisioning cloud resources, monitoring and observability, and developer experience, among others.

1.2.1   *The Kubernetes adoption journey*

It is fundamental that, no matter which tools platform teams choose, we abstract all the complexity and all the glue code we write to make these tools work together from the teams consuming these tools. Remember that application development teams, testing teams, and operations teams, among others, have different priorities and concerns. As part of the Kubernetes adoption journey, we must be we must be aware that not all the teams consuming these tools to be experts on Kubernetes.

Extending Kubernetes with your custom extensions is one way to make Kubernetes work for your organization-specific challenges. Remember that no matter which tools you write or install in your Kubernetes clusters, the operations teams will need to run them in your production environments and keep them running at scale. Each new tool or extension you write will require training the consumer teams to understand how these tools work and for which scenarios they were designed. It is quite easy to end up in a situation where you have chosen 10 different tools that need to be integrated, and glue code needs to be written. Platform teams always evaluate the trade-offs between writing glue code, rewriting a more tailored solution for their use case, or extending existing tools. I strongly recommend you get familiar with the tools in the CNCF landscape (https://landscape.cncf.io) to avoid going in a direction where every tool you use is custom-made for your organization, meaning that you will need to maintain internally all these tools in the long run.

Abstracting away complexity is a key part of building platforms. A clear contract with your teams specifying what the platform can do for them is crucial to successful platform engineering initiatives. These contracts are exposed as APIs that teams can interact with programmatically, using a dashboard, or via automation.

Figure 1.11 shows a typical Kubernetes adoption journey toward platform engineering. The journey starts by adopting Kubernetes as the target platform to run your workloads, followed by researching and selecting tools, usually from the CNCF Landscape. When initial tools are selected, your platform starts to shape up, and some investment is needed to configure and make these tools work for your teams. Finally, all these configurations and tools selected can be hidden behind a friendlier platform API, allowing end users to focus on their workflows instead of trying to understand every detail about the tools and glue code forming the platform.

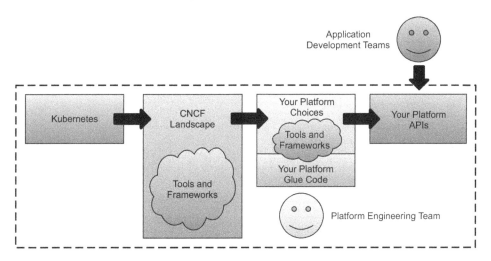

Figure 1.11 Platform journey on Kubernetes

Going through this journey, we can define platforms as how we encode the knowledge it takes to provide our development teams with all the workflows they need to be productive. The operational knowledge and the decisions on the tools used to implement these workflows are encapsulated behind a contract materialized as the platform APIs. These APIs can use the Kubernetes APIs to provide a declarative approach, but this is optional. Some platforms hide that the platform uses Kubernetes, which can also reduce the cognitive load from teams interacting with it.

While I've tried to cover from a very high level what a platform is, I prefer to delegate all the formal definitions to working groups in the cloud-native space that are in charge of defining and keeping terms updated. I strongly suggest you check the App Delivery TAG - Platform Working Group from the CNCF white paper on platforms (https://tag-app-delivery.cncf.io/whitepapers/platforms/), which takes on the work of trying to define what platforms are.

Their current definition, at the time of writing this book, reads as follows: "A platform for cloud-native computing is an integrated collection of capabilities defined and presented according to the needs of the platform's users. It is a cross-cutting layer that ensures a consistent experience for acquiring and integrating typical capabilities and services for a broad set of applications and use cases. A good platform provides consistent user experiences for using and managing its capabilities and services, such as web portals, project templates, and self-service APIs."

In this book, we will embark on this journey of building an example platform by looking at the available cloud-native tools to see how they can provide different platform capabilities. But where do we find these tools? Do these tools work together? How do we choose between different alternatives? Let's take a quick look at the CNCF Landscape.

1.2.2 *The CNCF Landscape puzzle*

Keeping up with cloud provider services is a full-time job, and each cloud provider hosts a yearly conference and minor events to announce what is new and shiny. In the Kubernetes and cloud native space, you can expect the same. The CNCF landscape is continuously expanding and evolving. As you can see in figure 1.12, the landscape is huge and very difficult to read at first sight.

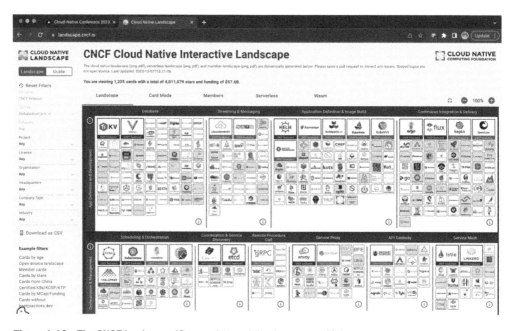

Figure 1.12   The CNCF landscape (Source: https://landscape.cncf.io)

A significant difference compared to cloud provider-offered services is the public and community-driven maturity model that each project in the CNCF must follow to obtain the graduated status. Each project's maturity journey is independent of any cloud provider, and you, as an individual or as an organization, can influence where the project is going or how fast it gets there.

While cloud providers have defined the cloud's shape, most are now involved in CNCF projects pushing for these open initiatives to succeed. They are working on tools that can be used across cloud providers, removing barriers and allowing innovation in the open instead of behind each cloud provider's door. Figure 1.13 shows how Kubernetes enabled the cloud native innovation ecosystem to flourish outside cloud providers. Cloud providers haven't stopped offering new, more specialized services, but in the last five years, we have seen a shift toward improved collaborations across cloud providers and software vendors to develop new tools and innovation in the open.

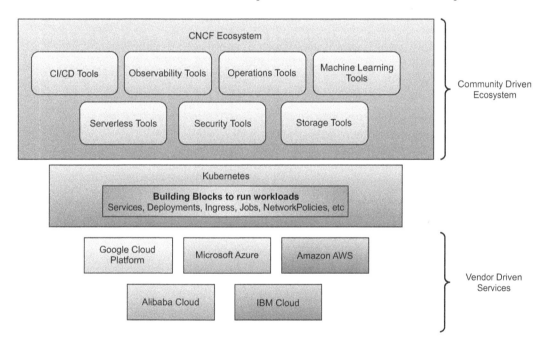

Figure 1.13   Kubernetes enabling a multi-cloud cloud-native ecosystem

A common denominator from most CNCF-hosted projects is that they all work with Kubernetes, extending it and solving high-level challenges closer to development teams. The CNCF has reached a point where more and more tools are being created to simplify development tools and workflows. Interestingly, most of these tools don't focus just on developers. They also enable operation teams and system integrators to glue projects together and define new developer experiences native to Kubernetes. Development teams don't need to worry about the tooling and integrations required for their day-to-day workflows. The increased maturity level of the communities involved in the CNCF landscape and this push to simplify how development teams interact with all these tools gave birth to the conversations around platform engineering. The next section will explore these conversations, why you can't buy a platform, and how we will explore this large ecosystem in the rest of this book.

1.3   *Platform engineering*

In the same way that cloud providers have internal teams defining which new services will be offered, how these services are going to scale, and which tools and APIs need to be exposed to their customers, it became clear that organizations can benefit from having their internal platform engineering teams. These teams help enable development teams by deciding the tool selection that makes sense to best solve software delivery problems and speed up the process.

A common trend is having a dedicated platform engineering team to define these APIs and make platform-wide decisions. The platform team collaborates with development teams, operations teams, and cloud provider experts to implement tools that meet the needs of the workflows application teams. Besides having a dedicated platform engineering team, a key cultural change promoted by the book *Team Topologies* (https://teamtopologies.com/) is to treat the platform itself as an internal product and your development teams as customers. This is not new, but it pushes the platform team to focus on these internal development teams' satisfaction while using the platform's tools.

Figure 1.14 shows how application development teams (App Dev Teams) can focus on working on new features using their preferred tools while the Platform Team creates Golden Paths (to production), which all the work produced by these teams to validate the functionality and deliver these changes to our organization customers/end users.

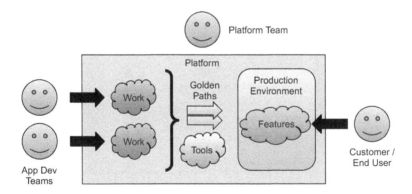

Figure 1.14   Platform teams take the work done by developers safely to production.

This relationship between the platform and development teams creates synergy, focusing on improving the entire organization's software delivery practices. By creating Golden Paths, the platform doesn't stop on the day-to-day development tasks. Still, it also aims to automate how the changes made by development teams reach our organization's end customers/consumers.

By adding visibility to the whole process, you can help the entire organization understand and see how teams produce new features and when those features will be available to our end users. This can be very valuable business decisions, marketing, and for planning in general.

1.3.1 Why can't I just buy a platform?

Unfortunately, you can't buy an off-the-shelf platform to solve all your organization's needs. As we discussed, you can buy one or more cloud provider services, but your internal teams will need to figure out which services and how they must be combined to solve specific problems. The exercise of figuring out which tools and services fit your organization's needs and compliance requirements and how to encapsulate these decisions behind interfaces that teams can consume using a self-service approach is usually something you can't buy.

There are tools designed with this situation in mind that try to enable platform teams to do less gluing by implementing a set of out-of-the-box workflows or having a very opinionated set of tools they support. Tools in this category that are also heavily using and extending Kubernetes are Red Hat OpenShift (https://www.redhat.com/en/technologies/cloud-computing/openshift) and VMware Tanzu (https://tanzu.vmware.com/tanzu). These tools are very attractive to Chief Technology Officers (CTOs) and architects because they cover most topics they need solutions for, such as CI/CD, operations, developer tooling, and frameworks. Based on my experience, while these tools are helpful in many scenarios, platform teams require flexibility in their chosen tools to fit their existing practices. At the end of the day, if you buy these tools, your teams will also need to spend time learning them, which is why these tools like Red Hat OpenShift and VMware Tanzu are sold with consulting services, which is another cost to factor into the equation. For medium and large organizations, adopting and adapting these opinionated off-the-shelf tools might require changes in well-defined workflows and practices that are already well-known to your teams. For smaller and less-mature organizations, these tools can save a lot of time by reducing the number of choices that teams will face when getting started with new initiatives, but the cost of these tools and services might be too high for a young organization.

Figure 1.15 shows how the journey changes depending on which tools the platform team chooses. These Kubernetes distributions (OpenShift, Tanzu, among others) can limit the number of choices the platform teams can make, but they can also save time and come with services such as training and consulting that your teams can rely on.

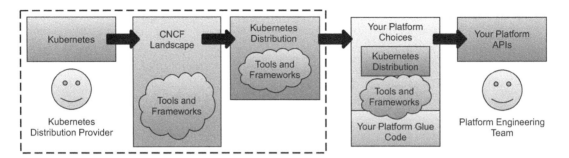

Figure 1.15   Building platforms on top of Kubernetes distributions

No matter if you are already a customer of these tools, you will still be in charge of building a platform on top of these tools. If you have Red Hat OpenShift or VMware Tanzu available to your teams, I strongly encourage you to familiarize yourself with the tools they support and their design choices and decisions. Aligning with the tools you have and consulting with their architects might help you find shortcuts to build your layers on top of these tools.

A word of caution: It is crucial to notice that these tools can be considered Kubernetes distributions. Distributions in the same sense as Linux distributions mean that I expect more and more distributions to appear, tackling different challenges and use cases. Tools like K0s and MicroK8s for IoT and edge cases are other examples. While you can adopt any of these distributions, ensure they align with your organization's goals.

Because I want to keep this book as practical as possible, we will look at a simple application we will use to go on our journey in the next section. We will not build a generic platform for a generic use case. We will build an example platform demonstrating the concepts covered in the previous sections. Having a concrete example you can run, experiment with, and change should help you map the topics discussed to your day-to-day challenges. The application introduced in the next section highlights the challenges you will face while creating, building, and maintaining distributed applications in most business domains. Hence, the example platform we will build to support this application should map to the challenges you will face in your business domain.

1.4   *The need for a walking skeleton*

In the Kubernetes ecosystem, it is common to need to integrate at least 10 or more projects or frameworks to deliver a simple PoC (proof of concept). This work can cover topics such as building projects into containers that can run inside Kubernetes and routing traffic to the REST endpoints provided by each service. If you want to experiment with new projects to see if they fit into your ecosystem, build a PoC to validate your understanding of how this new project/framework works and how it will save you and your team time.

For this book, I have created a simple "walking skeleton." This cloud-native application goes beyond being a simple PoC and allows you to explore how different architectural patterns can be applied. It also lets you test how different tools and frameworks can be integrated without changing your projects for experimentation. I've preferred the term "walking skeleton" instead of "proof of concept" or "demo application", as the term walking skeleton reflects more closely the intention of the application introduced in this section.

The primary purpose of this walking skeleton is to highlight how to solve very specific challenges from an architectural point of view, the requirements that your applications will need, and the delivery practices' angle. You should be able to map how these challenges are solved in the sample cloud-native application to your specific domain. Challenges will not always be the same, but I want to highlight the principles behind each proposed solution and the approach taken to guide your decisions.

With this walking skeleton, you can also figure out the minimum viable product you need and deploy it quickly to a production environment where you can improve it. By taking the walking skeleton to a production environment, you can gain valuable insights into what you will need for other services and from an infrastructure perspective. It can also help your teams understand what it takes to work with these projects and how and where things can go wrong.

The technology stack used to build the walking skeleton is unimportant. It is more important to understand how the pieces fit together and what tools and practices can enable each team behind a service (or a set of services) to evolve safely and efficiently.

1.4.1 Building a Conference application

Throughout this book, you will be working with a Conference application. This Conference application can be deployed in different environments to serve different events. This application relies on containers, Kubernetes, and tools that will work across any major cloud providers and on-prem Kubernetes installations.

Figure 1.16 shows what the application's main page looks like.

Figure 1.16 Conference application home page

The Conference application allows users to manage conference events, and it provides a basic landing page, an Agenda page where all the approved talks will be listed, and a Call for Proposals form where potential speakers can submit their talk proposals. The application also allows conference organizers to do admin tasks, such as reviewing submitted proposals and approving or rejecting them (see figure 1.17).

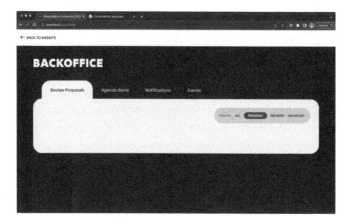

Figure 1.17   Conference application Back Office page

This application is composed of a set of services that have different responsibilities. Figure 1.18 shows the main components of the application that you control—in other words, the services that you and your team will be changing and delivering.

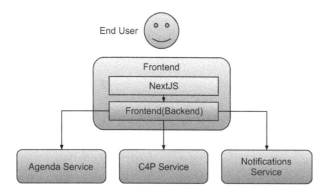

Figure 1.18   Conference application services. The end user interacts with the frontend that routes requests to all the backend services.

The team has created these services to implement a basic walking skeleton with functionality that demonstrates business value. Here is a brief description of each service:

- *Frontend:* This service is the main entry point for your users to access the application. For this reason, the service hosts a NextJS application (HTML, JavaScript, and CSS files) that the client's browser will download. The client-side application interacts with a backend service that accepts the requests from the browser and routes each request to one or more backend services.

- *Agenda service:* This service deals with listing all the talks that were approved for the conference. This service needs to be highly available during the conference dates, because the attendees will be hitting this service several times during the day to move between sessions.

- *Call for Proposals (C4P):* This service contains the logic to deal with Call for Proposals use case (C4P for short) when the conference is being organized. This functionality allows potential speakers to submit talk proposals that the conference organizers will review and decide which ones to include in the conference agenda.

- *Notifications service:* This service enables the conference organizers to send notifications to attendees and speakers.

Figure 1.19 shows the Call for Proposals flow that was selected by the team to build the walking skeleton and validate their assumptions about how the Conference application will work. By implementing this use case end to end, the team can validate its chosen technology stack and architectural assumptions.

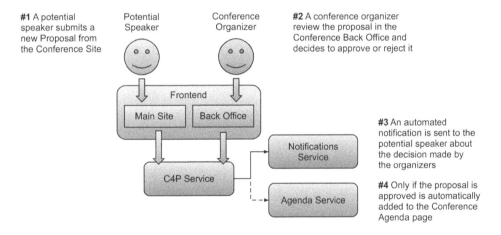

Figure 1.19   Call for Proposals use case

After implementing the basics of the Call for Proposals use case, the team can decide what use case to implement next. Do the conference organizers need to manage sponsors? Do the speakers need a dedicated profile page? Adding new features or services should be straightforward because the base building blocks are in place.

While looking at how these use cases are implemented, you need to consider also how to coordinate across teams when new use cases will be implemented or when changes need to be introduced. To improve collaboration, you need visibility, and you need to understand how the application is working.

You also need to consider the operation side of this cloud-native application. You can imagine there will be a period when the application will open the Call for Proposals request for potential speakers to submit proposals, then closer to the conference date, open the attendee registration page, etc.

Throughout this book, I will encourage you to experiment by adding new services and implementing new use cases. In chapter 2, when you deploy the application to a Kubernetes cluster, you will inspect how these services are configured to work, how the data flows between the different services, and how to scale the services.

By playing around with a fictional application, you are free to change each service's internals, use different tools and compare results or even have different versions of each service to try in parallel. Each service provides all the resources needed to deploy these services to your environment. In chapters 3 and 4, we will go deeper into each service to understand how to build and deploy each service so teams can change the current behavior and create and deploy new releases.

Before deploying this cloud-native conference application, it is important to mention some of the main differences with bundling all these functionalities in a single monolithic application.

But what about if the Conference application was created using a monolith approach? Let's briefly discuss what the main differences would be.

1.4.2   *Differences between a monolith and a distributed set of services*

Understanding the differences between having a single monolithic application and a fully distributed set of services is critical to grasping why the increased complexity is worth the effort. If you are still working with monolithic applications that you want to split up to use a distributed approach, this section highlights the main differences you will encounter.

Figure 1.20 shows a monolithic application implementing the same use case discussed before, but in this scenario, different teams working on different features will share the same codebase. There are no explicit requirements for strong interfaces between internal services when developing a monolithic application. It's optional to separate the logic of different functionalities in well-encapsulated modules. The lack of interfaces and overlap between functionality pushes the teams making changes on the application to have complex coordination strategies to ensure that features don't conflict and that changes can be merged in the codebase.

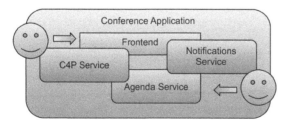

Figure 1.20   In a monolith application, all the logic to implement different use cases are bundled together. This push different teams to work on the same codebase and requires them to have complex coordination practices to avoid conflicting changes.

Functionally wise, they are the same and you can do the same amount of use cases, but the monolith application presented some drawbacks that you might be experiencing with your monolith applications already. The following points highlight the benefits of the cloud-native application that we will use in this book and some disadvantages associated with a parallel-universe alternative monolithic implementation:

- *Now services can evolve independently, teams are empowered to go faster, and there is no bottleneck at the codebase level:* In the monolithic application, there is a single source code repository for different teams to work on, there was a single continuous integration pipeline for the project which was slow, and teams were using feature branches that caused problems with complex merges.

- *Now the application can scale differently for different scenarios:* From a scalability perspective, each service can be scaled depending on the load level it experiences. With the monolith application, the operations team can only create new instances of the entire application if it need to scale just a single functionality. Fine-grained control over how different functionalities are scaled can be a significant differentiator for your use case, but you must do your due diligence.

- *The cloud-native version is much more complex, because it is a distributed system:* It uses the flexibility and characteristics of the cloud infrastructure much better, allowing the operation teams to use tools to manage this complexity and the day-to-day operations. Creating your in-house mechanism to operate large applications was much more common when building monolithic applications. In cloud-native environments, there are a lot of tools provided by cloud providers and open-source projects that can be used to operate and monitor cloud-native applications.

- *Welcome polyglotism:* Each service can be built using a different programming language or different frameworks. With the monolith, application developers were stuck in old versions of libraries, because changing or upgrading a library usually involved large refactoring, and the whole application needed to be tested to guarantee that the application will not break. In a cloud-native approach, services are not forced to use a single technology stack. This allowed teams to be more autonomous in choosing their tools, which can speed up delivery times in some situations.

- *All or nothing with the monolith:* If the monolith application went down, the entire application is down, and users couldn't access anything. With the cloud-native version, users can still access the application even if services are down. The example walking skeleton shows how to support degraded services by adopting popular tools. By using Kubernetes, which was designed to monitor your services and take action in case a service is misbehaving, the platform will try to self-heal your applications.

- *Each conference event required a different version of the monolith:* When dealing with different events, each conference required a version of the monolith slightly different from the other events. This causes divergent codebases and duplication of the entire project. Most of the changes done for a conference were lost when the event was done. In the cloud-native approach, we promote reusability by having fine-grained services that can be swapped, avoiding duplication of the whole application.

While the monolith application is much more straightforward to operate and develop than the cloud-native application, the remainder of the book focuses on understanding and reducing the complexity of building a distributed application. We'll do that by adopting the right tools and practices, which will unlock your teams to be more independent and efficient while promoting resiliency and robustness to your applications.

If you are currently working with a monolith application, I hope this book helps you to compare different approaches and introduces you to the tools and practices that are required for building distributed applications.

1.4.3   *Our walking skeleton and building platforms*

Now that we have a simple application that our customers will be using, we can focus on understanding all the tools our teams will need to improve these services continuously. The platforms we will cover in this book are those organizations that will build for domain-specific purposes, not generic ones. By creating our walking skeleton for a specific scenario, we can mimic a platform that optimizes tools and workflows to improve how software gets delivered for those teams. Our walking skeleton is not a simple "Hello World" application, so it allows for more experimentation, writing more complex features, and using tools to make the application more robust.

We will now embark on a cloud-native journey. First, we will look into how distributed applications run on top of Kubernetes, what Kubernetes provides, and its challenges. Right after that, we will start looking into tools that will extend the basic Kubernetes features to assist us in building, deploying, and running our cloud-native applications.

Later on, in chapter 6, after evaluating some of the challenges of building and delivering distributed applications, we will build our *platform walking skeleton* that will help teams create new features to work with the existing application in a safe environment, where they can do their day-to-day work without conflicting with other teams. Once we have our platform walking skeleton, we will build and offer higher-level platform capabilities to enable our teams to be more productive and reduce their need to understand the complexity of Kubernetes and all the tools we will discuss in this book.

Finally, to close the book, we will look at how to measure how good the platforms that we are building are. As with any software, we need to measure it to ensure that new tools or changes we introduce make things better and not worse.

This journey will push us to make hard decisions and choices that will become critical for our platform engineering practices. The following list covers the main milestones in this journey without going into the details of the specific tools covered in each chapter.

- *Chapter 2: Cloud-native application challenges:* After getting the Conference application up and running in a Kubernetes cluster, we will analyze the main and most common challenges you will face when working on and running cloud-native applications on top of Kubernetes. In this chapter, you will inspect the application from a runtime perspective and try to break it in different ways to see how it behaves when things go wrong.

- *Chapter 3: Service pipelines: Building cloud-native applications:* Once the application is up and running, you and your teams will change the application's services to add new features or fix bugs. This chapter covers what it takes to build these application services, including the latest changes using service pipelines to create a release of the artifacts needed to deploy these new versions into live environments.

- *Chapter 4: Environment pipelines: Deploying cloud-native applications:* If we sort out how to package and release new versions of our services, then we need to have a clear strategy on how to promote these new versions to different environments so they can be tested and validated before facing real customers. This chapter covers the concept of environment pipelines and a popular trend in the cloud-native community called GitOps to configure and deploy applications across different environments.

- *Chapter 5: Multi-cloud (app) infrastructure:* Your applications can't run in isolation. Application services need application infrastructure components, such as databases, message brokers, identity services, etc., to work. This chapter focuses on how to provision the components that our application's services need using a multi-cloud and Kubernetes-native approach.

- *Chapter 6: Let's build a platform on top of Kubernetes:* Once we understand how the application runs, how it is built and deployed, and how it connects to cloud infrastructure, we will focus our attention on abstracting the complexity introduced by all the tools that we are using from the teams making changes to the application. We don't want our development teams to get distracted setting up cloud-provider accounts, configuring the servers where the build pipelines will run, or worrying about where their environment is running. Welcome to the platform engineering team!

- *Chapter 7: Platform capabilities I: Shared application concerns:* How can we reduce friction and dependencies between application and operation teams? How can we decouple even further the logic of our applications from the components that these applications need to run? This chapter covers a set of platform capabilities that enable application developers to focus on writing code. The platform team can concentrate on deciding how to wire all the components required by the application and then expose simple and standardized APIs that developers can consume.

- *Chapter 8: Platform capabilities II: Enabling teams to experiment:* Now that we have a platform that takes care of provisioning environments for our teams to do their work, what else can the platform do for the application development teams? If you enable your teams to run more than a single version of your application's services simultaneously, new features or fixes can be rolled out incrementally.

Having room for experimentation allows the organization to find issues sooner and reduces each release's associated stress. This chapter covers how to implement different release strategies for your cloud-native applications.

- *Chapter 9: Measuring your platforms:* Platforms are as good as the improvements they bring to the organization. We need to measure our platform performance to see how well it's doing, because we should use a continuous improvement approach to ensure that the tools we use are helping our teams deliver faster and more efficiently. This chapter focuses on using the DORA metrics to understand how well the organization is delivering software and how platform changes can improve the throughput of our delivery pipelines.

Now that you know what is coming, let's deploy our cloud-native Conference application.

Summary

- (Cloud) platforms provide a set of services for teams to build their domain-specific applications.
- Platforms usually offer three main features: APIs, dashboards, and SDKs for different teams to use whatever fits their workflows.
- Cloud platforms provide a pay-as-you-go model to consume hardware and software. The higher you go up the stack, the more expensive the service will be.
- Kubernetes offers the basic building blocks to build platforms on top in a way that we can remain independent of the underlying cloud provider and even deploy our platforms on-premises.
- The Cloud Native and Computing Foundation promotes and fosters collaborations between open-source projects in the cloud-native space. Keeping track of what is going on in these communities is a full-time job.
- Platform engineering on Kubernetes (specifically for this book) helps manage the complexity of choosing which tools and practices teams need to adopt to be more efficient at delivering software that will run on top of Kubernetes.

Cloud-native application challenges

2

This chapter covers

- Working with a cloud-native application running in a Kubernetes cluster
- Choosing between local and remote Kubernetes clusters
- Understanding the main components and Kubernetes resources
- Understanding the challenges of working with cloud-native applications

When I want to try something new, a framework, a new tool, or just a new application, I tend to be impatient; I want to see it running immediately. Then, when it is running, I want to dig deeper and understand how it works. I break things to experiment and validate that I understand how these tools, frameworks, or applications work internally. That is the sort of approach we'll take in this chapter!

To have a cloud-native application up and running, you will need a Kubernetes cluster. In this chapter, you will work with a local Kubernetes cluster using a project called KinD (Kubernetes in Docker, https://kind.sigs.k8s.io/). This local cluster will allow you to deploy applications locally for development and experimentation. To install a set of microservices, you will use Helm, a project that helps package, deploy, and distribute Kubernetes applications. You will install the walking skeleton services introduced in chapter 1, which implements a Conference application.

Once the services for the Conference application are up and running, you will inspect its Kubernetes resources to understand how the application was architected and its inner workings by using kubectl. Once you get an overview of the main pieces inside the application, you will jump ahead to try to break the application, finding common challenges and pitfalls that your cloud-native applications can face. This chapter covers the basics of running cloud-native applications in a modern technology stack based on Kubernetes, highlighting the good and the bad that come with developing, deploying, and maintaining distributed applications. The following chapters tackle these associated challenges by looking into projects whose main focus is to speed up and make more efficient the delivery of your projects.

2.1 Running our cloud-native applications

To understand the innate challenges of cloud-native applications, we need to be able to experiment with a simple example that we can control, configure, and break for educational purposes. In the context of cloud-native applications, "simple" cannot be a single service, so for simple applications we will need to deal with the complexities of distributed applications such as networking latency, resilience to failure on some of the applications' services, and eventual inconsistencies. To run a cloud-native application, in this case, the walking skeleton introduced in chapter 1, you need a Kubernetes cluster. Where this cluster is going to be installed and who will be responsible for setting it up are the first questions that developers will have. It is quite common for developers to want to run things locally, on their laptop or workstation, and with Kubernetes, this is possible—but is it optimal? Let's analyze the advantages and disadvantages of running a local cluster against other options.

2.1.1 Choosing the best Kubernetes environment for you

This section doesn't cover a comprehensive list of all the available Kubernetes flavors, but it focuses on common patterns in how Kubernetes clusters can be provisioned and managed. There are three possible alternatives—all of them with advantages and drawbacks:

- *Local Kubernetes in your laptop/desktop computer:* I tend to discourage people from running Kubernetes on their laptops. As you will see in the rest of the book, running your software in similar environments to production is highly recommended to avoid problems that can be summed up as "but it works on my laptop." These problems are mostly caused by the fact that when you run Kubernetes on your laptop, you are not running on top of a real cluster of machines. Hence, there are no network round-trips and no real load balancing.
  - *Pros:* Lightweight, fast to get started, good for testing, experimenting, and local development. Good for running small applications.

- *Cons:* Not a real cluster, it behaves differently, and has reduced hardware to run workloads. You will not be able to run a large application on your laptop.
- *On-premise Kubernetes in your data center:* This is a typical option for companies with private clouds. This approach requires the company to have a dedicated team and hardware to create, maintain, and operate these clusters. If your company is mature enough, it might have a self-service platform that allows users to request new Kubernetes clusters on demand.
  - *Pros:* A real cluster on top of real hardware will behave closer to how a production cluster will work. You will have a clear picture of which features are available for your applications to use in your environments.
  - *Cons:* It requires a mature operation team to set up clusters and give credentials to users, and it requires dedicated hardware for developers to work on their experiments.
- *Managed service Kubernetes offering in a cloud provider:* I tend to be in favor of this approach, because using a cloud provider service allows you to pay for what you use, and services like Google Kubernetes Engine (GKE), Azure AKS, and AWS EKS are all built with a self-service approach in mind, enabling developers to spin up new Kubernetes clusters quickly. There are two primary considerations:

  1 You need to choose one cloud provider and have an account with a big credit card to pay for what your teams will consume. This might involve setting up some caps in the budget and defining who has access. By selecting a cloud provider, you might be in a vendor lock-in situation if you are not careful.
  2 Everything is remote, and for developers and other teams that are used to work locally, this is too big of a change. It takes time for developers to adapt, because the tools and most of the workloads will run remotely. This is also an advantage, because the environments used by your developers and the applications that they are deploying are going to behave as if they were running in a production environment.
  - *Pros:* You are working with real (fully fledged) clusters. You can define how many resources you need for your tasks, and when you are done, you can delete them to release resources. You don't need to invest in hardware up front.
  - *Cons:* You need a potentially big credit card, and you need your developers to work against remote clusters and services.

A final recommendation is to check the following repository, which contains free Kubernetes credits in major cloud providers: https://github.com/learnk8s/free -kubernetes. I've created this repository to keep an updated list of these free trials that you can use to get all the examples in the book up and running on top of real infrastructure. Figure 2.1 summarizes the information contained in the previous bullet points.

| Developers are used to work locally. | | These are in-house clusters but they feel remote to developers. | | These are fully remote setups, developers need to get used to new workflows. |

Local

Pros
- Lightweight
- Fast to get started
- Good for local development
- Good for testing (CI)
- Good for small applications

Cons
- Limited capacity
- It doesn't behave as a real cluster
- Good network bandwidth is required to download containers to your laptop

On Premises

Pros
- Real cluster on top of real machines
- It behaves closer to a Production Environment
- Provide a remote environment for development teams to work

Cons
- Requires you to have and maintain dedicated hardware
- Requires a mature team to provision the cluster and distribute credentials
- It might lack integrations and extra features provided by cloud providers
- Difficult to scale up if you require a large number of clusters

Cloud Provider

Pros
- Fully fledged managed clusters
- You don't need to deal with hardware
- Easy to scale and manage
- Extra services provided (backup, app infrastructure, security, etc.)
- Pay-as-you-go model

Cons
- Difficult to estimate costs, you might need a big credit card to pay for what you use
- Possible vendor lock-in
- Cloud-Provider specific expertise required

Figure 2.1   Kubernetes cluster Local vs. Remote setups.

While these three options are all valid and have drawbacks, in the next sections, you will use Kubernetes KinD (Kubernetes in Docker, https://kind.sigs.k8s.io/) to deploy the walking skeleton introduced in chapter 1 in a local Kubernetes environment running on your laptop/pc. Check the step-by-step tutorial located at https://github.com/salaboy/platforms-on-k8s/tree/main/chapter-2#creating-a-local-cluster-with-kubernetes-kind to create your local KinD cluster that we will use to deploy our walking skeleton, the Conference application.

Notice that the tutorial creates a local KinD cluster that simulates having three nodes and a special port mapping to allow our Ingress controller to route incoming traffic that we will send to http://localhost.

2.1.2   *Installing the walking skeleton*

To run containerized applications on top of Kubernetes, you will need to have each of the services packaged as a container image, plus you will need to define how these containers will be configured to run in your Kubernetes cluster. To do so, Kubernetes allows you to define different kinds of resources (using YAML format) to configure how your containers will run and communicate with each other. The most common kinds of resources are:

- *Deployments:* Declaratively define how many replicas of your container need to be up for your application to work correctly. Deployments also allow us to choose which container (or containers) we want to run and how these containers must be configured (using environment variables).

- *Services:* Declaratively define a high-level abstraction to route traffic to the containers created by your deployments. It also acts as a load balancer between the replicas inside your deployments. Services enable other services and applications inside the cluster to use the service name instead of the physical IP address of the containers to communicate, providing what is known as service discovery.

- *Ingress:* Declaratively define a route for routing traffic from outside the cluster to services inside the cluster. Using Ingress definitions, we can expose the services that are required by client applications running outside the cluster.

- *ConfigMap/secrets:* Declaratively define and store configuration objects to set up our service instances. Secrets are considered sensitive information that should have protected access.

These YAML files will be complex and hard to manage if you have large applications with tens or hundreds of services. Keeping track of the changes and deploying applications by applying these files using `kubectl` becomes a complex job. It is beyond the scope of this book to cover a detailed view of these resources, and other resources are available such as the official Kubernetes documentation page (https://kubernetes.io/docs/concepts/workloads/). In this book, we will concentrate on how to deal with these resources for large applications and the tools that can help us with that task. The following section provides an overview of the tools to package and install components into your Kubernetes cluster.

PACKAGING AND INSTALLING KUBERNETES APPLICATIONS

There are different tools to package and manage your Kubernetes applications. Most of the time, we can separate these tools into two main categories: templating engines and package managers. You will probably need both kinds of tools for real-life scenarios to get things done. Let's discuss these two kinds of tools: why would you need a templating engine? What kind of packages do you want to manage?

A templating engine allows you to reuse the same resource definitions in different environments where applications might require slightly different parameters. The textbook example of the need to template your resources is database URLs. If your service needs to connect to different database instances in different environments, such as the testing database in the testing environment and the production database in the production environment, you want to avoid maintaining two copies of the same YAML file but with different URLs. Figure 2.2 shows how you can now add variables to the YAML files, and the engine will then find and replace these variables with different values depending on where you want to use the final (rendered) resource.

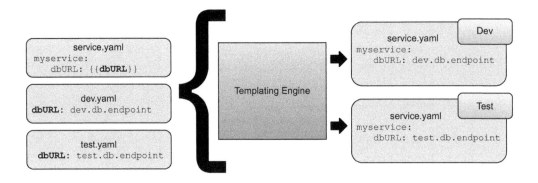

Figure 2.2   Templating engines render YAML resources by replacing variables.

Using a templating engine can save you a lot of time maintaining different copies of the same file, because when files start to pile up, maintaining them becomes a full-time job. There are several tools in the community to deal with templating Kubernetes files. Some tools just deal with YAML files, and some other tools are more targeted to Kubernetes resources specifically. Some projects that you should check out are:

- *Kustomize:* https://kustomize.io/
- *Carvel YTT:* https://carvel.dev/ytt/
- *Helm Templates:* https://helm.sh/docs/chart_best_practices/templates/#helm

Now, what do you do with all these files? It is quite a natural urge to organize these files in logical packages. If you are building an application that is composed of different services, it might make sense to group all the resources related to a service inside the same directory or even in the same repository that contains the source code for that service. You also want to make sure that you can distribute these files to the teams deploying these services to different environments, and you quickly realize that you need to version these files in some way. This versioning might be related to the version of your service itself or with a high-level logical aggregation that makes sense for your application. When we talk about grouping, versioning, and distributing these resources, we are describing the responsibility of a package manager. Developers and operations teams are already used to working with package managers no matter the technology stack they use. Maven/Gradle for Java, NPM for NodeJS, APT-GET for Linux/Debian/Ubuntu packages, and more recently, containers and container registries for cloud-native applications. So, what does a package manager for YAML files look like? What are the package manager's main responsibilities?

As a user, a package manager allows you to browse available packages and their metadata to decide which package you want to install. Once you have decided which package you want to use, you should be able to download it and then install it. Once the package is installed, you would expect, as a user, to be able to upgrade to a newer version of the package when it becomes available. Upgrading/updating a package requires manual intervention, meaning that as a user, you will explicitly tell the package manager to upgrade the installation of a certain package to a newer (or latest) version.

From a package provider's point of view, a package manager should offer a convention and structure to create packages and a tool to package the files you want to distribute. Package managers deal with versions and dependencies, meaning that if you create a package, you must associate a version number with it. Some package managers use the *semver* (semantic versioning) approach, which uses three numbers to describe the package maturity (1.0.1 where these numbers represent the major, minor, and patch versions). A package manager doesn't need to provide a centralized package repository, but they often do. This package repository is in charge of hosting packages for users to consume. Central repositories are useful because they provide access to developers with thousands of packages ready to be used. Some examples of these central repositories are Maven Central, NPM, Docker Hub, GitHub Container Registry, etc. These repositories are in charge of indexing the package's metadata (which can include versions, labels, dependencies, and short descriptions) to make them searchable by users. These repositories also deal with access control to have public and private packages, but at the end of the day, the main responsibility of the package repository is to allow package producers to upload packages and package consumers to download packages from them (see figure 2.3).

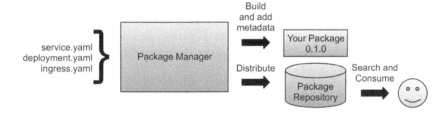

Figure 2.3 Package Managers' responsibilities: build, package, and distribute

When we talk about Kubernetes, Helm is a very popular tool that provides both a package manager and a templating engine. But there are others worth looking into, such as:

- Imgpkg (https://carvel.dev/imgpkg/), which uses Container registries to store the packages.
- Kapp (https://carvel.dev/kapp/), which provides higher-level abstractions to group resources as applications.
- Tools like Terraform and Pulumi that allow you to manage infrastructure as code.

In the following section, we will look at using Helm (http://helm.sh) to install the Conference application into our Kubernetes cluster.

2.2   *Installing the Conference application with a single command*

Let's install the Conference application introduced in chapter 1, section 1.4 into our Kubernetes cluster using Helm. This Conference application allows conference organizers to receive proposals from potential speakers, evaluate these proposals, and keep an updated agenda with the approved submissions for the event. We will use this application throughout the book to exemplify the challenges that you will face while building real-life applications.

> **NOTE**   For the complete list of steps, follow the step-by-step tutorial located at https://github.com/salaboy/platforms-on-k8s/tree/main/chapter-2. It includes all the prerequisites to run the commands described in this section, such as creating a cluster and installing the command-line tools needed for the examples to work.

This application was built as a walking skeleton, which means it is not a complete application but has all the pieces required for the "Call for Proposals" flow to work. These services can be iterated further to support other flows and real-life scenarios. In the following sections, you will install the application into the cluster and interact with it to see how it behaves when it runs on top of Kubernetes. Let's install the application with the following line:

```
helm install conference oci://docker.io/salaboy/conference-app --version
v1.0.0
```

You should see the output similar to listing 2.1.

Listing 2.1   Helm installed the chart conference-app version 1.0.0

```
> helm install conference oci://docker.io/salaboy/conference-app --version
➥v1.0.0
Pulled: registry-1.docker.io/salaboy/conference-app:v1.0.0
Digest:
sha256:e5dd1a87a867fd7d6c6caecef3914234a12f23581c5137edf63bfd9add7d5459
NAME: conference
LAST DEPLOYED: Mon Jun 26 08:19:15 2023
NAMESPACE: default
STATUS: deployed
REVISION: 1
TEST SUITE: None
NOTES:
Cloud-Native Conference Application v1.0.0
Chart Deployed: conference-app - v1.0.0
Release Name: conference
For more information visit: https://github.com/salaboy/platforms-on-k8s
Access the Conference Application Frontend by running
➥'kubectl port-forward svc/frontend -n default 8080:80'
```

> **NOTE**   Since Helm 3.7+ you can package and distribute Helm Charts as OCI container images, the URL for the Helm Chart contains oci:// because this chart is hosted in Docker Hub, where the application containers are stored. Before Helm supported OCI images, you needed to manually add and fetch packages from a Helm Chart Repository, which used tar files to distribute these charts.

`helm install` creates a Helm release, which means that you have created an application instance, in this case, the instance is called conference With Helm, you can deploy multiple instances of the application if you want to. You can list Helm releases by running:

```
helm list
```

The output should look like figure 2.4.

```
salaboy@salaboys-MacBook-Pro chapter-2 % helm list
NAME          NAMESPACE      REVISION      UPDATED                                    STATUS      CHART                       APP VERSION
conference    default        1             2023-10-02 17:50:54.019418 +0800 CST       deployed    conference-app-v1.0.0 v1.0.0
salaboy@salaboys-MacBook-Pro chapter-2 %
```

Figure 2.4   List Helm releases

> **NOTE**   If instead of using `helm install` you run `helm template oci://docker.io/salaboy/conference-app --version v1.0.0`. Helm will output the YAML files, which will apply against the cluster. There are situations where you might want to do that instead of `helm install`, for example, if you want to override values that the Helm Charts don't allow you to parameterize or apply any other transformations before sending the request to Kubernetes.

2.2.1   *Verifying that the application is up and running*

Once the application is deployed, containers will be downloaded to run on your laptop, which can take a while. Depending on your internet connection, the process can take up to 10 minutes because Kafka, PostgreSQL, and Redis will be downloaded alongside the application's containers. The RESTARTS columns show how often the container has been restarted due to an error. In distributed applications, this is normal, as components might depend on each other, and when they are started at the same time, connections can fail. By design, applications should be able to recover from problems, and Kubernetes will automatically restart a failing container.

You can monitor the progress by listing all the pods running in your cluster, once again, using the `-owide` flag to get more information:

```
kubectl get pods -owide
```

The output should look like figure 2.5.

```
salaboy@salaboys-MacBook-Pro chapter-2 % kubectl get pods -owide
NAME                                                          READY   STATUS    RESTARTS        AGE     IP            NODE           NOMINATED NODE   READINESS GATES
conference-agenda-service-deployment-746bddcdb4-5nzsn         1/1     Running   1 (4h43m ago)   4h44m   10.244.1.5    dev-worker2    <none>           <none>
conference-c4p-service-deployment-67bc96879c-cjknm            1/1     Running   4 (4h43m ago)   4h44m   10.244.3.7    dev-worker3    <none>           <none>
conference-frontend-deployment-797fc494c4-hgjv4               1/1     Running   1 (4h43m ago)   4h44m   10.244.3.6    dev-worker3    <none>           <none>
conference-kafka-0                                            1/1     Running   0               4h44m   10.244.2.12   dev-worker     <none>           <none>
conference-notifications-service-deployment-f76c4578f-8brqb   1/1     Running   2 (4h43m ago)   4h44m   10.244.2.10   dev-worker     <none>           <none>
conference-postgresql-0                                       1/1     Running   0               4h44m   10.244.1.9    dev-worker2    <none>           <none>
conference-redis-master-0                                     1/1     Running   0               4h44m   10.244.1.8    dev-worker2    <none>           <none>
salaboy@salaboys-MacBook-Pro chapter-2 %
```

Listing 2.5   Listing application pods

Something that you might notice in the list of pods is that we are not only running the application's services, but we are also running Redis, PostgreSQL, and Kafka, because the C4P (Call for Proposals) and Agenda services need persistent storage. The application will be using Kafka to exchange asynchronous messages between services. Besides the services, we will have these two databases and a message broker (Kafka) running inside our Kubernetes cluster.

In the output shown in figure 2.5 you need to pay attention to the READY and STATUS columns, where 1/1 in the READY column means that one replica of the container is running, and one is expected to be running. As you can see the RESTART column is showing 7 for the Call for Proposals Service (`conference-c4p-service`). This is because the service depends on Redis to be up and running for the service to be able to connect to it. While Redis is bootstrapping the application will try to connect, and if it fails, it will try to keep reconnecting. As soon as Redis is up, the service will connect to it. The same applies to Kafka and PostgreSQL. To quickly recap, our application services, the databases, and the message broker that we are running are shown in figure 2.6.

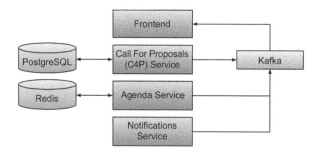

Figure 2.6   Application services, databases, and message broker

Notice that Pods can be scheduled in different nodes. You can check this in the NODE column; this is Kubernetes efficiently using the cluster resources. If all the Pods are up and running, you've made it! The application is now up and running, and you can access it by pointing your favorite browser to `http://localhost`.

If you are interested in Helm and building your own Conference application Helm Chart, I recommend you to check the source code provided with the tutorials: https://github.com/salaboy/platforms-on-k8s/tree/main/conference-application/helm/conference-app.

2.2.2   *Interacting with your application*

In the previous section, we installed the application into our local Kubernetes cluster. In this section, we will quickly interact with the application to understand how the services interact to accomplish a simple use case: Receiving and approving proposals. Remember that you can access the application by pointing your browser to `http://localhost`. The Conference application should look like figure 2.7.

**Figure 2.7
Conference
landing page**

If you switch to the Agenda section now, you should see something like figure 2.8.

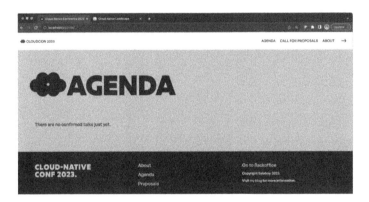

**Figure 2.8
Conference empty
Agenda when we
first install the
application**

The application's Agenda page lists all the talks scheduled for the conference. Potential speakers can submit proposals that the conference organizers will review. When you start the application for the first time, there will be no talks on the agenda, but you can now go ahead and submit a proposal from the Call from Proposals section. Check figure 2.9.

**Figure 2.9
Submitting a
proposal for
organizers to
review**

Notice that there are four fields (Title, Description, Author, and Email) in the form to submit a proposal. Fill in all the fields and submit by clicking the Submit Proposal button at the bottom of the form. The organizers will use this information to evaluate your proposal and get in touch with you via email if your proposal gets approved or rejected. Once the proposal is submitted, you can go to the Back Office (click the arrow pointing to the right at the top menu) and check the Review Proposals tab, where you can Approve or Reject submitted proposals. You will be acting as a conference organizer on this screen; see figure 2.10.

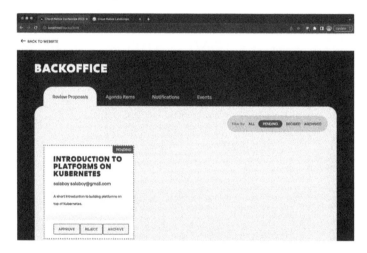

Figure 2.10   Conference organizers can Accept or Reject incoming proposals

Approved proposals will appear on the Main Agenda page. Attendees who visit the page at this stage can glance at the conference's main speakers. Figure 2.11 shows our freshly approved proposal in the Agenda section of the main conference page.

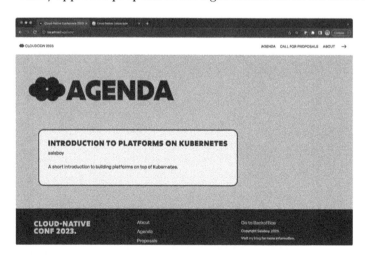

Figure 2.11   Your proposal is now live on the agenda!

At this stage, the potential speaker should have received an email about the approval or rejection of their proposal. You can check this by looking at the notification service logs, using `kubectl` from your terminal; see figure 2.12 for the output of the command:

```
kubectl logs -f conference-notifications-service -deployment-<POD_ID>
```

chapter-2 — kubectl logs -f conference-notifications-service-deployment-f76c4578f-8brqb — 152×25
2023/10/02 14:39:29 "GET http://10.244.2.10:8080/health/readiness HTTP/1.1" from 10.244.2.1:45332 - 200 12B in 134.834µs
2023/10/02 14:39:30
To: salaboy@gmail.com
Subject: Your proposal Introduction to Platforms on Kubernetes was accepted
Body: We are happy to inform that your proposal: `53254302-a4b1-4066-9784-07fc0c1136f0` with title: `Introduction to Platforms on Kubernetes` was accep
ted
We will send further instructions closer to your presentation date.
You session has been published into the conference website: e9a89841-16f5-4b82-bd81-1a19a81f7792
Thanks and see you soon.
- The Conference Organizers -
2023/10/02 14:39:31 "POST http://notifications-service.default.svc.cluster.local/notifications/ HTTP/1.1" from 10.244.3.7:35892 - 200 744B in 1.0107265s
2023/10/02 14:39:31 Notification Sent - Event emitted to Kafka: {a2df2af6-e5ab-46db-8e69-49296d89ef06 53254302-a4b1-4066-9784-07fc0c1136f0 e9a89841-16f5
-4b82-bd81-1a19a81f7792 Introduction to Platforms on Kubernetes salaboy@gmail.com true Your proposal Introduction to Platforms on Kubernetes was accept
ed We are happy to inform that your proposal: `53254302-a4b1-4066-9784-07fc0c1136f0` with title: `Introduction to Platforms on Kubernetes` was accepted
We will send further instructions closer to your presentation date.
You session has been published into the conference website: e9a89841-16f5-4b82-bd81-1a19a81f7792
Thanks and see you soon.
- The Conference Organizers -
}
2023/10/02 14:39:39 "GET http://10.244.2.10:8080/health/liveness HTTP/1.1" from 10.244.2.1:45710 - 200 12B in 60.792µs

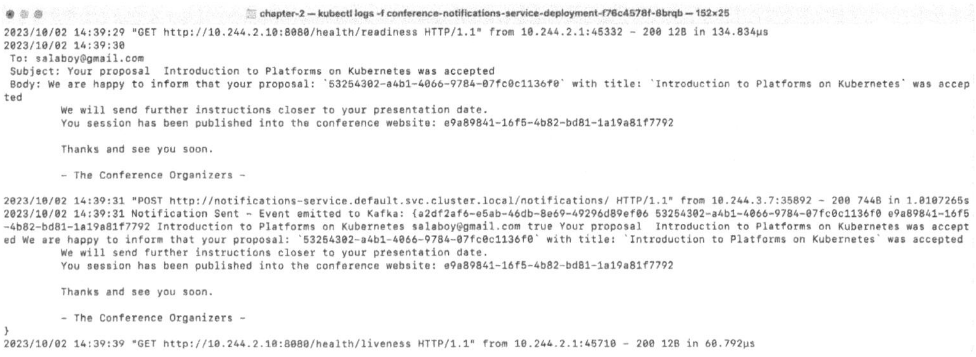

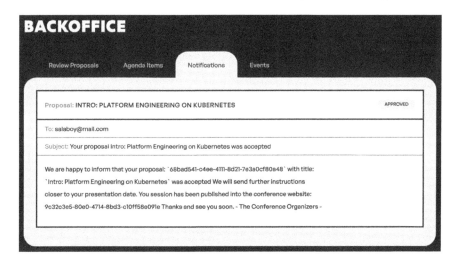

Figure 2.12 Notifications service logs (emails and events)

These logs show two important aspects of the application. First, notifications are sent via emails to potential speakers. The organizers need to keep track of these communications. On the conference Back Office page, you can find the Notifications tab, where the content of the notifications is shown to the organizers (see figure 2.13).

BACKOFFICE
Review Proposals
Agenda Items
Notifications
Events
Proposal: INTRO: PLATFORM ENGINEERING ON KUBERNETES
APPROVED
To: salaboy@mail.com
Subject: Your proposal Intro: Platform Engineering on Kubernetes was accepted
We are happy to inform that your proposal: `68bad541-c4ee-4111-8d21-7e3a0cf80a48` with title: `Intro: Platform Engineering on Kubernetes` was accepted We will send further instructions closer to your presentation date. You session has been published into the conference website: 9c32c3e5-80e0-4714-8bd3-c10ff58e091e Thanks and see you soon. - The Conference Organizers -

Figure 2.13 Notifications displayed in the Back Office

The second aspect displayed here is Events. All services from this application are emitting events when relevant actions are performed. The notification service is emitting an event, in this case to Kafka, for every notification that is being sent. This allows other services and applications to integrate with the application services asynchronously. Figure 2.14 shows the Events section of the Back Office.

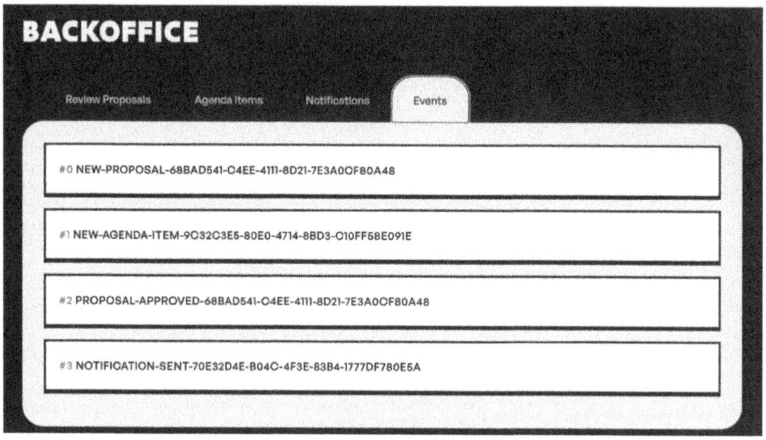

Figure 2.14   All service events in the Back Office

Figure 2.14 shows all events emitted by the application services; notice that you can see all the meaningful operations being performed by the services to fulfill the Call for Proposals flow (New Proposal > New Agenda Item > Proposal Approved > Notification Sent).

If you made it so far, congrats, the Conference application is working as expected. I encourage you to submit another proposal and reject it, to validate that the correct notification and events are sent to the potential speaker.

In this section, you installed the Conference application using Helm. Then we verified that the application is up and running and that potential speakers can submit proposals, while conference organizers can approve or reject these proposals. The decisions will send notifications to potential speakers via email.

This simple application allows us to demonstrate a basic use case that we can now expand and improve to support real users. We have seen that installing a new instance of the application is quite simple. We used Helm to install a set of services that are connected as well as some infrastructural components such as Redis, PostgreSQL, and in the next section, we will go deeper into understanding what we have installed and how the application is working.

2.3 Inspecting the walking skeleton

If you have been using Kubernetes for a while, you probably know all about `kubectl`. Because this application version uses native Kubernetes deployments and services, you can inspect and troubleshoot these Kubernetes resources using `kubectl`.

Usually, instead of just looking at the pods running (with `kubectl get pods`), to understand and operate the application, you will be looking at services and deployments. Let's explore the deployment resources first.

2.3.1 Kubernetes deployments basics

Let's start with deployments. Deployments in Kubernetes are in charge of containing the recipe for running our containers. Deployments are also in charge of defining how containers will run and how they will be upgraded to newer versions when needed. By looking at the deployment details, you can get very useful information, such as:

- The *container* that this deployment is using. Notice that this is just a simple Docker container, meaning that you can even run this container locally if you want to with `docker run`. This is fundamental to troubleshooting problems.
- The number of *replicas* required by the deployment. For this example, it is set to 1, but you will change this in the next section. More replicas add more resiliency to the application, because these replicas can go down. Kubernetes will spawn new instances to keep the number of desired replicas up at all times.
- The *resource allocation* for the container. Depending on the load and the technology stack that you used to build your service, you will need to fine-tune how many resources Kubernetes you allow your container to use.
- The status of the *readiness* and *liveness probes*. Kubernetes, by default, will monitor the health of your container. It does that by executing two probes: 1) The "readiness probe" checks if the container is ready to answer requests, and 2) The "liveness probe" checks if the main process of the container is running.
- The rolling updates strategy defines how our Pods will be updated to avoid downtime for our users. With the `RollingUpdateStrategy`, you can define how many replicas are allowed while triggering and updating to a newer version.

First, let's list all the available deployments with:

```
kubectl get deployments
```

The output should look like listing 2.2.

Listing 2.2 Listing your application's deployments

```
NAME                                          READY   UP-TO-DATE   AVAILABLE
conference-agenda-service-deployment          1/1     1            1
conference-c4p-service-deployment             1/1     1            1
conference-frontend-deployment                1/1     1            1
conference-notifications-service-deployment   1/1     1            1
```

2.3.2 Exploring deployments

In the following example, you will describe the Frontend deployment. You can describe each deployment in more detail with `kubectl describe deploy conference-fron-tend-deployment` (see listing 2.3).

Listing 2.3 Describing a deployment to see its details

> **Shows the replicas available for this deployment. This gives you a quick indication about the state of your deployment.**

```
> kubectl describe deploy conference-frontend-deployment
Name:                   conference-frontend-deployment
Namespace:              default
CreationTimestamp:      Tue, 27 Jun 2023 08:21:21 +0100
Labels:                 app.kubernetes.io/managed-by=Helm
Annotations:            deployment.kubernetes.io/revision: 1
                        meta.helm.sh/release-name: conference
                        meta.helm.sh/release-namespace: default
Selector:               app=frontend
Replicas:               1 desired | 1 updated | 1 total | 1 available
StrategyType:           RollingUpdate
MinReadySeconds:        0
RollingUpdateStrategy:  25% max unavailable, 25% max surge
Pod Template:
  Labels:  app=frontend
  Containers:
   frontend:
    Image:       salaboy/frontend-go...
    Port:        8080/TCP
    Host Port:   0/TCP
    ...
    ...
    Environment:
      AGENDA_SERVICE_URL:         agenda-service.default.svc.cluster.local
      C4P_SERVICE_URL:            c4p-service.default.svc.cluster.local
      NOTIFICATIONS_SERVICE_URL:  notifications-service.default.svc.cluster.
local
      KAFKA_URL:                  conference-kafka.default.svc.cluster.local
      POD_NODENAME:                (v1:spec.nodeName)
      POD_NAME:                    (v1:metadata.name)
      POD_NAMESPACE:               (v1:metadata.namespace)
      POD_IP:                      (v1:status.podIP)
      POD_SERVICE_ACCOUNT:         (v1:spec.serviceAccountName)
    Mounts:                       <none>
  Volumes:                        <none>
Conditions:
  Type           Status  Reason
  ----           ------  ------
  Available      True    MinimumReplicasAvailable
  Progressing    True    NewReplicaSetAvailable
OldReplicaSets:  <none>
NewReplicaSet:   conference-frontend-deployment-<ID> (1/1 replicas created)
```

The container image, including the name and tag used for this service.

The environment variables used to configure this container.

> **Events shows us relevant information about our Kubernetes resources—in this case, when the replica was created.**

```
Events:
  Type     Reason            Age   From                  Message
  ----     ------            ----  ----                  -------
  Normal   ScalingReplicaSet 48m   deployment-controller Scaled up replica
➥set conference-frontend-deployment-59d988899 to 1
```

Listing 2.3 shows that describing deployments in this way is very helpful if for some reason the deployment is not working as expected. For example, if the number of replicas required is not met, describing the resource will give you insights into where the problem might be. Always check at the bottom for the events associated with the resource to get more insights about the resource status. In this case, the deployment was scaled to have one replica 48 minutes ago.

As mentioned before, deployments are also responsible for coordinating version or configuration upgrades and rollbacks. The deployment update strategy is set by default to "Rolling ," which means that the deployment will incrementally upgrade pods one after the other to minimize downtime. An alternative strategy called `Recreate` can be set, which will shut down all the pods and create new ones.

In contrast with pods, deployments are not ephemeral; hence, if you create a `Deployment`, it will be there for you to query no matter if the containers under the hood are failing. By default, when you create a deployment resource, Kubernetes creates an intermediate resource for handling and checking the deployment–requested replicas.

2.3.3 ReplicaSets

Having multiple replicas of your containers is an important feature to scale your applications. If your application is experiencing loads of traffic from your users, you can easily scale up the number of replicas of your services to accommodate all the incoming requests. Similarly, if your application is not experiencing a large number of requests, these replicas can be scaled down to save resources. The object created by Kubernetes is called `ReplicaSet`, and it can be queried by running:

```
kubectl get replicaset
```

The output should look like listing 2.4.

Listing 2.4 Listing the deployment's ReplicaSets

```
> kubectl get replicasets
NAME                                                    DESIRED   CURRENT   READY
conference-agenda-service-deployment-7cc9f58875         1         1         1
conference-c4p-service-deployment-76dfc94444            1         1         1
conference-frontend-deployment-59d988899                1         1         1
conference-notifications-service-deployment-7cbcb8677b  1         1         1
```

These `ReplicaSet` objects are fully managed by the deployment's resource, and usually, you shouldn't need to deal with them. ReplicaSets are also essential when dealing with rolling updates, and you can find more information about this topic at https://kubernetes.io/docs/tutorials/kubernetes-basics/update/update-intro/. You will be performing updates to the application with Helm in later chapters, where these mechanisms will kick in.

If you want to change the number of replicas for a deployment, you once again can use `kubectl` to do so:

```
> kubectl scale --replicas=2 deployments/<DEPLOYMENT_ID>
```

You can try this out with the Frontend deployment:

```
> kubectl scale --replicas=2 deployments/conference-frontend-deployment
```

If we now list the application pods, we will see that there are two replicas for the frontend service:

```
conference-frontend-deployment-<ID>-8gpgn  1/1      Running   7 (53m ago)   59m
conference-frontend-deployment-<ID>-z4c5c  1/1      Running   0             13s
```

This command changes the deployment resource in Kubernetes and triggers the creation of a second replica for the Frontend deployment. Increasing the number of replicas of your user-facing services is quite common because it is the service that all users will hit when visiting the conference page.

If we access the application right now, as end users we will not notice any difference, but every time we refresh, a different replica might serve us. To make this more evident, we can turn on a feature that is built into the Frontend service, which shows us more information about the application containers. You can enable this feature by setting an environment variable:

```
kubectl set env deployment/conference-frontend-deployment
➥FEATURE_DEBUG_ENABLED=true
```

Notice that when you change the deployment object configuration (anything inside `spec.template.spec` block) the rolling update mechanism of the Deployment resource will kick in. All the existing pods managed by this deployment will be upgraded to have the new specification(in this example to include the new `FEATURE_DEBUG_ENABLED` environment variable). This upgrade, by default, will start a new pod with the new specification and wait for it to be ready before terminating the old version of the pod. This process will be repeated until all the pods (replicas for the deployment) are using the new configuration.

If you access the application again in your browser (you might need to access using Incognito Mode if the browser cached the website), in the Back Office section, there is a new Debug tab. You can see the Pod Name, Pod IP, the Namespace, and the Node name where the Pod is running for all services (figure 2.15).

Figure 2.15   First replica of the Frontend answering your request (running on Node Name: dev-worker)

If you wait for 3 seconds, the page will automatically refresh, and you should see the second replica answering this time, if not wait for the next cycle (figure 2.16).

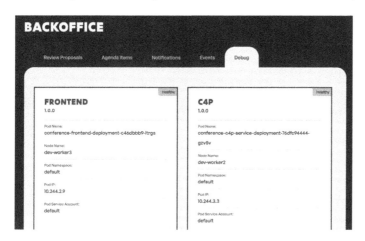

Figure 2.16   Second replica of the Frontend answering your request (running on Node Name: dev-worker3)

By default, Kubernetes will load-balance the requests between the replicas. Being able to scale by just changing the number of replicas, there is no need to deploy anything new, Kubernetes will provision a new pod (with a new container in it) to deal with more traffic. Kubernetes will also make sure that there is the amount of desired replicas at all times. You can test this by deleting one pod and watching how Kubernetes recreates it automatically. For this scenario, you need to be careful, because the web application frontend is executing several requests to fetch the HTML, CSS, and JavaScript libraries; hence, each of these requests can land in a different replica.

2.3.4 Connecting services

We have looked at deployments, which are in charge of getting our containers up and running and keeping them that way, but so far, these containers can only be accessed inside the Kubernetes cluster. If we want other services to interact with these containers, we need to look at another Kubernetes resource called `Service`. Kubernetes provides an advanced service-discovery mechanism that allows services to communicate with each other by just knowing their names. This is essential for connecting many services without knowing IP addresses of Kubernetes pods that can change over time, as they can be upgraded, rescheduled to a different node, or just restarted with a new IP address when something goes wrong.

2.3.5 Exploring services

To expose your containers to other services, you need to use a `Kubernetes Service` resource. Each application service defines this `Service` resource, so other services and clients can connect to them. In Kubernetes, services will be in charge of routing traffic to your application containers. These services represent a logical name that you can use to abstract where your containers run. If you have multiple replicas of your containers, the service resource will be in charge of load balancing the traffic among all the replicas. You can list all the services by running:

```
kubectl get services
```

After running the command, you should see something like listing 2.5.

Listing 2.5   Listing application's services

```
NAME                         TYPE        CLUSTER-IP       PORT(S)
agenda-service               ClusterIP   10.96.90.100     80/TCP
c4p-service                  ClusterIP   10.96.179.86     80/TCP
conference-kafka             ClusterIP   10.96.67.2       9092/TCP
conference-kafka-headless    ClusterIP   None        9092/TCP,9094/TCP,9093/TCP
conference-postgresql        ClusterIP   10.96.121.167    5432/TCP
conference-postgresql-hl     ClusterIP   None             5432/TCP
conference-redis-headless    ClusterIP   None             6379/TCP
conference-redis-master      ClusterIP   10.96.225.138    6379/TCP
frontend                     ClusterIP   10.96.60.237     80/TCP
kubernetes                   ClusterIP   10.96.0.1        443/TCP
notifications-service        ClusterIP   10.96.65.248     80/TCP
```

And you can also describe a service to see more information about it with:

```
kubectl describe service frontend
```

This should give you something like we see in listing 2.6. Services and deployments are linked by the Selector property, highlighted in the following image. In other words, the service will route traffic to all the pods created by a deployment containing the label `app=frontend`.

Listing 2.6   Describing the Frontend service

```
Name:               frontend
Namespace:          default
Labels:             app.kubernetes.io/managed-by=Helm
Annotations:        meta.helm.sh/release-name: conference
                    meta.helm.sh/release-namespace: default
Selector:           app=frontend            ◄
Type:               ClusterIP
IP Family Policy:   SingleStack
IP Families:        IPv4
IP:                 10.96.60.237
IPs:                10.96.60.237
Port:               <unset>  80/TCP
TargetPort:         8080/TCP
Endpoints:          10.244.1.6:8080,10.244.2.9:8080
Session Affinity:   None
Events:             <none>
```

The selector used to match a service and a deployment.

2.3.6   Service discovery in Kubernetes

By using services, if your application service needs to send a request to any other service, it can use the Kubernetes service's name and port; in most cases, you can use port 80 if you are using HTTP requests, so you only need to use the service name. If you look at the source code of the services, you will see that HTTP requests are created against the service name; no IP addresses or Ports are needed.

Finally, if you want to expose your services outside the Kubernetes cluster, you need an Ingress resource. As the name represents, this Kubernetes resource is in charge of routing traffic from outside the cluster to services that are inside the cluster. Usually, you will not expose multiple services, limiting the entry points for your applications.

You can get all the available Ingress resources by running the following command:

```
kubectl get ingress
```

The output should look like listing 2.7.

Listing 2.7   Listing the application's Ingress resources

```
NAME                          CLASS   HOSTS   ADDRESS     PORTS   AGE
conference-frontend-ingress   nginx   *       localhost   80      84m
```

And then you can describe the Ingress resource in the same way as you did with other resource types to get more information about it:

```
kubectl describe ingress conference-frontend-ingress
```

You should expect the output to look like listing 2.8.

Listing 2.8   Describing the Ingress resource

```
Name:              conference-frontend-ingress
Labels:            app.kubernetes.io/managed-by=Helm
Namespace:         default
Address:           localhost
Ingress Class:     nginx
Default backend:   <default>                       All traffic going to '/' will go to
Rules:                                                  the frontend:80 service.
  Host         Path  Backends
  ----         ----  --------
    *
               /    frontend:80 (10.244.1.6:8080,10.244.2.9:8080)  ◄──────────┘
Annotations:   meta.helm.sh/release-name: conference
               meta.helm.sh/release-namespace: default
               nginx.ingress.kubernetes.io/rewrite-target: /
Events:        <none>
```

As you can see, Ingress also uses the service's name to route traffic. For this to work, you need an Ingress controller, like we installed when we created the KinD cluster. If you are running in a cloud provider, you might need to install an Ingress controller.

The following spreadsheet is a community resource created to keep track of the different options of Ingress controllers that are available for you to use: http://mng .bz/K9Bn.

With Ingresses, you can configure a single entry-point and use path-based routing to redirect traffic to each service you need to expose. The previous Ingress resource in listing 2.8 routes all the traffic sent to / to the frontend service. Notice that Ingress rules are pretty simple, and you shouldn't add any business logic routing at this level.

2.3.7   *Troubleshooting internal services*

Sometimes, it is important to access internal services to debug or troubleshoot services that are not working. For such situations, you can use the kubectl port-forward command to temporarily access services that are not exposed outside of the cluster using an Ingress resource. For example, to access the Agenda service without going through the Frontend you can use the following command:

```
kubectl port-forward svc/agenda-service 8080:80
```

You should see the following output (listing 2.9) and make sure that you don't kill the command.

Listing 2.9   kubectl port-forward allows you to expose a service for debugging purposes

```
Forwarding from 127.0.0.1:8080 -> 8080
Forwarding from [::1]:8080 -> 8080
```

And then using your browser, use curl in a different tab or any other tool to point to http://localhost:8080/service/info to access the exposed Agenda service. The following listing shows how you can `curl` the Agenda service info endpoint and print a pretty/colorful JSON payload with the help of `jq`, which you must install separately

---

Listing 2.10 curl localhost:8080 to access Agenda service using port-forward

```
> curl -s localhost:8080/service/info | jq --color-output
{
  "Name": "AGENDA",
  "Version": "1.0.0",
  "Source": "https://github.com/salaboy/platforms-on-k8s/tree/main/
              conference-application/agenda-service",
  "PodName": "conference-agenda-service-deployment-7cc9f58875-28wrt",
  "PodNamespace": "default",
  "PodNodeName": "dev-worker3",
  "PodIp": "10.244.2.2",
  "PodServiceAccount": "default"
}
```

In this section, you have inspected the main Kubernetes resources that were created to run your application's containers inside Kubernetes. By looking at these resources and their relationships, you can troubleshoot problems when they arise.

For everyday operations, the `kubectl` command line tool might not be optimal, and different dashboards can be used to explore and manage your Kubernetes workloads, such as k9s (https://k9scli.io/), the Kubernetes dashboard (https://kubernetes.io/docs/tasks/access-application-cluster/web-ui-dashboard/) and Skooner (https://github.com/skooner-k8s/skooner).

2.4 *Cloud-native application challenges*

In contrast to a monolithic application, which will go down entirely if something goes wrong, cloud-native applications shouldn't crash if a service goes down. Cloud-native applications are designed for failure and should keep providing valuable functionality in the case of errors. A degraded service while fixing problems is better than having no access to the application. In this section, you will change some of the service configurations in Kubernetes to understand how the application will behave in different situations.

In some cases, application/service developers will need to make sure that they build their services to be resilient and Kubernetes or the infrastructure will solve some concerns.

This section covers some of the most common challenges associated with cloud-native applications. I find it useful to know what are the things that are going to go wrong in advance rather than when I am already building and delivering the application. This is not an extensive list; it is just the beginning to make sure that you don't get stuck with problems that are widely known. The following sections will exemplify and highlight these challenges with the Conference application:

- *Downtime is not allowed*: If you are building and running a cloud-native application on top of Kubernetes, and you are still suffering from application downtime, then you are not capitalizing on the advantages of the technology stack that you are using.
- *Service's built-in resiliency*: Downstream services will go down, and you need to ensure that your services are prepared for that. Kubernetes helps with dynamic service discovery, but that is not enough for your application to be resilient.
- *Dealing with the application state is not trivial*: We must understand each service's infrastructural requirements to allow Kubernetes to scale up and down our services efficiently.
- *Inconsistent data*: A common problem of working with distributed applications is that data is not stored in a single place and tends to be distributed. The application will need to be ready to deal with cases where different services have different views of the state of the world.
- *Understanding how the application is working (monitoring, tracing, and telemetry)*: Having a clear understanding of how the application is performing and that it is doing what it is supposed to be doing is essential for quickly finding problems when things go wrong.
- *Application security and identity management*: Dealing with users and security is always an afterthought. For distributed applications, having these aspects clearly documented and implemented early on will help you to refine the application requirements by defining "who can do what and when."

Let's start with the first of the challenges: Downtime is not allowed.

2.4.1 Downtime is not allowed

When using Kubernetes, we can easily scale up and down our services' replicas. This is a great feature when your services were designed based on the assumption that the platform will scale them by creating new copies of the containers running the service. So, what happens when the service is not ready to handle replication or when no replicas are available for a given service?

Let's scale up the Frontend service to have two replicas running. To achieve this, you can run the following command:

```
kubectl scale --replicas=2 deployments/conference-frontend-deployment
```

If one of the replicas stops running or breaks for any reason, Kubernetes will try to start another one to ensure that two replicas are up all the time. Figure 2.17 shows two Frontend replicas serving traffic to the user.

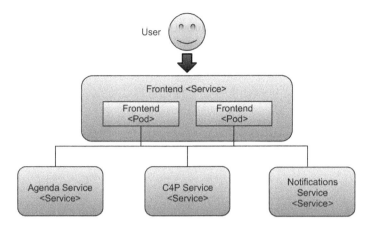

Figure 2.17 **By having two replicas of the Frontend container running, we allow the application to tolerate failures and also to increase the number of concurrent requests that the application can handle.**

You can quickly try this self-healing feature of Kubernetes by killing one of the two pods of the application Frontend. You can do this by running the following commands, as shown in listings 2.11 and 2.12.

Listing 2.11 Checking that the two replicas are up and running

```
> kubectl get pods
NAME                                                READY   STATUS    RESTARTS     AGE
conference-agenda-service-deployment-<ID>           1/1     Running   7 (92m ago)  100m
conference-c4p-service-deployment-<ID>              1/1     Running   7 (92m ago)  100m
conference-frontend-deployment-<ID>                 1/1     Running   0            25m
conference-frontend-deployment-<ID>                 1/1     Running   0            25m
conference-kafka-0                                  1/1     Running   0            100m
conference-notifications-service-deployment-<ID>    1/1     Running   7 (91m ago)  100m
conference-postgresql-0                             1/1     Running   0            100m
conference-redis-master-0                           1/1     Running   0            100m
```

Now, copy one of the two Pods Id and delete it:

```
> kubectl delete pod conference-frontend-deployment-c46dbbb9-ltrgs
```

Then list the pods again (listing 2.12).

Listing 2.12 A new replica is automatically created as soon as one goes down

```
> kubectl get pods

NAME                                                READY   STATUS            RESTARTS     AGE
conference-agenda-service-deployment-<ID>           1/1     Running           7 (92m ago)  100m
conference-c4p-service-deployment-<ID>              1/1     Running           7 (92m ago)  100m
conference-frontend-deployment-<NEW ID>             0/1     ContainerCreating 0            1s
conference-frontend-deployment-<ID>                 1/1     Running           0            25m
conference-kafka-0                                  1/1     Running           0            100m
conference-notifications-service-deployment-<ID>    1/1     Running           7 (91m ago)  100m
conference-postgresql-0                             1/1     Running           0            100m
conference-redis-master-0                           1/1     Running           0            100m
```

You can see how Kubernetes (the ReplicaSet, more specifically) immediately creates a new pod when it detects only one running. While this new pod is being created and started, you have a single replica answering your requests until the second one is up and running. This mechanism ensures that at least two replicas answer your users' requests. Figure 2.18 shows that the application still works, because we still have one pod serving requests.

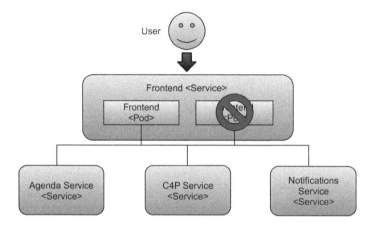

Figure 2.18   If one of the instances fails, Kubernetes will automatically kill and recreate that instance. But at least the other running container can keep answering requests.

If you have a single replica and kill the running pod, you will have downtime in your application until the new container is created and ready to serve requests. You can revert to a single replica with the following:

```
> kubectl scale --replicas=1 deployments/conference-frontend-deployment
```

Go ahead and try this out. Delete only the replica available for the Frontend pod:

```
> kubectl delete pod <POD_ID>
```

Figure 2.19 shows the application is not working anymore, because there are no Frontend pods to serve incoming requests from users.

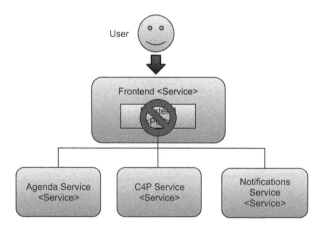

Figure 2.19   With a single replica being restarted, there is no backup to answer user requests. If there is no replica available to serve your users' requests, you will experience downtime. This is exactly what we want to avoid.

After killing the pod, try to access the application by refreshing your browser (http://localhost). You should see "503 Service Temporarily Unavailable" in your browser, because the Ingress controller (not shown in the previous figure for simplicity) cannot find a replica running behind the Frontend service. If you wait for a bit, you will see the application come back up. Figure 2.20 shows the 503 "Service Temporarily Unavailable" being returned by the NGINX Ingress controller component that was in charge of routing traffic to the Frontend service.

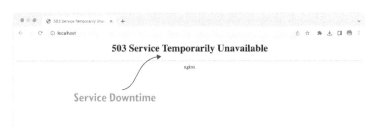

Figure 2.20 With a single replica being restarted, there is no backup to answer user requests

This error message is quite tricky, because the application takes about a second to get restarted and to be fully functional, so if you didn't manage to see it, you can try to downscale the frontend service to zero replicas with `kubectl scale --replicas=0 deployments/conference-frontend-deployment` to simulate downtime.

This behavior is expected, because the Frontend service is a user-facing service. If it goes down, users will not be able to access any functionality, so having multiple replicas is recommended. From this perspective, the Frontend service is the most important service of the entire application, since our primary goal for our applications is to avoid downtime.

In summary, pay special attention to user-facing services exposed outside of your cluster. Whether they are user interfaces or just APIs, ensure you have as many replicas as needed to deal with incoming requests. Having a single replica should be avoided for most use cases besides development.

2.4.2 Service's resilience built-in

But now, what happens if the other services go down? For example, the Agenda service, is just in charge of listing all the accepted proposals to the conference attendees. This service is also critical, because the Agenda List is right there on the main page of the application. So, let's scale the service down:

```
kubectl scale --replicas=0 deployments/conference-agenda-service-deployment
```

Figure 2.21 shows how the application can keep working, even if one of the services is misbehaving.

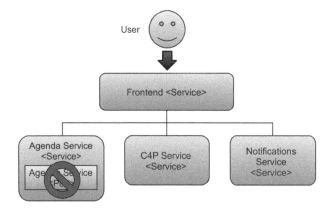

Figure 2.21   No pods for the Agenda service. If a service is failing, the user should be able to keep using the application with limited functionality.

Right after running this command, the container will be killed, and the service will not have any container answering its requests. Try refreshing the application in your browser, you should see a cached response as shown in figure 2.22.

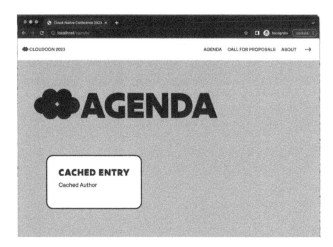

Figure 2.22   If the Agenda service has no replica running, the Frontend is wise enough to show the user some cached entries.

As you can see, the application is still running, but the Agenda service is not available right now. Check the Debug tab in the Back Office section, which should show that the Agenda service is unhealthy (figure 2.23).

Figure 2.23 If in Debug mode, the Back Office should show the unhealthy services.

You can prepare your application for such scenarios; in this case, the Frontend has a cached response to at least show something to the user. If, for some reason, the Agenda service is down, at least the user will be able to access other services and other sections of the application. From the application perspective, it is important not to propagate the error back to the user. The user should be able to keep using other application services, for example, the Call for Proposals form, until the Agenda service is restored.

You need to pay special attention when developing services that will run in Kubernetes, as now your service is responsible for dealing with errors generated by downstream services. This is important to ensure that errors or services going down don't bring your entire application down. Simple mechanisms such as cached responses will make your applications more resilient and allow you to incrementally upgrade these services without worrying about bringing everything down. For our conference scenario, having a CronJob that periodically caches the agenda entries might be enough. Remember, downtime is not allowed.

Let's now switch to talking about dealing with the state in our applications and how it is critical to understand how our application's services handle the state from a scalability point of view. Since we will be talking about scalability, data consistency is the challenge we will try to solve next.

2.4.3 *Dealing with the application state is not trivial*

Let's scale up the agenda service again to have a single replica:

```
> kubectl scale --replicas=1 deployments/conference-agenda-service-deployment
```

If you have created proposals before, you will notice that as soon as the Agenda service goes back up, you see the accepted proposals again on the Agenda page. This works only because both the Agenda service and C4P Service store all the proposals and agenda items in external databases (PostgreSQL and Redis). In this context, external means outside of the pod memory. What will happen if we scale the Agenda service up to two replicas? See listing 2.13.

```
> kubectl scale --replicas=2 deployments/conference-agenda-service-deployment
NAME                                                      READY   STATUS    AGE
conference-agenda-service-deployment-<ID>                 1/1     Running   2m30s
conference-agenda-service-deployment-<ID>                 1/1     Running   22s
conference-c4p-service-deployment-<ID>                    1/1     Running   150m
conference-frontend-deployment-<ID>                       1/1     Running   8m55s
conference-kafka-0                                        1/1     Running   150m
conference-notifications-service-deployment-<ID>          1/1     Running   150m
conference-postgresql-0                                   1/1     Running   150m
conference-redis-master-0                                 1/1     Running   150m
```

Figure 2.24 shows the Agenda service running two replicas of the service concurrently.

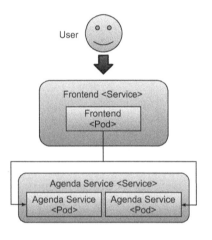

**Figure 2.24
Two replicas can now deal with more traffic. The requests being forwarded by the Frontend can be answered by the two available replicas, allowing the application to handle more load.**

With two replicas dealing with your user requests, now the Frontend will have two instances to query. Kubernetes will do the load balancing between the two replicas, but your application will have no control over which replica the request hits. Because we are using a database to back up the data outside of the pod's context, we can scale the replicas to many pods dealing with the application demand. Figure 2.25 shows how the Agenda service relies on Redis to store the application state, while the Call for Proposals uses PostgreSQL to do the same.

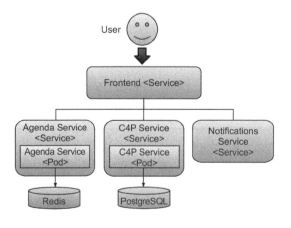

Figure 2.25   Both data-sensitive services use persistent stores. Delegating state storage to external components, make your service stateless and easier to scale.

One of the limitations of this approach is the number of database connections that your database supports in its default configuration. If you keep scaling up the replicas, always consider reviewing the database connection pool settings to ensure that your database can handle all the connections created by all the replicas. But for the sake of learning, let's imagine that we don't have a database, and our Agenda service keeps all the agenda items in memory. How would the application behave if we started scaling up the Agenda service pods? Figure 2.26 shows the hypothetical case of having in-memory data inside our applications.

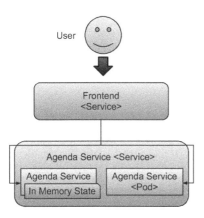

**Figure 2.26
What would happen
if the Agenda service
keeps the state in-
memory? If state is
kept in memory it is
quite hard to share
across replicas. This
makes scaling the
service much harder.**

By scaling these services up, we have found a problem with the design of one of the application services. The Agenda service is keeping the state in-memory, and that will affect the scaling capabilities from Kubernetes. For this kind of scenario, when Kubernetes balances the requests across different replicas, the Frontend service will receive different data depending on which replica processed the request.

When running existing applications in Kubernetes, you will need to deeply understand how much data they are keeping in-memory because this will affect how you can scale them up. For web applications that keep HTTP sessions and require sticky sessions (subsequent requests going to the same replica), you need to set up HTTP session replication to get this working with multiple replicas. This might require more components being configured at the infrastructure level, such as a cache.

Understanding your service requirements will help you plan and automate your infrastructural requirements, such as databases, caches, message brokers, etc. The more complex the application gets, the more dependencies on these infrastructural components it will have.

As we have seen before, we have installed Redis and PostgreSQL as part of the application Helm Chart. This is usually not a good idea because databases and tools like message brokers will need special care from the operation team, who can choose not to run these services inside Kubernetes. We will expand on this topic in chapter 4 where we go deeper into how to deal with infrastructure when working with Kubernetes and cloud providers.

2.4.4   *Dealing with inconsistent data*

Having stored data in a relational data store like PostgreSQL or a NoSQL approach like Redis doesn't solve the problem of having inconsistent data across different stores. Because these stores should be hidden away by the service API, you will need to have mechanisms to check that the data that the services are handling is consistent. In distributed systems, it is quite common to talk about "eventual consistency," meaning that eventually the system will be consistent. Having eventual consistency is better than not having consistency at all. For this example, we can build a simple check mechanism that once in a while (imagine once a day) checks for the accepted talks in the Agenda service to see if they have been approved in the Call for Proposals service. If there is an entry that the Call hasn't approved for the Proposal Service (C4P), then we can raise some alerts or send an email to the conference organizers (figure 2.27).

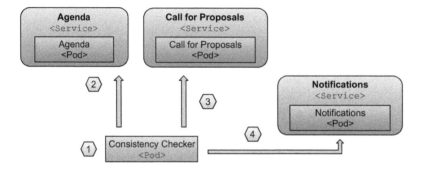

Figure 2.27   Consistency checks can run as CronJobs. We can execute checks against the application services on fixed intervals to make sure that the state is consistent. For example: (1) every day at midnight we query the Agenda Service (2) to verify that the published sessions are approved in the (3) Call For Proposals Service and a corresponding notification has been sent by the (4) Notifications Service.

In figure 2.27, we can see how a CronJob (1) will be executed every X period, depending on how important it is for us to fix consistency problems. Then it will query the Agenda service public APIs (2) to check which accepted proposals are being listed and compare that with the Call for Proposals service approved list (3). Finally, if any inconsistency is found, an email can be sent using the Notifications service public APIs (4).

Think of the simple use case this application was designed for; what other checks would you need? One that immediately comes to mind is verifying that emails were sent correctly for Rejected and Approved proposals. For this use case, emails are really important, and we need to ensure those emails are sent to our accepted and rejected speakers.

2.4.5   *Understanding how the application is working*

Distributed systems are complex beasts, and fully understanding how they work from day one can help you save time when things go wrong. This has pushed the monitoring, tracing, and telemetry communities hard to develop solutions that help us understand how things are working at any given time.

The https://opentelemetry.io/ OpenTelemetry community has evolved alongside Kubernetes, and it can now provide most of the tools you will need to monitor how your services are working. As stated on their website, "You can use it to instrument, generate, collect, and export telemetry data (metrics, logs, and traces) for analysis to understand your software's performance and behavior." Figure 2.28 shows a common use case where services all push metrics, traces, and logs to a centralized place that stores and aggregates the information so it can be displayed in dashboards or used by other tools.

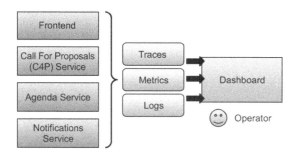

Figure 2.28   Aggregating observability from all our services in a single place reduces the cognitive load on the teams responsible for keeping the application up and running.

It is important to notice that OpenTelemetry focuses on both the behavior and performance of your software, because they will both affect your users and user experience. From the behavior point of view, you want to make sure that the application is doing what it is supposed to do, and by that, you will need to understand which services are calling which other services or infrastructure to perform tasks.

Using Prometheus and Grafana allows us to see the service telemetry and build domain-specific dashboards to highlight certain application-level metrics, for example, the amount of Approved vs. Rejected proposals over time, as shown in figure 2.29.

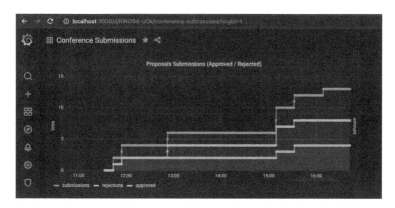

Figure 2.29   Monitoring telemetry data with Prometheus and Grafana

From the performance point of view, you need to ensure that services are respecting their Service Level Agreements (SLAs), which means that they are taking only a short time to answer requests. If one of your services misbehaves and takes more than usual, you want to know.

For tracing, you must modify your services to understand the internal operations and their performance. OpenTelemetry provides drop-in instrumentation libraries in most languages to externalize service metrics and traces. Figure 2.30 shows the OpenTelemetry architecture, where you can see the OpenTelemetry collector receiving information from each application agent, but also from shared infrastructure components.

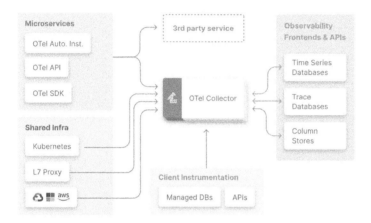

Figure 2.30   OpenTelemetry architecture and library (Source: https://opentelemetry.io/docs/)

The recommendation here is if you are creating a walking skeleton, ensure it has Open-Telemetry built-in. If you push monitoring to later stages of the project, it will be too late, things will go wrong, and finding out who is responsible will take too much time.

2.4.6   *Application security and identity management*

If you have ever built a web application, you know that providing identity management (user accounts and user identity) plus authentication and authorization is quite an endeavor. A simple way to break any application (cloud-native or not) is to perform actions you are not supposed to do, such as deleting all the proposed presentations unless you are a conference organizer.

This also becomes challenging in distributed systems, because authorization and user identity must be propagated across different services. In distributed architectures, it is quite common to have a component that generates requests on behalf of a user instead of exposing all the services for the user to interact directly. In our example, the Frontend service is this component. Most of the time, you can use this external-facing component as the barrier between external and internal services. For this reason, it is quite common to configure the Frontend service to connect with an authorization and authentication provider commonly using the OAuth2 protocol. Figure 2.31 shows the Frontend service interacting with an identity management service, which is responsible for connecting to an Identity Provider (Google, GitHub, your internal LDAP server) to validate the user credentials as well as to provide roles or group memberships that define what the user can and can't do in different services. The Frontend service handles the login flow (authentication and authorization), but only the context is propagated to the backend services once that is done.

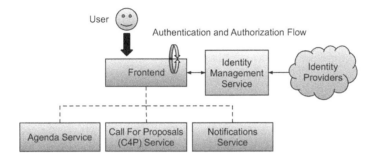

Figure 2.31 **Identity management: The Role/Group is propagated to the backend services.**

On the identity management front, you have seen that the application doesn't handle users or their data, which is good for regulations such as GDPR. We might want to allow users to use their social media accounts to log in to our applications without the need for them to create separate accounts. This is usually known as social login.

Some popular solutions bring both OAuth2 and identity management together, such as Keycloak (https://www.keycloak.org/) and Zitadel (https://zitadel.com/opensource). These open-source projects provide a one-stop-shop for single sign-on solutions and advanced identity management. In the case of Zitadel, it also provides a managed service that you can use if you don't want to install and maintain an SSO and identity management component inside your infrastructure.

The same is true with tracing and monitoring. If you are planning to have users (and you will probably do, sooner or later), including single sign-on and identity management into the walking skeleton will push you to think about the specifics of "who will be able to do what," refining your use case even more.

2.4.7 Other challenges

In the previous sections, we have covered a few common challenges you will face while building cloud-native applications, but these are not all. Can you think of other ways of breaking this first version of the application?

Notice that tackling the challenges discussed in this chapter will help, but there are other challenges related to how we deliver a continuously evolving application composed of a growing number of services.

2.5   *Linking back to platform engineering*

In previous sections, we have covered many topics. We reviewed options for packaging and distributing Kubernetes applications, and then installing our walking skeleton in a Kubernetes cluster using Helm. We tested the application functionality by interacting with it, and finally, we jumped into analyzing common cloud-native challenges that teams will face when building distributed applications.

But you might be wondering how all these topics relate to the title of this book, continuous delivery, and platform engineering in general. In this section, we will make more explicit connections to the topics introduced in chapter 1.

First, the intention behind creating a Kubernetes cluster and running an application on top of it was to ensure we cover Kubernetes built-in mechanisms for resilience and scaling up our application services. Kubernetes provides the building blocks to run our applications with zero downtime, even when we are constantly updating them. This allows us, Kubernetes users, to release new versions of our components more frequently, because we are not supposed to stop the entire application from updating one of its parts. In chapter 8 we will see how Kubernetes' built-in mechanisms can be extended to implement different release strategies.

If you are not using the capabilities offered by Kubernetes to keep releasing software in front of your customers, then you need to raise a red flag. Quite often, this can be due to old practices from before Kubernetes that are getting in the way, lack of automation, or not having clearly defined contracts between services that block dependent services from being released independently. We will touch on this topic several times in future chapters because this is a fundamental principle when trying to improve your continuous delivery practice and something that the platform engineering team needs to prioritize.

In this chapter, we have also seen how to install a cloud-native application using a package manager that encapsulates the configuration files required to deploy our application. These configuration files (Kubernetes resources expressed as YAML files) describe our application topology and contain links to the containers used by each application's service. These YAML files also contain configuration for each service, such as the environment variables to configure each service. Packaging and versioning these configuration files allows us to easily create new application instances in different environments, which we will cover in chapter 4.

I highly recommend the book *Grokking Continuous Delivery* by Christie Wilson (Manning Publications, 2018) if you want to get more insights into the continuous delivery aspects of how configuration as code can help you deliver more software reliably.

Because I wanted to make sure that you have an application to play around with and because we needed to cover Kubernetes built-in mechanisms, I've made a conscious decision to start with an already packaged application that can be easily deployed into any Kubernetes cluster (no matter if it is running locally or in a cloud provider). We can identify two different phases. One we haven't covered yet is how to produce these packages that can be deployed to any Kubernetes cluster, and the second, which we started playing with, is when we run this application in a concrete cluster (we can consider this cluster an environment, maybe a development environment), as shown in figure 2.32.

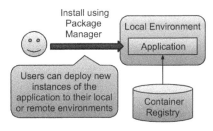

Figure 2.32
Applications' lifecycle from building and packaging to running inside an environment

It is important to understand that the steps executed for our local environment will work for any Kubernetes cluster, no matter the cluster size and location. While each cloud provider will have its own security and identity mechanisms, the Kubernetes APIs and resources we created when we installed our application Helm Chart to the cluster will be the same. If you now use Helm templating capabilities to fine-tune your application (for example, resource consumptions and network configurations) for the target environment, you can easily automate these deployments to any Kubernetes cluster.

Before moving on, let's be clear that pushing developers to configure application instances might not be the best use of their time. A developer accessing the production environment that users/customers are accessing might also not be optimal. We want to ensure that developers are focused on building new features and improving our application. Figure 2.33 shows how we should be automating all the steps involved in building, publishing, and deploying the artifacts that developers are creating, making sure that they can focus on adding features to the application instead of manually dealing with packaging, distributing, and deploying new versions when they are ready. This is the primary focus of this chapter.

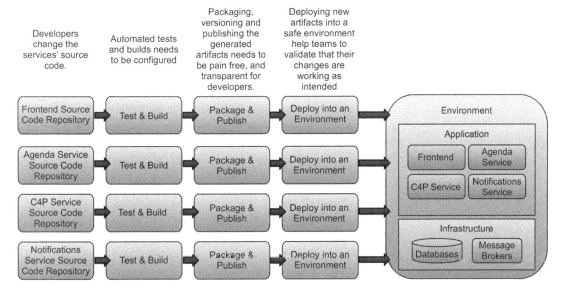

Figure 2.33 Developers can focus on building features, but the platform team needs to automate the entire process after changes are made.

Understanding the tools we can use to automate the path from source code changes to running software in a Kubernetes cluster is fundamental to enabling developers to focus on what they do best "code new features." Another big difference we will tackle is that cloud-native applications are not static. As you can see in the previous diagram, we will not install a static application definition. We want to release and deploy new versions of the services as they become available.

Manually installing applications is error-prone; manually changing configurations in our Kubernetes clusters can make us end up in situations where we don't know how to replicate the current state of our application in a different environment. Hence in chapters 3 and 4, we will talk about automation using what is commonly known as pipelines.

In the next chapter, we will cover a more dynamic aspect of our distributed application with pipelines to deliver new versions of our services. Chapter 4 will explore how we can manage our environments using Kubernetes-based GitOps tools.

Summary

- Choosing between local and remote Kubernetes clusters requires serious considerations:
  - You can use Kubernetes KinD to bootstrap a local Kubernetes cluster to develop your application. The main drawback is that your cluster is limited by your local resources (CPU and memory) and is not a real cluster of machines.
  - You can have an account in a cloud provider and do all development against a remote cluster. The main drawback of this approach is that most developers are not used to working remotely all the time and that someone needs to pay for the remote resources.
- Package managers, like Helm, help you to package, distribute, and install your Kubernetes applications. In this chapter, you installed an application into a Kubernetes cluster with a single command line.
- Understanding which Kubernetes resources are created by your application gives you an idea about how the application will behave when things go wrong and what extra considerations are needed in real-life scenarios.
- Even with very simple applications, you will face challenges that you will have to tackle one at a time. Knowing these challenges ahead of time helps you to plan and architect your services with the right mindset.
- Having a walking skeleton helps you to try different scenarios and technologies in a controlled environment. In this chapter, you have experimented with:
  - Scaling up and down your services to see first-hand how the application behaves when things go wrong.
  - Keeping state is hard, and we will need dedicated components to do this efficiently.

- – Having at least two replicas for our services minimizes downtime. Making sure that the user-facing components are always up and running guarantees that even when things go wrong, the user will be able to interact with parts of the application.
  - – Having fallbacks and built-in mechanisms to deal with problems when they arise makes your application more resilient.
- If you have followed the linked step-by-step tutorial, you now have hands-on experience creating a local Kubernetes cluster, installing an application, scaling up and down services, and, most importantly, checking that the application is running as expected.

Service pipelines: Building
cloud-native applications

This chapter covers

- Discovering the components for delivering cloud-native applications
- Learning the advantages of creating and standardizing service pipelines
- Using Tekton, Dagger, and GitHub Actions to build cloud-native applications

In the previous chapter, you installed and interacted with a simple distributed Conference application composed of four services. This chapter covers what it takes to continuously deliver each component using the *pipeline* concept as a delivery mechanism. This chapter describes and shows in practice how each of these services can be built, packaged, released, and published so they can run in your organization's environments.

This chapter introduces the concept of *service pipelines*. The service pipeline takes all the steps to build your software from source code until the artifacts are ready to run. This chapter is divided into two main sections:

- What does it take to deliver a cloud-native applications continuously?
- Service pipelines
  - What is a service pipeline?
  - Service pipelines in action using:
    - Tekton, a Kubernetes native pipeline engine
    - Dagger to code your pipelines, and then run everywhere
    - Should I use Tekton, Dagger, or GitHub Actions?

3.1 *What does it take to deliver cloud-native applications continuously?*

When working with Kubernetes, teams are now responsible for more moving pieces and tasks involving containers and how to run them in Kubernetes. These extra tasks don't come for free. Teams must learn to automate and optimize the steps required to keep each service running. Tasks that were the responsibility of the operations teams are now becoming more and more the responsibility of the teams in charge of developing each of the individual services. New tools and new approaches give developers the power to develop, run, and maintain the services they produce. The tools that we will look at in this chapter are designed to automate all the tasks involved to go from source code to a service that is up and running inside a Kubernetes cluster. This chapter describes the mechanisms to deliver software components (our application services) to multiple environments where these services will run. But before jumping into the tools, let's take a quick look at the challenges that we are facing.

Building and delivering cloud-native applications present significant challenges that teams must tackle:

- *Dealing with different team interactions when building different pieces of the application:* This requires coordination between teams and ensuring that services are designed so that the team responsible for a service is not blocking other teams' progress or their ability to keep improving their services.
- *We need to support upgrading a service without breaking or stopping all the other running services:* If we want to achieve continuous delivery, services should be upgraded independently without the fear of bringing down the entire application. This teams to think about how backward compatible the new version is and whether the new version can run alongside the old version to avoid big bang upgrades.
- *Storing and publishing several artifacts per service that can be accessed/downloaded from different environments, which might be in different regions:* If we are working in a cloud environment, all servers are remote, and all produced artifacts need to be accessible for each of these servers to fetch. If you are working on an on-premise setup, all the repositories for storing these artifacts must be provisioned, configured, and maintained in-house.

- *Managing and provisioning different environments for various purposes such as development, testing, Q&A, and production:* If you want to speed up your development and testing initiatives, developers and teams should be able to provision these environments on demand. Having environments configured as close as possible to the real production environment will save you a lot of time catching errors before they hit your live users.

As we saw in the previous chapter, the main paradigm shift when working with cloud-native applications is that our application has no single code base. Teams can work independently on their services, but this requires new approaches to compensate for the complexities of working with a distributed system. If teams worry and waste time every time a new service needs to be added to the system, we are doing things wrong. End-to-end automation is necessary for teams to feel comfortable adding or refactoring services. This automation is usually performed by what is commonly known as pipelines. As shown in figure 3.1, these pipelines describe what needs to be done to build and run our services, and usually, they can be executed without human intervention.

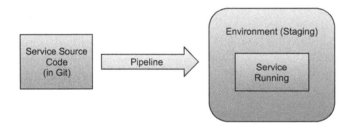

Figure 3.1   We use the concept of a pipeline to transform source code into an artifact that can run inside an environment.

You can even have pipelines to automate the creation of a new service or add new users to your identity management solution. But what are these pipelines doing exactly? Do we need to create our pipelines from scratch? How do we implement these pipelines in our projects? Do we need one or more pipelines to achieve this?

Section 3.2 is focused on using pipelines to build solutions that can be copied, shared, and executed multiple times to produce the same results. Pipelines can be created for different purposes, and it is common to define them as a set of steps (one after the other in sequence) that produce a set of expected outputs. Based on these outputs, these pipelines can be classified into different groups.

Most pipeline tools allow you to define pipelines as a collection of tasks (also known as steps or jobs) that will run a specific job or script to perform a concrete action. These steps can be anything, from running tests, copying code from one place to another, deploying software, provisioning virtual machines, creating users, etc.

Pipeline definitions can be executed by a component known as the *pipeline engine*, which is responsible for picking up the pipeline definition to create a new pipeline instance that runs each task. The tasks will be executed one after the other in sequence, and each task execution might generate data that can be shared with the following task. If there is an error in any of the steps involved with the pipeline, the pipeline stops, and the pipeline state will be marked as an error (failed). If there are no errors, the pipeline execution (also known as pipeline instance) can be marked as successful. Depending on the pipeline definition and whether the execution was successful, we should verify that the expected outputs were generated or produced.

In figure 3.2, we can see the pipeline engine picking up our pipeline definition and creating different instances that can be parameterized differently for different outputs. For example, Pipeline Instance 1 finished correctly, while Pipeline Instance 2 failed to execute all the tasks included in the definition. Pipeline Instance 3, in this case, is still running.

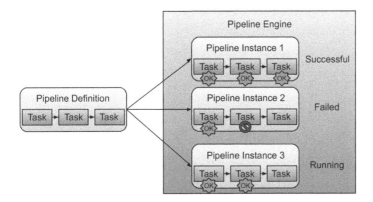

Figure 3.2 **A pipeline definition can be instantiated by a pipeline engine multiple times, and it describes what needs to be done. The pipeline engine creates pipeline Instances, which run the tasks included in the pipeline definition. These pipeline instances can fail or run for longer periods of time depending on the tasks that they are performing. As a user, you can always ask the pipeline engine the status of a particular pipeline instance and its tasks.**

As expected, with these pipeline definitions we can create loads of different automation solutions, and it is common to find tools that build more specific solutions on top of a pipeline engine or even hide the complexity of dealing with a pipeline engine to simplify the user experience. In the following sections, we will look for examples of different tools, some more low-level and flexible, and some higher level, more opinionated, and designed to solve a very concrete scenario.

But how do these concepts and tools apply to delivering cloud-native applications? For cloud-native applications, we have very concrete expectations about how to build, package, release, and publish our software components (services) and where these should be deployed. In the context of delivering cloud-native applications, we can define two main kinds of pipelines:

- *Service pipelines:* These take care of the building, unit testing, packaging, and distributing (usually to an artifact repository) of our software artifacts.

- *Environment pipelines:* These take care of deploying and updating all the services in a given environment, such as staging, testing, production, etc., usually consuming what needs to be deployed from a source of truth.

Chapter 3 focuses on service pipelines, while chapter 4 focuses on tools that help us to define environment pipelines using a more declarative approach known as GitOps.

By separating the build process (service pipeline) and the deployment process (environment pipeline), we give more control to the teams responsible for promoting new versions in front of our customers. Service and environment pipelines are executed on top of different resources and with different expectations. The following section goes into more detail about the steps that we commonly define in our service pipelines. Chapter 4 covers what is expected of environment pipelines.

3.2 Service pipelines

A service pipeline defines and executes all the steps required to build, package, and distribute a service artifact so it can be deployed into an environment. A service pipeline is not responsible for deploying the newly created service artifact, but it can be responsible for notifying interested parties that there is a new version available for the service.

You can share the same pipeline definition for different services if you standardize how your services must be built, packaged, and released. Try to avoid pushing each of your teams to define a completely different pipeline for each service, because they will probably reinvent something that has already been defined, tested, and improved by other teams. A considerable amount of tasks need to be performed, and a set of conventions that, when followed, can reduce the time required to perform the whole process.

The name *service pipeline* refers to the fact that each of our application's services will have a pipeline that describes the tasks required for that particular service. If the services are similar and they are using a similar technology stack, it makes sense for the pipelines to look quite similar. One of the main objectives of these service pipelines is to contain enough detail to run without any human intervention, automating all the tasks in the pipeline end to end.

Service pipelines can be used as a mechanism to improve the communication between the development team that is creating a service and the operations team that is running that service in production. Development teams expect these pipelines to run and notify them if there is any problem with the code they are trying to build. If there are no errors, they will expect one or more artifacts to be produced as part of the pipeline execution. Operations teams can add all the checks to these pipelines to ensure the produced artifacts are production ready. These checks can include policy and conformance checks, signing, security scanning, and other requirements that validate that the produced artifacts are up to the standards expected to run in the production environment.

NOTE It is tempting to think about creating a single pipeline for the entire application (collection of services), as we did with monolith applications. However, that defeats the purpose of independently updating each service at its own pace. You should avoid situations with a single pipeline defined for a set of services, because it will block your ability to release services independently.

3.3 Conventions that will save you time

Service pipelines can be more opinionated on their structure and reach. By following some of these strong opinions and conventions, you can avoid pushing your teams to define every little detail and discover these conventions by trial and error. The following approaches have been proven to work:

- *Trunk-based development:* The idea here is to ensure that what you have in the *main* branch of your source code repository is always ready to be released. You don't merge changes that break this branch's build and release process. You only merge if the changes you are merging are ready to be released. This approach also includes using feature branches, which allow developers to work on features without breaking the main branch. When the features are done and tested, developers can send pull requests (change requests) for other developers to review and merge. This also means that when you merge something to the main branch, you can automatically create a new release of your service (and all the related artifacts). This creates a continuous stream of releases generated after each new feature is merged into the main branch. Because each release is consistent and has been tested, you can then deploy this new release to an environment that contains all the other services of your application. This approach enables the team behind the service to move forward and keep releasing without worrying about other services.

- *Source code and configuration management:* There are different approaches to dealing with software and the configuration needed to run the software we are producing. When we talk about services and distributed applications, there are two different schools of thought:

  - *One service/one repository/one pipeline:* You keep your service source code and all the configurations that need to be built, packaged, released, and deployed in the same repository. This allows the team behind the service to push changes at any pace they want without worrying about other services' source code. It is a common practice to have the source code in the same repository where you have the `Dockerfile` describing how the Docker image should be created and the Kubernetes manifest required to deploy the service into a Kubernetes cluster. These configurations should include the pipeline definition that will be used to build and package your service.

  - *Mono repository:* Alternatively, use a mono repository approach where a single repository is used, and different pipelines are configured for different directories inside the repository. While this approach can work, you need to ensure that your teams are not blocking each other by waiting for each other's pull requests to merge.

- *Consumer-driven contract testing:* Your service uses contracts to run tests against other services. Unit testing an individual service shouldn't require having other services up and running. By creating consumer-driven contracts, each service can test its functionality against other APIs. If any downstream service is released, a new contract is shared with all the upstream services so they can run their tests against the new version.

There are two books that I strongly recommend:

- *Continuous Delivery: Reliable Software Releases through Build, Test, and Deployment Automation* by Jez Humble and David Farley (Addison-Wesley Professional, 2010)
- *Grokking Continuous Delivery* by Christie Wilson (Manning Publications, 2022)

Most of the tools mentioned in these books allow you to implement these practices for efficient delivery. If we take these practices and conventions into account, we can define the responsibility of a service pipeline as follows: *A service pipeline transforms source code to one or a set of artifacts that can be deployed in an environment.*

3.4 *Service pipeline structure*

With this definition in mind, let's take a look at what tasks are included in service pipelines for cloud-native applications that will run on Kubernetes:

- *Register to receive notifications about changes in the source code repository main branch:* (Source version control system, nowadays a Git repository.) If the source code changes, we need to create a new release. We create a new release by triggering the service pipeline. This is usually implemented using webhooks or a pull-based mechanism that checks if new changes were submitted.
- *Clone the source code from the repository:* To build the service, we need to clone the source code into a machine that has the tools to build/compile the source code into a binary format that can be executed.
- *Create a new tag for the new version to be released:* Based on trunk-based development, a new release can be created every time a change happens. This will help us to understand what is being deployed and what changes were included in each new release.
- *Build and test the source code:*
  - As part of the build process, most projects will execute unit tests and break the build if there are any failures.
  - Depending on our technology stack, we will need tools available for this step, for example, compilers, dependencies, linters (static source code analyzers), etc.

- Tools like CodeCov, which measures how much of the code is being covered by tests, are used to block changes from being merged if a coverage threshold is not met.
- Security scanners are also used to evaluate vulnerabilities on our application dependencies. If a new CVE (Common Vulnerabilities and Exposures) is found, the change can be blocked too.

- *Publish the binary artifacts into an artifact repository:* We need to make sure that these binaries are available for other systems to consume, including the next steps in the pipeline. This step involves copying the binary artifact to a different location over the network. This artifact will share the same version of the tag created in the repository, providing us with traceability from the binary to the source code used to produce it.

- *Building a container image:* If we are building cloud-native services, we must build a container image. The most common way of doing this today is using Docker or other container alternatives. This step requires the source code repository to have, for example, a `Dockerfile` defining how this container image needs to be built and the mechanism to build (builder) the container image. Some tools like CNCF Buildpacks (https://buildpacks.io) save us from having a `Dockerfile` and can automate the container-building process. Having the right tools for the job is essential, because multiple container images might need to be generated for different platforms. For a released service, we might have more than one container image, for example, one for `amd64` and one for `arm64` platforms. All the examples in this book are built for these two platforms.

- *Publish the container image into a container registry:* In the same way that we published the binary artifacts generated when building our service source code, we need to publish our container image into a centralized location where others can access it. This container image will have the same version as the tag created in the repository and the binary published. This helps us see which source code will run when you run the container image.

- *Lint, verify, and optionally package YAML files for Kubernetes deployments (Helm can be used here):* If you are running these containers inside Kubernetes, you need to manage, store, and version a Kubernetes manifest that defines how the containers are going to be deployed into a Kubernetes cluster. If you use a package manager such as Helm, you can version the package with the same version used for the binaries and the container image. My rule for packaging YAML files goes as follows: "If you have enough people trying to install your services (open-source project or very large globally distributed organization), you might want to package and version your YAML files. If you only have a few teams and environments to handle, you can probably distribute the YAML files without using a packaging tool."

- *(Optional) Publish these Kubernetes manifests to a centralized location:* If you are using Helm, it makes sense to push these Helm packages (called Charts) to a centralized location. This will allow other tools to fetch these Charts so they can be deployed in any number of Kubernetes clusters. As we saw in chapter 2, these Helm Charts can now be distributed as OCI container images to a container registry.

- *Notify interested parties about the new version of the service:* If we are trying to automate from a source to a service running, the service pipeline can send notifications to all the interested services that might be waiting for new versions to be deployed. These notifications can be pull requests to other repositories, events to an event bus, emails to the teams interested in these releases, etc. A pull-based approach can also work, where an agent constantly monitors the artifact repository (or container registry) to see if new versions are available for a given artifact.

Figure 3.3 shows the steps described in the previous bullet points as a sequence of steps. Most pipeline tools will have a visual representation that allows you to see which steps will be executed.

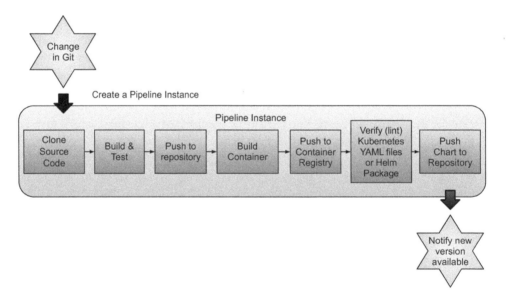

Figure 3.3   Service pipelines automate all the steps required to produce artifacts that can run in multiple environments. Service pipelines are often triggered by changes in source code, but are not in charge of deploying the created artifacts in a specific environment. They can notify other components about these new versions.

The outcome of this pipeline is a set of artifacts that can be deployed to an environment to have the service up and running. The service needs to be built and packaged in a way that does not depend on any specific environment. The service can depend on other services to work in the environment, such as infrastructural components like databases, message brokers, or other downstream services.

No matter the tool that you choose to use to implement these pipelines, you should be looking at the following characteristics:

- Pipelines run automatically based on changes (if you follow trunk-based development, one pipeline instance is created for every change in the repository's main branch).

- Pipelines executions will notify about the success or failure state with clear messages. This includes having easy ways to find, for example, the why and where the pipeline failed or how much time it takes to execute each step.

- Each pipeline execution has a unique `id` that we can use to access the log and the parameters that were used to run the pipeline, so we can reproduce the setup that was used to troubleshoot problems. Using this unique `id`, we can also access the logs created by all the steps in the pipeline. By looking at the pipeline execution, we should also be able to find all the produced artifacts and where those were published.

- Pipelines can also be triggered manually and configured with different parameters for special situations. For example, to test a work-in-progress feature branch.

Let's now deep dive into the concrete details of what a service pipeline will look like in real life.

3.4.1 *Service pipeline in real life*

In real life, a service pipeline will run every time you merge changes to the main branch of your repository. This is how it should work if you follow a trunk-based development approach:

- When you merge changes to your main branch, this service pipeline runs and creates a set of artifacts using the latest code base. If the service pipeline succeeds, our artifacts will be releasable. We want to ensure that our main branch is always in a releasable state, so the service pipeline that runs on top of the main branch must always succeed. If, for some reason, this pipeline is failing, the team behind the service needs to switch the focus to fixing the problem as soon as possible. In other words, teams shouldn't merge code into your main branch that breaks its service pipeline. We must also run a pipeline in our feature branches to do that.

- For each of your feature branches, a very similar pipeline should run to verify that the changes in the branch can be built, tested, and released against the main branch. In modern environments, the concept of GitHub pull requests is used to run these pipelines to make sure that before merging any pull request, a pipeline validates the changes.

- It is common that after merging a set of features to the main branch, and because we know that the main branch is releasable at all times, the team in charge of the service decides to tag a new release. In Git, a new tag (a pointer to a specific commit) is created based on the main branch. The tag name is commonly used to represent the version of the artifact that the pipeline will create.

Figure 3.4 shows the pipelines configured for the main branch and a generic pipeline to validate feature branches only when pull requests are created. Multiple instances of these pipelines can be triggered to validate new changes continuously.

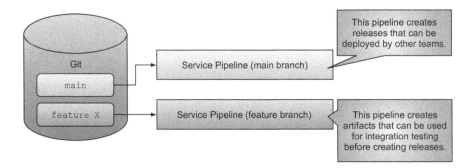

Figure 3.4   Service pipelines for main branch and feature branches

The service pipeline shown in figure 3.4 represents the most common steps you must execute every time you merge something to the main branch. Still, there are also some variations of this pipeline that you might need to run under different circumstances. Different events can kick off a pipeline execution, and we can have slightly different pipelines for different purposes, such as:

- *Validate a change in a feature branch:* This pipeline can execute the same steps as the pipeline in the main branch, but the artifacts generated should include the branch name, maybe as a version or as part of the artifact name. Running a pipeline after every change might be too expensive and not needed all the time, so you should decide based on your needs.
- *Validate a pull request (PR)/change request:* The pipeline will validate that the pull request/change request changes are valid and that artifacts can be produced with the recent changes. Usually, the result of the pipeline can be notified back to the user in charge of merging the PR and also block the merging options if the pipeline is failing. This pipeline is used to validate that whatever is merged into the main branch is valid and can be released. Validating pull requests and change requests can be an excellent option to avoid running pipelines for every change in the feature branches. When the developer(s) is ready to get feedback from the build system, it can create a PR that will trigger the pipeline. The pipeline would be retriggered if developers made changes on top of the pull request.

Despite minor differences and optimizations that can be added to these pipelines, the behavior and produced artifacts are mostly the same. These conventions and approaches rely on the pipelines executing enough tests to validate that the produced service can be deployed to an environment.

3.4.2   *Service pipeline requirements*

This section covers the infrastructural requirements for service pipelines to work and the contents of the source repository required for the pipeline to do its work.

Let's start with the infrastructural requirements that a service pipeline needs to work:

- *Webhooks for source code change notifications:* First, it needs access to register webhooks to the Git repository with the service's source code, so a pipeline instance can be created when a new change is merged into the main branch.

- *Artifact repository available and valid credentials to push the binary artifacts:* Once the source code is built, we need to push the newly created artifact to the artifact repository where all artifacts are stored. This requires configuring an artifact repository with valid credentials to push new artifacts.

- *Container registry and valid credentials to push new container images:* In the same way as we need to push binary artifacts, we need to distribute our docker containers, so Kubernetes clusters can fetch the images when we want to provision a new instance of a service. A container registry with valid credentials is needed to accomplish this step.

- *Helm Chart repository and valid credentials:* Kubernetes manifest can be packaged and distributed as Helm Charts. If you are using Helm, you must have a Helm Chart repository and valid credentials to push these packages.

Figure 3.5 shows the most common external systems a pipeline instance will interact with. From a Git repository to artifact repositories and container registries, the team maintaining these pipelines must ensure that the right credentials are in place and that these components are reachable (from a network perspective) from where the pipelines are running.

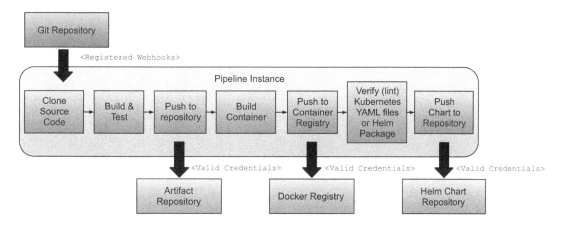

Figure 3.5 **Running pipelines requires a lot of infrastructure to be in place. This includes maintaining services and repositories, creating users and credentials, and making sure that these services (repositories) are accessible from remote locations.**

For service pipelines to do their job, the repository containing the service's source code also needs to have a `Dockerfile` or the ways to produce a container image and the necessary Kubernetes manifest to deploy the service into Kubernetes.

Figure 3.6 shows a possible directory layout of our service source code repository, which includes the source (src) directory containing all the files that will be compiled into binary format. The `Dockerfile` is used to build our container image for the service, and the Helm Chart directory contains all the files to create a Helm chart that can be distributed to install the service into a Kubernetes cluster. You can decide between having a Helm Chart per service or a single Helm Chart for all the application services.

Figure 3.6 shows the service layout, including the Helm Chart definition. This can help to package and distribute services independently. If we include everything needed to build, package, and run our service into a Kubernetes cluster, the service pipeline needs to run after every change in the main branch to create a new service release.

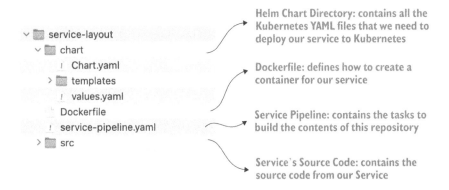

Figure 3.6   The service source code repository needs to have all the configurations for the service pipeline to work.

In summary, service pipelines are responsible for building our source and related artifacts to be deployed into an environment. As mentioned, service pipelines are not responsible for deploying the produced service into a live environment. The environment pipeline's responsibility is covered in the next chapter.

3.4.3   *Opinions, limitations, and compromises around service pipelines*

No "one size fits all" solution exists for creating our service pipelines. In real life, you must make compromises depending on your requirements. Before looking at tools like Tekton, Dagger, and GitHub Actions, let me quickly touch on some practical aspects I've seen teams fighting with. Here is a short and non-comprehensive list of things to consider when designing your service pipelines:

- *Avoid strict rules and opinions to define where service pipelines start and end:* For example, your services might not need to be packaged as Helm Charts, as mentioned in the previous sections. If there are not enough cases when you want to install an isolated service—for example, your service depends heavily on other services—removing that step from the service pipeline and the chart definition from the service repository might make a lot of sense.
- *Understand the lifecycle of your components and artifacts:* Depending on how often services change and their dependencies, service pipelines can be linked together to

build a set of services together. Mapping these relationships and understanding the needs of the teams operating these services will give you the right granularity to create your service pipelines. For example, you can enable your teams to keep releasing new container images for new versions of the services that they are working on, but a different team controls the cadence and release of the Helm Charts that bundle all the application services together.

- *Find what works best for your organization:* Optimize end-to-end automation based on business priorities. If a critical service is causing delays to be released and deployed, focus on having the service pipeline ready and fully functional before trying to cover other services. There is no point in creating generic solutions that might take a while to figure out that your organization suffers 80% of the cases with a single service.

- *Do not create unnecessary steps until they are required:* I've heavily mentioned tools like Helm in this book to package and distribute Kubernetes manifest, but I am not suggesting that is the way to go. I've used Helm as an example tool that is widely adopted, but you might be in a situation where you don't need to package your Kubernetes manifest for distribution. Your service pipeline shouldn't have that step if that's the case. If the need arises later, you can extend your service pipelines to include more steps.

Let's now jump to see some tools in this space.

3.5 Service pipelines in action

There are several pipeline engines out there, even fully managed services like GitHub Actions (https://github.com/features/actions) and several well-known CI (continuous integration) managed services that will provide loads of integrations for you to build and package your application's services.

In the following sections, we will examine two projects: Tekton and Dagger. These projects provide you with the tools to work with cloud-native applications and, as we will see in chapter 6, enable platform teams to package, distribute, and reuse the organization's specific knowledge built over time. Tekton (https://tekton.dev) was designed as a pipeline engine for Kubernetes. Because Tekton is a generic pipeline engine, you can create any pipeline with it. On the other hand, a much newer project called Dagger (https://dagger.io) was designed to run everywhere. We will contrast Tekton and Dagger with GitHub actions.

3.5.1 Tekton in action

Tekton was initially created as part of the Knative project (https://knative.dev) from Google. (We will look more into Knative in chapter 8). Tekton was initially called Knative Build, and later separated from Knative to be an independent project. Tekton's main characteristic is that it is a cloud-native pipeline engine designed for Kubernetes. This section will look into how to use Tekton to define service pipelines.

In Tekton, you have two main concepts: tasks and pipelines. In Tekton, the pipeline engine is a set of components that understand how to execute `Tasks` and `Pipelines` Kubernetes resources. Tekton, like most of the Kubernetes projects covered in this book, can be installed into your Kubernetes cluster. I strongly recommend you check their official documentation page, which explains the value of using a tool like Tekton at https://tekton.dev/docs/concepts/overview/.

> **NOTE**   I've included a set of step-by-step tutorials in this repository. You can start by looking at how to install Tekton in your cluster and the `tekton/hello -world/` example at https://github.com/salaboy/platforms-on-k8s/tree/main/ chapter-3/tekton.

When you install Tekton, you install a set of custom resource definitions, which are extensions to the Kubernetes APIs, that define tasks and pipelines. Tekton also installs the pipeline engine that knows how to deal with `Tasks` and `Pipelines` resources. Notice that after installing Tekton, you can also install the Tekton Dashboard and the `tkn` command-line interface tool.

Once you install the Tekton release, you will see a new namespace called `tekton -pipelines`, which contains the pipeline controller (the pipeline engine), and the pipeline webhook listener, which is used to listen for events coming from external sources, such as git repositories.

A task in Tekton will look like a normal Kubernetes resource, as shown in listing 3.1.

Listing 3.1   Simple Tekton task definition

```
apiVersion: tekton.dev/v1
kind: Task
metadata:
 name: hello-world-task
spec:
  params:
    - name: name
      type: string
      description: who do you want to welcome?
      default: tekton user
  steps:
    - name: echo
      image: ubuntu
      command:
        - echo
      args:
        - "Hello World: $(params.name)"
```

The name of the resource defined in metadata.name represents the task definition name.

We can use the params section to define which parameters can be configured for our task definition.

The Docker image called Ubuntu is going to be used for this task.

The command arguments (args) in this case are just a "Hello World: $(params.name)" string, which will use the Task parameter.

The command arguments (args) in this case are just a "Hello World" string; notice that you can send a list of arguments for more complex commands.

You can find the task definition in this repository, alongside a step-by-step tutorial to run it in your cluster: https://github.com/salaboy/platforms-on-k8s/blob/main/chapter-3/tekton/hello-world/hello-world-task.yaml.

Derived from this example, you can create a task for whatever you want, because you have the flexibility to define which container to use and which commands to run. Once you have the task definition, you need to make that available to Tekton by applying this file to the cluster with `kubectl apply -f task.yaml`. By applying the file into Kubernetes, we are only making the definition available to the Tekton components in the cluster, but the task will not run.

If you want to run this task, a task can be executed multiple times. Tekton requires you to create a TaskRun resource like the following listing.

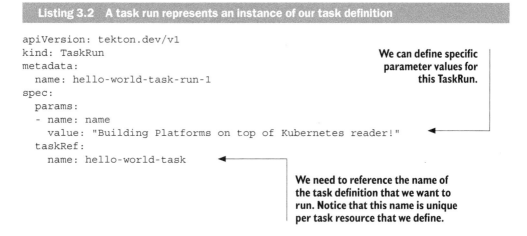

Listing 3.2   A task run represents an instance of our task definition

```
apiVersion: tekton.dev/v1
kind: TaskRun
metadata:
  name: hello-world-task-run-1
spec:
  params:
  - name: name
    value: "Building Platforms on top of Kubernetes reader!"
  taskRef:
    name: hello-world-task
```

We can define specific parameter values for this TaskRun.

We need to reference the name of the task definition that we want to run. Notice that this name is unique per task resource that we define.

The TaskRun resource can be found at https://github.com/salaboy/platforms-on-k8s/blob/main/chapter-3/tekton/hello-world/task-run.yaml.

If you apply this TaskRun to the cluster (`kubectl apply -f taskrun.yaml`), the pipeline engine will execute this task. You can take a look at the Tekton task in action by looking at the TaskRun resources in listing 3.3.

Listing 3.3   Get all TaskRun instances

```
> kubectl get taskrun
NAME                      SUCCEEDED    STARTTIME    COMPLETIONTIME
hello-world-task-run-1    True         66s          7s
```

If you list all the running pods, you will notice that each task creates a pod, as shown in listing 3.4.

Listing 3.4 List all the pods associated to TaskRuns

```
> kubectl get pods
NAME                                    READY   STATUS     AGE
hello-world-task-run-1-pod              0/1     Init:0/1   2s
```

And because you have a pod, you can tail the logs to see what the task is doing as in listing 3.5.

Listing 3.5 Accessing the TaskRun logs using the pod name

```
> kubectl logs -f hello-world-task-run-1-pod
Defaulted container "step-echo" out of: step-echo, prepare (init)
Hello World: Building Platforms on top of Kubernetes reader!
```

You just executed your first Tekton TaskRun. Congrats! But a single task is not interesting at all. If we can sequence multiple tasks together, we can create our service pipelines. Let's look at how we can build Tekton pipelines from this simple task example.

3.5.2 Pipelines in Tekton

A task can be helpful, but Tekton becomes interesting when you create sequences of these tasks using pipelines.

A pipeline is a collection of these tasks in a concrete sequence. The following pipeline uses the task definition that we defined earlier. It prints a message, fetches a file from a URL, and then reads its content, which is forwarded to our Hello World task, which prints a message.

Figure 3.7 shows a simple Tekton pipeline comprising three Tekton tasks.

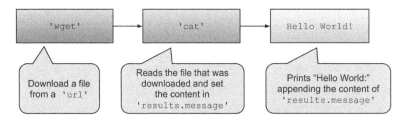

Figure 3.7 Simple Tekton pipeline using our Hello World task

In this simple pipeline, we are using an existing task definition (`wget`) from the Tekton Hub, which is a community repository hosting generic tasks, and then we are defining the `cat` task inline inside the pipeline to showcase Tekton flexibility, to finally use the `Hello World` task that we defined in the previous section.

Let's look at a simple service pipeline defined in Tekton (`hello-world-pipeline .yaml`). Don't be scared. This is a lot of YAML, I warned you. See listing 3.6.

Listing 3.6 Pipeline definition

```
apiVersion: tekton.dev/v1
kind: Pipeline
metadata:
  name: hello-world-pipeline
  annotations:
    description: |
      Fetch resource from internet, cat content and then say hello
spec:
  results:
  - name: message
    type: string
    value: $(tasks.cat.results.messageFromFile)
  params:
  - name: url
    description: resource that we want to fetch
    type: string
    default: ""
  workspaces:
  - name: files
  tasks:
  - name: wget
    taskRef:
      name: wget
    params:
    - name: url
      value: "$(params.url)"
    - name: diroptions
      value:
        - "-P"
    workspaces:
    - name: wget-workspace
      workspace: files
  - name: cat
    runAfter: [wget]
    workspaces:
    - name: wget-workspace
      workspace: files
    taskSpec:
      workspaces:
      - name: wget-workspace
      results:
        - name: messageFromFile
          description: the message obtained from the file
      steps:
```

Pipeline resources can define an array of results that are expected from the pipeline when they are executed. Tasks can set these results values when they are executed.

In the same way as tasks, we can define which parameters can be set by the user when running this pipeline. These pipeline parameters can be forwarded to individual tasks if needed.

We use a task reference to a task we didn't create. We need to make sure to install this task definition before creating a PipelineRun for this pipeline.

Pipelines and tasks allow the use of Tekton Workspaces to store persistent information. This can be used to share information between tasks. As each task is executed in its container, using persistent storage to share information is easy to set up.

We can define tasks inline the pipeline if we want to. This makes the pipeline file more complicated, but sometimes it is useful to have a task that just glues other tasks together, as is shown in this case. The only purpose of this task is to read the content of the downloaded file and make it available as a String for our Hello World task that doesn't accept a file.

```
    - name: cat
      image: bash:latest
      script: |
        #!/usr/bin/env bash
        cat $(workspaces.wget-workspace.path)/welcome.md |
➥tee /tekton/results/messageFromFile
  - name: hello-world
    runAfter: [cat]
    taskRef:
      name: hello-world-task
    params:
      - name: name
        value: "$(tasks.cat.results.messageFromFile)"
```

This also requires installing the "hello-world-task" definition in the cluster. Remember that you can always run "kubectl get tasks" to see which tasks are available.

We can use Tekton's powerful templating mechanism to provide the value for Hello World task. We are using a reference to the "cat" task results.

You can find the full pipeline definition at https://github.com/salaboy/platforms -on-k8s/blob/main/chapter-3/tekton/hello-world/hello-world-pipeline.yaml.

Before applying the pipeline definition, you need to install the `wget` Tekton task that was created and maintained by the Tekton community:

```
kubectl apply -f
➥https://raw.githubusercontent.com/tektoncd/catalog/main/task/wget/0.1/wget.yaml
```

Once again, you must apply this pipeline resource to your cluster for Tekton to know about: `kubectl apply –f hello-world-pipeline.yaml`.

As you can see in the pipeline definition, the `spec.tasks` field contains an array of tasks. These tasks need to be already deployed into the cluster, and the pipeline definition defines the sequence in which these tasks will be executed. These task references can be your tasks, or as in the example, they can come from the Tekton catalog, a repository containing community-maintained task definitions that you can reuse.

In the same way, because tasks need TaskRuns for the executions, you will need to create a PipelineRun for every time you want to execute your pipeline, as shown in the following listing.

> **Listing 3.7   PipelineRun represent an instance (execution) of our pipelines**

When we create a PipelineRun, we need to bound the workspaces defined in the pipeline definition to real storage. In this case a VolumeClaim is created requesting I Mb of storage for the PipelineRun to use.

```
apiVersion: tekton.dev/v1
kind: PipelineRun
metadata:
  name: hello-world-pipeline-run-1
spec:
  workspaces:
    - name: files
      volumeClaimTemplate:
        spec:
```

```
        accessModes:
        - ReadWriteOnce
        resources:
          requests:
            storage: 1M
    params:
    - name: url
      value:
➥"https://raw.githubusercontent.com/salaboy/salaboy/main/welcome.md"
    pipelineRef:
      name: hello-world-pipeline
```

The pipeline parameter "url" can be any URL that you want as soon because it is accessible from the PipelineRun context (meaning that it can reach the URL, and it is not behind a firewall).

As with tasks, we need to provide the name of the pipeline definition that we want to use for this PipelineRun.

You can find the PipelineRun resource at https://github.com/salaboy/platforms-on -k8s/blob/main/chapter-3/tekton/hello-world/pipeline-run.yaml.

When you apply this file to the cluster `kubectl apply -f pipeline-run.yaml`, Tekton will execute the pipeline by running all the tasks defined in the pipeline definition. When running this pipeline, Tekton will create one pod per task and three TaskRun resources. A pipeline is just orchestrating tasks, or in other words creating TaskRuns.

To check that the TaskRuns were created and that the pipeline executed successfully, see listing 3.8.

Listing 3.8 Getting task runs from the pipeline execution

```
> kubectl get taskrun
NAME                                     SUCCEEDED  STARTTIME  COMPLETIONTIME
hello-world-pipeline-run-1-cat           True       109s       104s
hello-world-pipeline-run-1-hello-world   True       103s       98s
hello-world-pipeline-run-1-wget          True       117s       109s
```

For each TaskRun, Tekton created a pod (listing 3.9).

Listing 3.9 Checking that all TaskRuns belonging to the pipeline have finished

```
> kubectl get pods
NAME                                         READY  STATUS     AGE
hello-world-pipeline-run-1-cat-pod           0/1    Completed  11s
hello-world-pipeline-run-1-hello-world-pod   0/1    Completed  5s
hello-world-pipeline-run-1-wget-pod          0/1    Completed  19s
```

Review the logs from the `hello-world-pipeline-run-1-hello-world-pod` to see what the task printed, as shown in listing 3.10.

Listing 3.10 Getting the logs from the last task

```
> kubectl logs hello-world-pipeline-run-1-hello-world-pod
Defaulted container "step echo" out of: step echo, prepare (init)
Hello World: Welcome, Internet traveler! Do you want to learn more about
Platforms on top of Kubernetes? Check this repository: https://github.com/
salaboy/platforms-on-k8s
```

You can always look at Tasks, TaskRuns, Pipelines, and PipelineRuns in the Tekton dashboard. To access the Tekton dashboard, if you installed it in your cluster, you need to first run:

```
> kubectl port-forward -n tekton-pipelines
➥services/tekton-dashboard 9097:9097
```

Figure 3.8 shows the Tekton dashboard user interface, where we can explore our task and pipeline definitions as well as trigger new task and pipeline runs and explore the logs that each task outputs.

Figure 3.8   Our PipelineRun execution in the Tekton dashboard

If required, you can find a step-by-step tutorial on how to install Tekton in your Kubernetes cluster and how to run the service pipeline at the following repository: https://github.com/salaboy/platforms-on-k8s/blob/main/chapter-3/tekton/hello-world/README.md.

At the end of the tutorial, you will find links to more complex pipelines I've defined for each Conference application service. These pipelines are more complex because they require access to external services, credentials to publish artifacts and container images, and the rights to do some privileged actions inside the cluster. Check this section of the tutorial if you are interested in more details: https://github.com/salaboy/platforms-on-k8s/tree/main/chapter-3/tekton#tekton-for-service-pipelines.

3.5.3   *Tekton advantages and extras*

As we have seen, Tekton is super flexible and allows you to create advanced pipelines, and it includes other features, such as:

- Input and output mappings to share data between tasks
- Event triggers that allow you to listen for events that will trigger pipelines or tasks
- A command-line tool to easily interact with tasks and pipelines from your terminal
- A simple dashboard to monitor your pipelines and task executions (figure 3.9)

Figure 3.9 Tekton dashboard—a user interface for monitoring your pipelines

Figure 3.9 shows the community-driven Tekton dashboard, which you can use to visualize the execution of your pipelines. Remember that because Tekton was built to work on top of Kubernetes, you can monitor your pipelines using `kubectl` as with any other Kubernetes resource. Still, nothing beats a user interface for less technical users.

But now, if you want to implement a service pipeline with Tekton, you will spend quite a bit of time defining tasks, the pipeline, how to map inputs and outputs, defining the right events listener for your Git repositories, and then going more low-level into defining which docker images you will use for each task. Creating and maintaining these pipelines and their associated resources can become a full-time job, and for that, Tekton launched an initiative to define a catalog where tasks (pipelines and resources are planned for future releases) can be shared. The Tekton catalog is available at https://github.com/tektoncd/catalog.

With the help of the Tekton catalog, we can create pipelines that reference tasks defined in the catalog. In the previous section, we used the `wget` task downloaded from this catalog; you can find a full description of the `wget` task at https://hub.tekton.dev/tekton/task/wget. Hence, we don't need to worry about defining them. You can also visit https://hub.tekton.dev, which allows you to search for task definitions and provides detailed documentation about installing and using these tasks in your pipelines (figure 3.10).

Tekton Hub and the Tekton catalog allow you to reuse tasks and pipelines created by a large community of users and companies. I strongly recommend you check out the Tekton Overview page, which summarizes the advantages of using Tekton, including who should use Tekton and why: https://tekton.dev/docs/concepts/overview/.

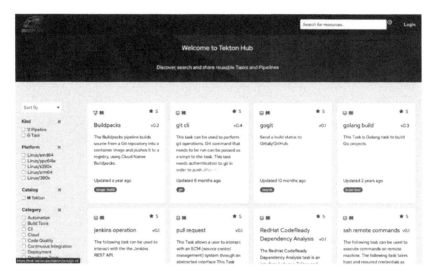

Figure 3.10   Tekton Hub is a portal to share and reuse tasks and pipeline definitions

Tekton is quite a mature project in the cloud-native space, but it also presents some challenges:

- You need to install and maintain Tekton running inside a Kubernetes cluster. You don't want your pipelines running right beside your application workloads, so you might need a separate cluster.
- There is no easy way to run a Tekton pipeline locally. For development purposes, you rely on having access to a Kubernetes cluster to run a pipeline manually.
- You need to know Kubernetes to define and create tasks and pipelines.
- While Tekton provides some conditional logic, it is limited by what you can do in YAML and using a declarative approach of Kubernetes.

We will now jump into a project called Dagger that was created to mitigate some of these points, not to replace Tekton but to provide a different approach to solving everyday challenges when building complex pipelines.

3.5.4   *Dagger in action*

Dagger (https://dagger.io) was born with one objective: "to enable developers to build pipelines using their favorite programming language that they can run everywhere." Dagger only relies on a container runtime to run pipelines that can be defined using code that every developer can write. Dagger currently supports Go, Python, TypeScript, and JavaScript SDKs, but the team behind Dagger is quickly expanding to new languages.

Dagger is not focused on Kubernetes only. Platform teams must ensure that while teams use Kubernetes' powerful and declarative nature, also development teams can be productive and use the appropriate tool for the job. This short section will examine how Dagger compares with Tekton, where it can fit better, and where it can complement other tools.

If you are interested in getting started with Dagger, you can check these resources:

- *Dagger docs*: https://docs.dagger.io
- *Dagger Quickstart*: https://docs.dagger.io/648215/quickstart/
- *Dagger GraphQL playground*: https://play.dagger.cloud

Dagger, like Tekton, also has a pipeline engine, but this engine can work both locally and remotely, providing a unified runtime across environments. Dagger doesn't directly integrate with Kubernetes. This means that there are no Kubernetes CRDs or YAML involved. This can be important depending on the skills and preferences of the teams in charge of creating and maintaining these pipelines.

In Dagger, we define pipelines by writing code. Because pipelines are just code, these pipelines can be distributed using any code packaging tools. For example, if our pipelines are written in Go, we can use Go modules to import pipelines or tasks written by other teams. If we use Java, we can use Maven or Gradle to package and distribute our pipeline libraries to promote reuse.

Figure 3.11 shows how development teams can write pipelines using the Dagger SDKs and then use the Dagger engine to execute these pipelines using any OCI Container Runtime such as Docker or PodMan. It doesn't matter if you want to run your pipelines in your local development environment (your laptop with Docker for Mac or Windows), your continuous integration environment, or even inside Kubernetes. These pipelines will behave in the same way.

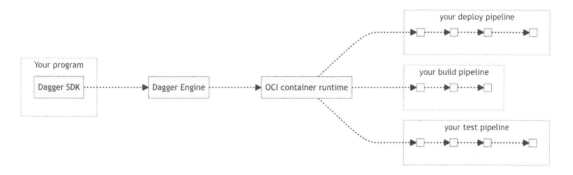

Figure 3.11 **Using your preferred programming language and its tools to write pipelines (Source: dagger.io)**

The Dagger pipeline engine is then in charge of orchestrating the tasks defined in the pipelines and optimizing what is requested by the container runtime used to execute each task. A significant advantage of the Dagger pipeline engine is that it was designed from the ground up to optimize how pipelines run. Imagine that you are building tons of services multiple times a day. You will not only keep your CPUs hot, but the amount of traffic downloading artifacts, again and again, becomes expensive—more if you are running on top of a cloud provider, which charges you based on consumption.

Dagger, similar to Tekton, uses containers to execute each task (step) in the pipeline. The pipeline engine optimizes the resource consumption by caching the results of previous executions, preventing you from re-executing tasks that were already executed using the same inputs. In addition, you can run the Dagger engine locally on your laptop/workstation or remotely, even inside a Kubernetes cluster.

When I compare Dagger to something like Tekton, with my developer background, I tend to like the flexibility of coding pipelines using a programming language I am familiar with. For developers to create, version and share code is easy, because I don't need to learn any new tools.

Instead of looking at a Hello World example, I wanted to show how a service pipeline would look in Dagger. So, let's look at how a service pipeline is defined using the Dagger Go SDK. The following code snippet shows a service pipeline defining the main goals we want to execute for each service. Take a look at the `buildService`, `test Service`, and `publishService` functions. These functions codify what it means to build, test, and publish each service. These functions use the Dagger client to execute actions inside containers that Dagger will orchestrate, as shown in listing 3.11.

> **Listing 3.11   Go application defining tasks using Dagger**

```go
func main() {
  var err error
  ctx := context.Background()

  if len(os.Args) < 2 {
    ...)
  }

  client := getDaggerClient(ctx)
  defer client.Close()
  switch os.Args[1] {
    case "build":
      if len(os.Args) < 3 {
        panic(...)
      }
      _, err = buildService(ctx, client, os.Args[2])

    case "test":
      err = testService(ctx, client, os.Args[2])
    case "publish":
      pv, err := buildService(ctx, client, os.Args[2])

      err = publishService(ctx, client, os.Args[2], pv, os.Args[3])
    case "all":
      pv, err := buildService(ctx, client, os.Args[2])

      err = testService(ctx, client, os.Args[2])
```

```
      err = publishService(ctx, client, os.Args[2], pv, os.Args[3])
   default:
     log.Fatalln("invalid command specified")

}
```

You can find the `service-pipeline.go` definition at https://github.com/salaboy/ platforms-on-k8s/blob/main/conference-application/service-pipeline.go.

By running `go run service-pipeline.go build notifications-service` Dagger will use containers to build our Go application source code and then build a container ready to be pushed to a container registry. If you look at the `buildService` function in listing 3.12, you will notice that it builds our service source code, in this case, looping over a list of target platforms (amd64 and arm64) to produce binaries for each of them. Once the binaries are produced, a container is created using the Dagger client `client.Container` function. Because we are defining each step programmatically, we can also define what needs to be cached for subsequent builds (using `client.CacheVolume`).

> **Listing 3.12 Tasks: Go code that uses Dagger built-in functions**

```
func buildService(ctx context.Context,
                  client *dagger.Client,
                  dir string) ([]*dagger.Container, error) {
  srcDir := client.Host().Directory(dir)

  platformVariants := make([]*dagger.Container, 0, len(platforms))
  for _, platform := range platforms {
    ctr := client.Container()
    ctr = ctr.From("golang:1.20-alpine")

    // mount in our source code
    ctr = ctr.WithDirectory("/src", srcDir)
    ctr = ctr.WithMountedCache("/go/pkg/mod", client.CacheVolume("go-mod"))
    ctr = ctr.WithMountedCache("/root/.cache/go-build",
    ➥ client.CacheVolume("go-build"))

    // mount in an empty dir to put the built binary
    ctr = ctr.WithDirectory("/output", client.Directory())

    // ensure the binary will be statically linked and thus executable
    // in the final image
    ctr = ctr.WithEnvVariable("CGO_ENABLED", "0")

    // configure go to support different architectures
    ctr = ctr.WithEnvVariable("GOOS", "linux")
    ctr = ctr.WithEnvVariable("GOARCH", architecture(platform))

    // build the binary and put the result at the mounted output directory
    ctr = ctr.WithWorkdir("/src")
    ctr = ctr.WithExec([]string{"go", "build","-o", "/output/app",".",})
    // select the output directory
    outputDir := ctr.Directory("/output")
```

```
// create a new container with the output and the platform label
binaryCtr := client.Container(dagger.ContainerOpts{Platform: platform}).
                 WithEntrypoint([]string{"./app"}).
                 WithRootfs(outputDir)
  platformVariants = append(platformVariants, binaryCtr)
}
return platformVariants, nil
}
```

These pipelines are written in Go and build Go applications, but nothing stops you from building other languages and using the necessary tools. Each task is just a container. Dagger and the open-source community will create all the basic building blocks, but each organization has to create domain-specific libraries to integrate with third-party or in-house/legacy systems. By focusing on enabling developers, Dagger lets you choose the right tool(s) to create these integrations. There is no need to write plugins, just code that can be distributed as any other library.

Try running the pipeline for one of the services or follow the step-by-step tutorial that you can find at https://github.com/salaboy/platforms-on-k8s/blob/main/chapter-3/dagger/README.md. If you run the pipeline twice, the second run will be almost instant since most steps are cached.

In contrast with Tekton, we are running the Dagger pipeline locally, not in a Kubernetes cluster, which has advantages. For example, we don't need a Kubernetes cluster to run and test this pipeline, and we don't need to wait for remote feedback. Developers can run these pipelinesby using a local container runtime (like Docker or Podman), including integration tests, before pushing any changes to the Git repository. Having fast feedback allows them to go faster.

But now, how does this translate to a remote environment? What if we want to run this pipeline remotely on a Kubernetes cluster? The good news is that it works the same: it is just a remote Dagger pipeline engine that will execute our pipelines. No matter where this remote pipeline engine is, running inside Kubernetes or as a managed service, our pipeline behavior and the caching mechanisms provided by the pipeline engine will behave the same way. Figure 3.12 shows how the execution will go if we install the Dagger pipeline engine inside Kubernetes and run the same pipelines.

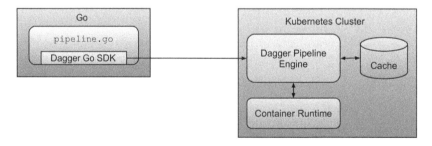

Figure 3.12   When configured against a remote Dagger Pipeline Engine, the Dagger SDK will collect and send the context for the pipeline to be executed remotely.

When the Dagger Pipeline Engine is installed in a remote environment such as a Kubernetes Cluster, virtual machine, or any other computing resource, we can connect and run our pipelines against it. The Dagger Go SDK takes all the context needed from the local environment and sends it to the Dagger Pipeline Engine to execute the tasks remotely. We don't need to worry about publishing our application source code online for the pipeline.

Check this step-by-step tutorial on how to run your Dagger pipelines on Kubernetes: https://github.com/salaboy/platforms-on-k8s/blob/main/chapter-3/dagger/README.md#running-your-pipelines-remotely-on-kubernetes.

As you can see, Dagger will use persistent storage (Cache) to cache all the builds and tasks to optimize performance and reduce pipeline running times. The operations team in charge of deploying and running Dagger inside Kubernetes will need to track how much storage is needed based on the pipelines the organization is running.

In this short section, we have seen how to use Dagger to create our service pipelines. We have seen that Dagger is very different from Tekton: you don't need to write your pipelines using YAML, you can write your pipelines in any supported programming language, you can run your pipelines locally or remotely using the same code, and you can distribute your pipelines using the same tools that you are using for your applications.

From a Kubernetes point of view, when you use a tool like Dagger, you lose the Kubernetes native approach of managing your pipelines as you manage your other Kubernetes resources. I see the Dagger community expanding in that direction if they get enough feedback and requests for that.

From a platform engineering perspective, you can create and distribute complex pipelines (and tasks) for your teams to use and extend using tools they already know. These pipelines will run the same way no matter where they are executed, making it an extremely flexible solution. Platform teams can take this flexibility to decide where to run these pipelines more efficiently (based on costs and resources) without complicating developers' lives, as they will always be able to run their pipelines locally for development purposes.

3.5.5 Should I use Tekton, Dagger, or GitHub Actions?

As you have seen, Tekton and Dagger provide us with the basic building blocks to construct unopinionated pipelines. In other words, we can use Tekton and Dagger to build service pipelines and almost every imaginable pipeline. With Tekton, we use the Kubernetes resource-based approach, scalability, and self-healing features. Using Kubernetes-native resources can be very helpful in integrating Tekton with other Kubernetes tools, such as managing and monitoring Kubernetes resources. Using the Kubernetes resource model, you can treat your Tekton pipelines and PipelineRuns as any other Kubernetes resource and reuse all the existing tooling.

With Dagger, we can define our pipelines using well-known programming languages and tools and run these pipelines everywhere (locally in our workstations in the same way as if we were running them remotely). This makes Tekton and Dagger perfect tools that platform builders can use to build more opinionated pipelines that development teams can use.

On the other hand, you can use a managed service such as GitHub Actions. You can look at how the service pipelines are configured using GitHub actions for all the projects mentioned here. For example, you can check the service pipeline for the notifications service at https://github.com/salaboy/platforms-on-k8s/blob/main/.github/workflows/notifications-service-service-pipelines.yaml.

This GitHub Action pipeline uses `ko-build` to build the service and then pushes the new container image to Docker Hub. Notice that this pipeline doesn't run any tests, and it uses a custom step (https://github.com/salaboy/platforms-on-k8s/blob/main/.github/workflows/notifications-service-service-pipelines.yaml#L17) to check if the code for the service was changed; only run the build and push to Docker Hub if there were changes to the service source code.

The advantage of using GitHub Actions is that you don't need to maintain the infrastructure running them or pay for the machines that run these pipelines (if your volume is small enough). But if you are running loads of pipelines and these pipelines are data-intensive, GitHub Actions will be costly.

For cost-related reasons or because you cannot run your pipelines in the cloud due to industry regulations, Tekton and Dagger shine in providing you with all the building blocks to compose and run complex pipelines. While Dagger is already focused on cost and runtime optimization, this is coming for Tekton and other pipeline engines.

It is important to note that you can integrate Tekton and Dagger with GitHub. For example, use Tekton Triggers (https://github.com/tektoncd/triggers/blob/main/docs/getting-started/README.md) to react to commits into a GitHub repository. You can also run Dagger inside a GitHub Action, enabling developers to run the same pipeline locally executed in GitHub Actions, which cannot be done easily out of the box.

Now that we have our artifacts and configurations ready to be deployed to multiple environments, let's look at what is commonly known as the GitOps approach for continuous deployment through environment pipelines.

3.6   *Linking back to platform engineering*

As part of your platform initiatives, you will need to help teams build their services in an automated way. Most of the time, a decision must be made to standardize how the services will be built and packaged across teams. If the platform team can provide a solution that is accessible to teams to try out locally or have the right environments to test before pushing changes to a Git repository, this will increase the velocity and feedback loop that these teams need to move with confidence. A separate setup might be needed to validate pull requests and alert teams if their repositories' main branch is unreleasable.

While GitHub Actions (and other managed services) are a popular solution, platform engineering teams might choose different tools or services based on their budgets and other platform-wide decisions (such as aligning with the Kubernetes APIs).

I've made conscious choices for this book's demos and step-by-step tutorials (https://github.com/salaboy/platforms-on-k8s/tree/main/chapter-3) that might differ greatly from your projects. First, because the complexity of the projects presented in this book is quite low, but also because to keep the resources organized and versioned to support future revisions, all the application service's source code is kept under a simple directory structure. This decision to have all the service's source code together in the same repository influences the shape of our service pipelines.

The service pipelines provided (both using Tekton and Dagger) receive as a parameter the directory of the repository that the user wants to build. If you set up webhooks to trigger pipelines on pull requests, you must filter where the changes are to see which service pipeline to run. This adds to the complexity of the entire setup. As suggested in previous sections, an alternative approach is to have one repository per service. This enables you to have custom service pipeline definitions per service (which can reuse generic tasks) and simple webhook definitions, as you know exactly what to run when changes are made. The main problem with having one repository per service is dealing with users and access, because adding new services will force you to create new repositories and ensure that developers have access to it.

Another big decision the platform team will need to make concerning service pipelines is where they start and end. For the examples provided here, the service pipelines start when a change is submitted and end after publishing the container images for each service. Service Pipelines for the walking skeleton services don't package and publish individual services Helm Charts. Figure 3.13 shows the responsibility of the service pipelines defined by the examples.

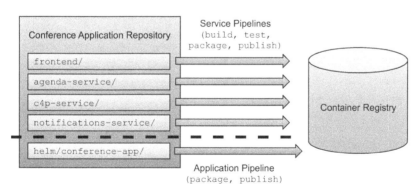

Figure 3.13 **The service pipelines and the application pipeline have different lifecycles.**

You need to ask yourself if having Helm Charts per service is a good idea or an overkill. You should have a clear understanding of who will consume these artifacts. Try answering questions to find a strategy that will work for your teams:

- Will you deploy your services individually, or will they always be deployed as a set?
- How often does your services change? Do you have services that change more often?

- How many teams are going to deploy these services?
- Are you creating an artifact that an open-source community will consume with many users deploying the services individually?

For the examples provided for this chapter, a separate application-level pipeline is provided to package and publish the Conference application Helm Chart.

The reason behind this decision was simple: every reader will install the application in a cluster, and I needed a simple way to enable that. If readers don't want to use Helm to install the application in their clusters, they can export the output of running the `helm template` command and apply the output using `kubectl`. Another important factor behind that decision is the lifecycle of the Helm Chart and the application's services. The shape of the application doesn't change much. The Helm Chart definition might only change if we need to add or remove a service. The service's code, however, changes a lot, and we want to enable the teams working on these services to keep adding changes to them.

Figure 3.14 shows two complementary approaches for service pipelines. The services running in the developer's environment provide fast feedback loops, and those running remotely produce artifacts that teams will use to deploy the same application across different environments.

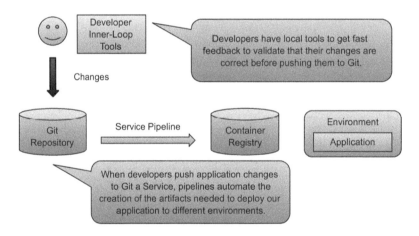

Figure 3.14   Local vs. remote service pipelines

Finally, none of the examples in this book provide configurations to tap into webhooks from the Git repositories besides those linked using GitHub actions. Pushing readers to get the right tokens and configuring this with multiple Git providers is not complex, but it would take me many pages to explain. Teams consuming these mechanisms wouldn't need to worry about dealing with the credentials needed for your service pipelines. As a platform team, automating access to credentials for development (and other) teams to just connect to services is fundamental to speed up their workflows.

Summary

- Service pipelines define how to go from source code to artifacts that can be deployed in multiple environments. Following trunk-based development and one service = one repository practices helps your teams standardize building and releasing software artifacts more efficiently.

- You need to find what works for your teams and applications. There is no one-size-fits-all solution, and compromises must be made. How often do your application's services change, and how do you deploy them into environments? Answering these questions can help you to define where your service pipelines start and end.

- Tekton is a pipeline engine designed for Kubernetes. You can use Tekton to design your custom pipelines and use all the shared tasks and pipelines openly available in the Tekton catalog. You can now install Tekton in your cluster and start creating pipelines.

- Dagger allows you to write and distribute pipelines using your favorite programming language. These pipelines can be executed in any environment, including your developer's laptops.

- Tools like GitHub Actions are very useful but can be expensive. Platform builders must look for tools that provide enough flexibility to build and distribute tasks that other teams can reuse and follow company guidelines. Enabling teams to run their pipelines locally is a big plus as it will improve their developer experience and their feedback times.

- If you followed the step-by-step tutorials, you gained hands-on experience in using Tekton and Dagger to create and run your service pipelines.

Environment pipelines: Deploying cloud-native applications

This chapter covers

- Deploying produced artifacts into environments
- Using environment pipelines and GitOps to manage environments
- Using Argo CD with Helm to deliver software efficiently

This chapter introduces the concept of *environment pipelines*. We cover the steps required to deploy the artifacts created by service pipelines into concrete running environments all the way to production. We will look into a common practice that has emerged in the cloud-native space called GitOps, which allows us to define and configure our environments using a Git repository. Finally, we will look at a project called Argo CD, which implements a GitOps approach for managing applications on top of Kubernetes. This chapter is divided into three main sections:

- Environment pipelines
- Environment pipelines in action using Argo CD
- Service + environment pipelines working together

4.1 Environment pipelines

We can build as many services as we want and produce new versions, but if these versions cannot flow freely across different environments to be tested and finally used by our customers, our organization will struggle to have a smooth end-to-end software delivery practice. Environment pipelines are in charge of configuring and maintaining our environments.

It is quite common for companies to have different environments for different purposes, for example, a staging environment where developers can deploy their latest versions of the services or a quality assurance (QA) environment where manual testing happens and one or more production environments, which are where the real users interact with our applications. These (staging, QA, and production) are just examples. There shouldn't be any hard limit on how many environments we can have. Figure 4.1 shows how a single release flows throughout different environments until it reaches production, where it is going to be live in front of our application's users.

Figure 4.1   Released service moving throughout different environments

Each environment (development, staging, QA, and production) will have one environment pipeline. These pipelines will be responsible for keeping the environment configuration in sync with the hardware running the live version of the environment. These environment pipelines use as the source of truth a repository that contains the environment configurations, including which services and which version of each service needs to be deployed (figure 4.2).

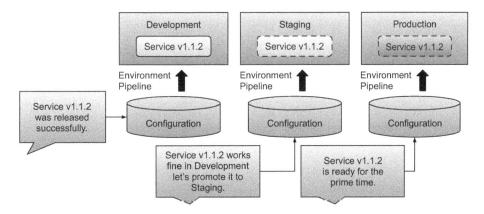

Figure 4.2   Promoting services to different environments means updating environment configurations

If you are using this approach, each environment will have its configuration repository. Promoting a newly released version means changing the environment configuration repository to add a new service or updating the configuration to point to the newly released version. Some organizations keep all sensitive environment configurations all together in a single repository; this helps with centralizing the credentials required to read and modify these configurations.

These configuration changes can be automated or require manual intervention. For more sensitive environments, such as the production environment, you might require different stakeholders to sign off before adding or updating a service.

But where do environment pipelines come from? And why wouldn't you have heard of them before? Before jumping into the details about what an environment pipeline would look like, we need to get a bit of background on why this matters in the first place.

4.1.1 *How did this work in the past, and what has changed lately?*

Traditionally, creating new environments was hard and costly. Creating new environments on demand wasn't a thing for these two reasons. First, the differences between the environment that a developer used to create an application and where the application ran for end users were completely different. These differences, not only in computing power, caused huge stress on operations teams responsible for running these applications. Depending on the environment's capabilities, they needed to fine-tune the application's configurations (that they didn't design). Second, tools for automating the provisioning and configuration of complex setups have become mainstream. With the help of containers and Kubernetes, there has been a standardization around how these tools are designed and work across cloud providers. These tools had reached a point where developers can codify infrastructure using their programming language of choice or rely on the Kubernetes API to create these definitions.

Before the rise of cloud–native applications, deploying a new application or a new version of an application required shutting down the server, running some scripts, copying some binaries, and then starting the server again with the new version running. After the server starts again, the application could fail to start. Hence more configuration tuning might be needed. Most of these configurations were done manually in the server itself, making it difficult to remember and keep track of what was changed and why.

As part of automating these processes, tools like Jenkins (https://www.jenkins.io/, a very popular pipeline engine) and/or scripts were used to simplify deploying new binaries. So instead of manually stopping servers and copying binaries, an operator can run a Jenkins Job defining which versions of the artifacts they wanted to deploy, and Jenkins will run the job notifying the operator about the output. This approach had two main advantages:

- Tools like Jenkins can have access to the environment's credentials, avoiding manual access to the servers by the operators.
- Tools like Jenkins log every job execution and the parameters, allowing us to keep track of what was done and the result of the execution.

While automating with tools like Jenkins was a big improvement compared to manually deploying new versions, there were still some problems, such as having fixed environments completely different from where the software was being developed and tested. We needed to specify how the environment is created and configured to the operating system's version and the software installed into the machines or virtual machines to reduce the difference between different environments. Virtual machines helped greatly with this task, because we can easily create two or more virtual machines configured similarly.

We can even give our developers these virtual machines to work. But now we have a new problem. We will need new tools to manage, run, maintain, and store our virtual machines. If we have multiple physical machines where we want to run virtual machines, we don't want our operations team to start these VMs in each server manually. Hence, we will need a hypervisor to monitor and run VMs in a cluster of physical computers.

Using tools like Jenkins and virtual machines (with hypervisors) were a huge improvement. Because we implemented some automation, operators didn't need to access servers or VMs to change configurations manually, and our environments were created using a configuration predefined in a fixed virtual machine configuration. Tools like Ansible (https://www.ansible.com/) and Puppet (https://www.puppet .com/) are built on top of these concepts.

Figure 4.3 shows Jenkins Jobs configured to create virtual machines that host our applications. But beware, these virtual machines host an entire operating system. All the tools bundled with that operating system will run beside your applications!

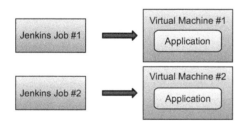

Figure 4.3 Jenkins Jobs or scripts encapsulated the operational knowledge of how to do deployments in an imperative way, defining step-by-step what needs to be done. This is a complex task, hard to maintain and modify, and very specific to the tool we're using. On the other hand, virtual machines are resource-intensive and not portable across cloud providers.

While this approach is still common in the industry, there is a lot of room for improvement, for example, in the following areas:

- Jenkins Jobs and scripts are imperative by nature, meaning they specify step-by-step what needs to be done. This has a great disadvantage, because if something changes—let's say a server is no longer there or requires more data to authenticate against a service—the logic of the pipeline will fail, and it will need to be manually updated.

- Virtual machines are heavy. Every time you start a virtual machine, you start a complete instance of an operating system. Running the operating system processes does not add any business value; the larger the cluster, the bigger the operating system overhead. On the VM's requirements, running VMs in developers' environments may not be possible.
- Environments' configurations are hidden and not versioned. Most of the environment configurations and how the deployments are done are encoded inside tools like Jenkins, where complex pipelines tend to grow out of control, making the changes very risky and migration to newer tools and stacks very difficult.
- Each cloud provider has a non-standard way of creating virtual machines. This can push us into a vendor lock-in situation. If we created VMs for Amazon Web Services, we could not run these VMs into the Google Cloud Platform or Microsoft Azure.

How are teams approaching this with modern tooling? That is an easy question. We now have Kubernetes and containers that aim to solve the overhead caused by VMs and the cloud-provider portability by relying on containers and the widely adopted Kubernetes APIs. Kubernetes also provides the building blocks to ensure we don't need to shut down our servers to deploy new applications or change their configurations. If we do things in the Kubernetes way, we shouldn't have any downtime in our applications.

But Kubernetes alone doesn't solve the process of configuring the clusters themselves. How we apply changes to their configurations, or the process and tooling involved into deploying applications to these clusters, also matter. That's why you might have heard about GitOps.

What is GitOps, and how does it relate to our environment pipelines? We'll answer that question next.

4.1.2   What is GitOps, and how does it relate to environment pipelines?

If we don't want to encode all of our operational knowledge in a tool like Jenkins, where it is difficult to maintain, change, and keep track of it, we need a different approach.

The term GitOps, defined by the CNCF's GitOps Working Group (https://opengitops.dev/), defines the process of creating, maintaining, and applying the configuration of our environments and applications declaratively using Git as the source of truth. OpenGitOps defines four core principles that we need to consider when we talk about GitOps:

1 *Declarative:* A system (https://github.com/open-gitops/documents/blob/v1.0.0/GLOSSARY.md#software-system) managed by GitOps must have its desired state expressed declaratively (https://github.com/open-gitops/documents/blob/v1.0.0/GLOSSARY.md#declarative-description). We have this covered if we use Kubernetes manifest, because we define what needs to be deployed and how that needs to be configured using declarative resources that Kubernetes will reconcile.

2 *Versioned and immutable:* The desired state is stored (https://github.com/open-gitops/documents/blob/v1.0.0/GLOSSARY.md#state-store) in a way that enforces

immutability and versioning and retains a complete version history. The Open GitOps initiative doesn't enforce the use of Git. As soon as our definitions are stored, versioned, and immutable, we can consider it as GitOps. This opens the door to storing files in, for example, S3 buckets, which are also versioned and immutable.

3 *Pulled automatically:* Software agents automatically pull the desired state declarations from the source. The GitOps software pulls the changes from the source periodically in an automated way. Users shouldn't worry about when the changes are pulled.

4 *Continuously reconciled:* Software agents continuously (https://github.com/open -gitops/documents/blob/v1.0.0/GLOSSARY.md#continuous) observe the system state and attempt to apply (https://github.com/open-gitops/documents/ blob/v1.0.0/GLOSSARY.md#reconciliation) the desired state. This continuous reconciliation helps us to build resilience in our environments and the entire delivery process, because we have components that are in charge of applying the desired state and monitoring our environments from configuration drifts. If the reconciliation fails, GitOps tools will notify us about the problems and keep trying to apply the changes until the desired state is achieved.

By storing the configuration of our environments and applications in a Git repository, we can track and version the changes we make. By relying on Git, we can easily roll back changes if these changes don't work as expected. GitOps covers the configuration storage and how these configurations are applied to the computing resources where the applications run.

GitOps was coined in the context of Kubernetes, but this approach is not new, because configuration management tools have existed for a long time. Instead, GitOps represents a refinement of these tried and tested approaches that can be applied to any software operation, not just Kubernetes. With the rise in popularity of cloud providers' tools for managing Infrastructure as Code, tools like Chef (https://www.chef.io/), Ansible (https://www.ansible.com/), Terraform (https://www.terraform.io/), and Pulumi (https://www.pulumi.com/) are loved by operations teams, because these tools allow them to define how to configure cloud resources and configure them together in a reproducible way. If you need a new environment, you just run this Terraform script or Pulumi app, and then voila, the environment is up and running. These tools are also equipped to communicate with the cloud provider's APIs to create Kubernetes clusters so that we can automate the creation of these clusters.

With GitOps, we manage configuration and rely on the Kubernetes APIs as the standard way to deploy our applications to Kubernetes clusters. With GitOps, we use a Git repository as the source of truth for our environment's internal configurations (Kubernetes YAML files) while removing the need to interact manually with the Kubernetes clusters to avoid configuration drifts and security problems. When using GitOps tools, we can expect to have software agents in charge of pulling from the source of truth (Git repository in this example) periodically and constantly monitoring the environment to provide a continuous reconciliation loop. This ensures that the GitOps tool will do its best to ensure that the desired state expressed in the repository is what we have in our live environments.

We can reconfigure any Kubernetes cluster to have the same configuration stored in our Git repository by running an environment pipeline. Figure 4.4 shows how these pieces fit together. On the left, we have Infrastructure as Code tools that can create cloud resources, including Kubernetes clusters and application infrastructure for our environments. Once the environment is set up, an environment pipeline using a GitOps approach can sync all the configurations for our environment into the target Kubernetes cluster, regularly checking that the configuration stored in Git is in sync with the cluster.

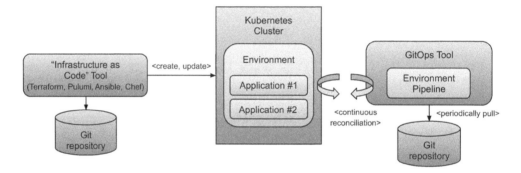

Figure 4.4   Infrastructure as Code, GitOps, and environment pipelines working together. Infrastructure as code tools run scripts to create cloud resources in a reproducible way. We can create our Kubernetes clusters to be all the same using these tools. GitOps tools run environment pipelines to continuously reconcile declarative configuration, which is stored in a versioned and immutable repository.

By separating the infrastructure and application concerns, our environment pipelines allow us to ensure that our environments are easy to reproduce and update whenever needed. By relying on Git as the source of truth, we can roll back our infrastructural and application changes as needed. It is also important to understand that because we are working with the Kubernetes APIs, our environment's definitions are now expressed in a declarative way, supporting changes in the context where these configurations are applied and letting Kubernetes deal with how to achieve the desired state expressed by these configurations.

Figure 4.5 shows these interactions, where operation teams only make changes to the Git repository that contains our environment configuration, and then a pipeline (a set of steps) is executed to ensure that this configuration is in sync with the target environment.

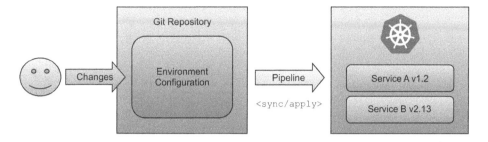

Figure 4.5 **Defining the state of the cluster using the configuration in Git (GitOps). Environment pipelines monitor configuration changes on a Git repository and apply those changes to the infrastructure (Kubernetes cluster) whenever a new change is detected. Following this approach allows us to roll back changes in the infrastructure by reverting commits on Git. We can also replicate the exact environment configuration by just running the same pipeline against another cluster.**

When you start using environment pipelines, you aim to stop interacting, changing, or modifying the environment's configuration manually, and all interactions are done exclusively by these pipelines. To give a very concrete example, instead of executing `kubectl apply -f` or `helm install` into our Kubernetes cluster, an operator will be in charge of running these commands based on the contents of a Git repository that has the definitions and configurations of what needs to be installed in the cluster.

In theory, an operator that monitors a Git repository and reacts to changes is all you need, but in practice, a set of steps is needed to ensure we have full control of what is deployed to our environments. Hence, thinking about GitOps as a pipeline helps us understand that for some scenarios, we will need to add extra steps to these pipelines triggered every time an environment configuration is changed.

Let's look at these steps with more concrete tools commonly found in real-life scenarios.

4.1.3 Steps involved in an environment pipeline

No matter what kind of applications you are deploying to different environments, environment pipelines usually include a set of predefined steps. Figure 4.6 shows these steps as a sequence, as most of the time these steps are defined inside scripts or encoded in tools that are in charge of checking that each step was executed correctly. Let's dig deeper into the details of these steps:

- *Reacting to changes in the configuration:* This can be done by polling or pushing:
  - *Polling for changes:* A component can pull the repository and check if there have been new commits since the last time it checked. If new changes are detected, a new environment pipeline instance is created.
  - *Pushing changes using webhooks:* If the repository supports webhooks, the repository can notify our environment pipelines that there are new changes to sync.

Remember, the GitOps principles state "pulled automatically," which means we can use webhooks, but we should not rely entirely on them for getting config change updates.

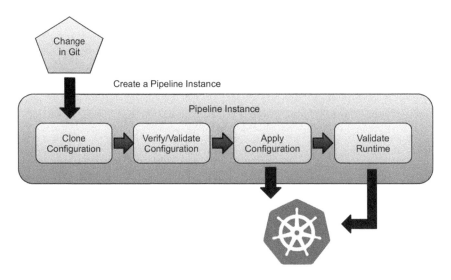

Figure 4.6   Environment pipeline for a Kubernetes environment

- *Clone the source code from the repository, which contains the desired state for our environment:* This step fetches the configuration from a remote Git repository that contains the environment configurations. Tools like Git fetch only the delta between the remote repository and what we have locally.

- *Apply the desired state to a live environment:* This usually includes doing a `kubectl apply -f` or a `helm install` command to install new versions of the artifacts. Notice that with both `kubectl` and `helm`, Kubernetes is smart enough to recognize where the changes are and only apply the differences. Once the pipeline has all the configurations locally accessible, it will use a set of credentials to apply these changes to a Kubernetes cluster. Notice that we can fine-tune the access rights that the pipelines have to the cluster to ensure they are not exploited from a security point of view. This also allows you to remove access from individual team members to the clusters where the services are deployed.

- *Verify that the changes are applied and that the state matches what is described inside the Git repository (deal with configuration drift):* Once the changes are applied to the live cluster, checking that the new versions of services are up and running is needed to identify if we need to revert to a previous version. It is quite simple if we need to revert changes, because all the history is stored in Git. Applying the previous version is just looking at the previous commit in the repository.

- *Validate that your workloads are working as expected:* Once the configurations are applied correctly, we need to validate that the applications deployed are working as expected and doing what they are supposed to do.

For the environment pipeline to work, a component that can apply the changes to the environment is needed, and it needs to be configured accordingly with the right access credentials. The main idea behind this component is to make sure that nobody will change the environment configuration by manually interacting with the cluster. This component is the only one allowed to change the environment configuration, deploy new services, upgrade versions, or remove services from the environment. For an environment pipeline to work, the following two considerations need to be met:

- The repository containing the desired state for the environment must have all the necessary configurations to create and configure the environment successfully.
- The Kubernetes cluster where the environment will run needs to be configured with the correct credentials for allowing the state to be changed by the pipelines.

The term *environment pipeline* refers to the fact that each environment will have a pipeline associated with it. Because multiple environments are usually required (development, staging, production) for delivering applications, each will have a pipeline in charge of deploying and upgrading the components running in them. By using this approach, promoting services between different environments is achieved by sending pull requests/change requests to the environment's repository. The pipeline will reflect the changes in the target cluster.

4.1.4 *Environment pipeline requirements and different approaches*

So, what are the contents of these environment's repositories? As you will see in figure 4.7, the contents of the environment repository are just the definition of which services need to be present in the environment. The environment pipeline then can just apply these Kubernetes manifests to the target cluster.

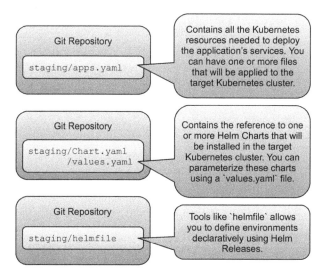

Figure 4.7 Environment configuration options

The first option (simple layout) is to store all the Kubernetes YAML files in a Git repository, and then the environment pipeline will just use `kubectl apply -f *` against the configured cluster. While this approach is simple, there is one big drawback: if you have your Kubernetes YAML files for each service in the service repository, then the environment repository will have these files duplicated, and they can go out of sync. Imagine if you have several environments, you must maintain all the copies in sync, which might become challenging.

The second option (using Helm Charts) is a bit more elaborate now that we are using Helm to define the state of the cluster. You can use Helm dependencies to create a parent chart that will include as dependencies all the services that should be present in the environment. If you do so, the environment pipeline can use `helm update .` to apply the chart into a cluster. Something I don't like about this approach is that you create one Helm release per change, and there are no separate releases for each service. This approach uses Helm dependencies to fetch each service definition, so a prerequisite for this approach is to have every service package as a Helm Chart.

The third option is to use a project called `helmfile` (https://github.com/helmfile/helmfile), designed for this very specific purpose, to define environment configurations. A `helmfile` allows you to declaratively define what Helm releases need to be present in our cluster. These Helm releases will be created when we run `helmfile sync`, having defined a `helmfile` containing the helm releases we want in the cluster.

Whether you use any of these approaches or other tools to do this, the expectation is clear. You have a repository with the configuration (one repository per environment or a directory per environment), and a pipeline is in charge of picking up the configuration and using a tool to apply it to a cluster.

It is common to have several environments (staging, QA, production), even allowing teams to create on-demand environments for running tests or day-to-day development tasks. If you use the "one environment per namespace" approach, as shown in figure 4.8, it is common to have a separate Git repository for each environment, because it helps keep access to environments isolated and secure. This approach is simple, but it doesn't provide enough isolation on the Kubernetes cluster, because Kubernetes Namespaces were designed for logical partitioning of the cluster. In this case, the staging environment will share with the production environment the cluster resources.

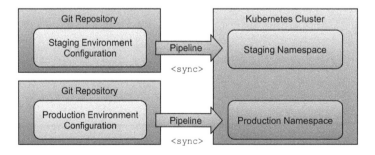

Figure 4.8   One environment per Kubernetes namespace approach. One strategy is to use namespaces for different environments. While this simplifies the configurations required for the pipelines to deploy services to different environments, namespaces don't provide strong isolation guarantees.

An alternative approach can be to use an entirely new cluster for each environment. The main difference is isolation and access control. By having a cluster per environment, you can be stricter in defining who and which components can deploy and upgrade things in these environments and have different hardware configurations for each cluster, such as multi-region setups and other scalability concerns that might not make sense to have in your staging and testing environments. Using different clusters, you can also aim for a multi-cloud setup, where different cloud providers can host different environments.

Figure 4.9 shows how you can use the namespace approach for development environments, which will be created by different teams and then have separated clusters for staging and production. The idea here is to have the staging and production cluster configured as similarly as possible, so applications deployed onto different environments behave the same.

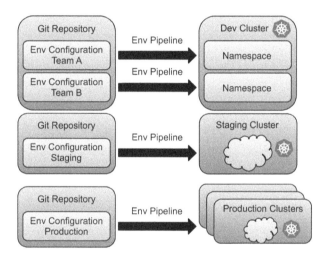

Figure 4.9 **Different environment configurations, based on requirements. A more realistic approach can use the same cluster for multiple teams doing day-to-day work, while more sensitive environments like staging and production are separated on their own clusters and Git repositories to store their configurations. For a service to be promoted to a new environment, a pull request needs to be submitted to the corresponding Git repository.**

Okay, but how can we implement these pipelines? Should we implement these pipelines using Tekton? In the next section, we will look at Argo CD (https://argo-cd .readthedocs.io/en/stable/), a tool that has encoded the environment pipeline logic and best practices into a very specific tool for continuous deployment.

4.2   *Environment pipelines in action*

You can implement an environment pipeline as described in the previous section using Tekton or Dagger. This has been done in projects like Jenkins X (https://jenkins-x .io), but nowadays, the steps for an environment pipeline are encoded in specialized tools for continuous deployment like Argo CD (https://argo-cd.readthedocs.io/en/ stable/).

In contrast with service pipelines, where we might need specialized tools to build our artifacts depending on which technology stack we use, environment pipelines for Kubernetes are well-standardized today under the GitOps umbrella. Considering that all our artifacts are being built and published by our service pipelines, we first need to create our environment Git repository, which will contain the environment configuration, including the services deployed to that environment.

Argo CD provides a very opinionated but flexible GitOps implementation. We will delegate all the steps required to deploy software into our environments to Argo CD. Argo CD can out-of-the-box monitor a Git repository that contains our environment(s) configuration and periodically apply the configuration to a live cluster. This enables us to remove manual interactions with the target clusters, which reduces configuration drifts as Git becomes our source of truth.

Using tools like Argo CD allows us to declaratively define what we want to install in our environments, while Argo CD is in charge of notifying us when something goes wrong or our clusters are out of sync. Argo CD is not limited to a single cluster, meaning our environment can live in separate clusters, even in different cloud providers. Figure 4.10 shows Argo CD managing different environments on different clusters, using different Git repositories as the source of truth to keep the configuration of each environment.

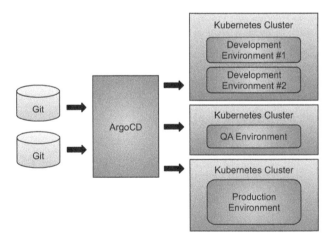

Figure 4.10   Argo CD will sync environments, configurations from Git to live clusters

In the same way that we now have separate service pipelines for each service, we can have separate repositories, branches, or directories to configure our environments. Argo CD can monitor repositories or directories inside repositories for changes to sync our environments configurations.

We will install Argo CD in our Kubernetes cluster for this example and configure our staging environment using a GitOps approach. For that, we need a Git repository that serves as our source of truth. You can follow a step-by-step tutorial located at https://github.com/salaboy/platforms-on-k8s/blob/main/chapter-4/README.md.

For installing Argo CD, I recommend you check their Getting Started guide that you can find at https://argo-cd.readthedocs.io/en/stable/getting_started/. This guide installs all the components required for Argo CD to work, so after finishing this guide, we should have all we need to get our staging environment going. It also guides you through the installation of the `argocd` CLI (Command-Line Interface), which sometimes is very handy. In the following sections, we will focus on the user interface, but you can access the same functionality using the CLI. Argo CD comes with a very useful user interface that lets you monitor how your environments and applications are doing and quickly find out if there are any problems.

The main objective of this section is to replicate what we did in section 2.1.3 in chapter 2, where we installed and interacted with the application, but here we aim to fully automate the process for an environment that will be configured using a git repository. Once again, we will use Helm to define the environment configuration as Argo CD provides an out-of-the-box Helm integration.

> **NOTE** Argo CD used a different nomenclature than the one we used here. In Argo CD you configure applications instead of environments. In the following screenshots, you will see that we will be configuring an Argo CD application to represent our staging environment. As there are no restrictions on what you can include in a Helm Chart, we will be using a Helm Chart to configure our Conference application into this environment.

4.2.1 Creating an Argo CD application

If you access the Argo CD user interface, you will see right in the top left corner of the screen the + New App button (figure 4.11).

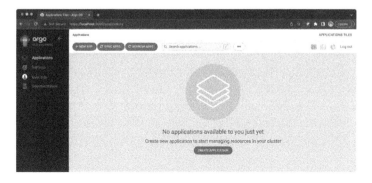

Figure 4.11 Argo CD user interface—new application creation

Go ahead and hit that button to see the application creation form. Besides adding a name and selecting a Project where our Argo CD application will live (we will select the `default` project), we will check the `Auto-Create Namespace` option, as shown in figure 4.12.

Figure 4.12   New application parameters, manual sync, and auto-create namespace

By associating our environment with a new namespace in our cluster, we can only use the Kubernetes RBAC mechanism to allow administrators to modify the Kubernetes resources in that namespace. Remember that by using Argo CD, we want to ensure that developers don't accidentally change the application configuration or manually apply configuration changes to the cluster. Argo CD will sync the resources defined in a Git repository. So where is that Git repository? That's exactly what we need to configure next (figure 4.13).

Figure 4.13   Argo CD application's configuration repository, revision, and path

As mentioned, we will use a directory inside the https://github.com/salaboy/platforms -on-k8s/ repository to define our staging environment. You should fork this repository (and then use your fork URL) to make any changes you want to the environment configuration. The directory that contains the environment configuration can be found under chapter-4/argo-cd/staging/. As shown in figure 4.14, you can also select between different branches and tags, allowing you to have fine-grain control of where the configuration is coming from and how that configuration evolves.

DESTINATION

Cluster URL
https://kubernetes.default.svc   URL ▾

Namespace
staging

Figure 4.14   Configuration destination, for this example, is the cluster where Argo CD is installed

The next step is to define where Argo CD will apply this environment configuration. We can use Argo CD to install and sync environments in different clusters, but for this example, we will be using the same Kubernetes cluster where we installed Argo CD and the `staging` namespace. There is an option for Argo CD to create this namespace for you, or you can create it manually when setting up the cluster and the permissions for different namespaces.

Finally, because it makes sense to reuse the same configuration for similar environments, Argo CD enables us to configure different parameters specific to this installation. Since we are using Helm and the Argo CD user interface is smart enough to scan the content of the repository/path we have entered, it knows it is dealing with a Helm Chart. If we were not using a Helm Chart, Argo CD allows us to set up environment variables as parameters for our configuration scripts (figure 4.15).

Figure 4.15   Helm configuration parameters for the staging environment

As you can see in the previous image, Argo CD also identified an empty values.yaml file inside the repository path that we have provided. If the values.yaml file had any parameters, the user interface will parse them and show them for you to validate. We can add more parameters to the `VALUES` text box to override any other chart (or sub-charts) configurations.

After we provide all this configuration, we are ready to hit the Create button at the top of the form. Argo CD will create the application and automatically sync the changes, as we selected the Automatic Sync option (figure 4.16).

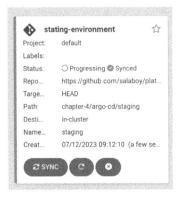

**Figure 4.16
Application
created and
automatically
synced**

If you click into the application, you will drill down to the application's full view, which shows you the state of all the resources associated with the application, as shown in figure 4.17.

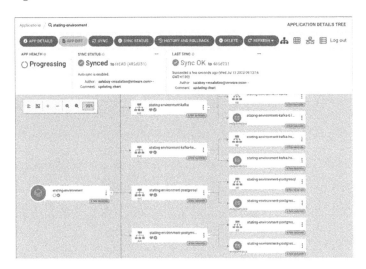

Figure 4.17   Our staging environment is healthy, and all the services are running.

If you are creating the environment in a local cluster or a real Kubernetes cluster, you should access the application and interact with it. Let's recap what we have achieved:

- We have installed Argo CD into our Kubernetes cluster. Using the provided Argo CD Dashboard (user interface), we have created a new Argo CD application for our staging environment.
- We have created our staging environment configuration in a Git repository hosted in GitHub, which uses a Helm Chart definition to configure our Conference application services and their dependencies (Redis, PostgreSQL, and Kafka).

- We have synced the configuration to a namespace (`staging`) in the same cluster where we installed Argo CD.

- Most importantly, we have removed the need for manual interaction against the target cluster. Theoretically, there will be no need to execute `kubectl` against the `staging` namespace.

For this setup to work, we need to make sure that the artifacts that the Helm Charts (and the Kubernetes resources inside them) are available for the target cluster to pull. I strongly recommend you follow the step-by-step tutorial (https://github.com/salaboy/platforms-on-k8s/tree/main/chapter-4) to get hands-on with Argo CD to understand how this tool works and how it can help your teams to continuously deploy their applications to multiple environments.

4.2.2 Dealing with changes the GitOps way

Imagine now that the team in charge of developing the user interface (`frontend`) decides to introduce a new feature. They create a pull request to the `frontend` repository. Once this pull request is merged with the `main`, the team can decide to create a new release for the service. The release process should include the creation of tagged artifacts using the release number. The creation of these artifacts is the responsibility of the service pipeline, as we saw in previous sections. Figure 4.18 shows how Argo CD, in this case, syncs the configuration changes from the staging configuration repository.

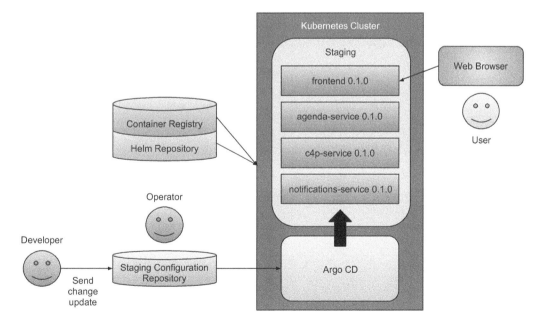

Figure 4.18 Components to set up the staging environment with Argo CD

Once we have the released artifacts, we can now update the environment. We can update the staging environment by submitting a pull request to our GitHub repository that can be reviewed before merging to the main branch, the branch we used to configure our Argo CD application. The changes in the environment configuration repository are going to be usually about:

- *Bumping up or reverting a service version:* For our example, this is as simple as changing the version of the chart of one or more services. Rolling back one of the services to the previous is as simple as reverting the version number in the environment chart or even reverting the commit that increased the version in the first place. Notice that reverting commits is always recommended, as rolling back to a previous version might also include configuration changes to the services that, if they are not applied, old versions might not work.

- *Adding or removing a service:* Adding a new service is a bit more complicated, because you will need to add both the chart reference and the service configuration parameters. For this to work, the chart definition needs to be reachable by the Argo CD installation. Suppose the service(s)' chart(s) are available, and the configuration parameters are valid. In that case, the next time we sync our Argo CD application, the new service(s) will be deployed to the environment. Removing services is more straightforward, because the moment you remove the dependency from the environment Helm Chart, the service will be removed from the environment.

- *Tweaking charts parameters:* Sometimes, we don't want to change any service version, and we might be trying to fine-tune the application parameters to accommodate performance or scalability requirements, monitoring configurations, or the log level for a set of services. These changes are also versioned and should be treated as new features and bug fixes.

We will quickly notice the differences if we compare this with manually installing Helm to install the application into the cluster. First, a developer might have the environment configuration on their laptop, making the environment very difficult to replicate from a different location. Changes to the environment configuration that are not tracked using a version control system will be lost, and we will not have any way to verify whether these changes are working in a live cluster. Configuration drifts are much more difficult to track down and troubleshoot.

This automated approach with Argo CD can open the door to more advanced scenarios. For example, we can create preview environments (figure 4.19) for our pull requests to test changes before they get merged and artifacts are released.

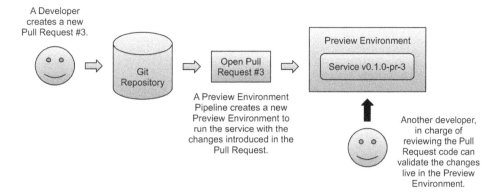

Figure 4.19 Preview environments for faster iterations

Using preview environments can help iterate faster and enable teams to validate changes before merging them into the project's main branch. Preview environments can also be notified when the pull request is merged, making an automated clean-up mechanism straightforward to implement.

> **NOTE**   Another important detail to mention when using Argo CD and Helm is that compared with using Helm Charts manually, where Helm will create release resources every time we update a chart in our cluster, Argo CD will not use this Helm feature. Argo CD takes the approach of using a Helm template to render the Kubernetes resources YAML, and then it applies the output using `kubectl apply`. This approach relies on the fact that everything is versioned in Git and allows the unification of different templating engines for YAML. In addition to some security benefits, this is key to enabling diffing in Argo CD, which allows us to specify which resources should be managed by Argo CD and which elements may be managed by different controllers.

Finally, to tie things together, let's see how service and environment pipelines interact to provide end-to-end automation, from code changes to deploying new versions into multiple environments.

4.3 *Service + environment pipelines*

Let's look at how service pipelines and environment pipeline connect. The connection between these two pipelines happens via pull/change requests to Git repositories, because the pipelines will be triggered when changes are submitted and merged (figure 4.20).

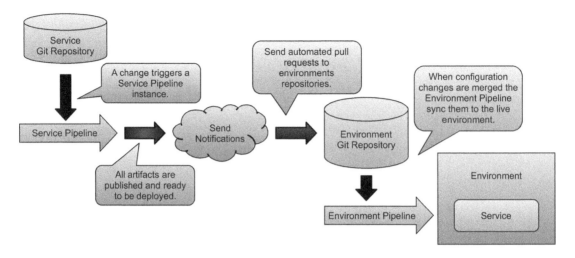

Figure 4.20   A service pipeline can trigger an environment pipeline via a pull request.

Developers, when they finish a new feature, create a pull/change request to the repository's main branch. This pull/change request can be reviewed and built by a specialized service pipeline. When this new feature is merged into the repository's main branch, a new instance of the service pipeline is triggered. This instance creates a new release and all the artifacts needed to deploy the service's new version into a Kubernetes cluster. As we saw in chapter 3, this includes a binary with the compiled source code, a container image, and Kubernetes Manifests that can be packaged using tools like Helm.

As the last step of the service pipeline, you can include a notification step that can notify the interested environments that there is a new version of a service that they are running available. This notification is usually an automated pull/change request into the environment's repository. Alternatively, you monitor (or subscribe to notifications) your artifact repositories, and when a new version is detected, a pull/change request is created to the configured environments.

The pull/change requests created to environment repositories can be automatically tested by a specialized environment pipeline. In the same way as we did with service pipelines, and for low-risk environments, these pull/change requests can be automatically merged without any human intervention.

By implementing this flow, we can enable developers to focus on fixing bugs and creating new features that will be automatically released and promoted to low-risk environments. Once the new versions are tested in environments like staging, and we know that these new versions or configurations are not causing any problems, a pull/change request can be created for the repository that contains the production environment configuration.

The more sensitive the environments are, the more required checks and validations. In this case, as shown in figure 4.21, to promote a new service version to the production environment, a new test environment will be created to validate and test the changes introduced in the pull/change request submitted. Once those validations are done, a manual sign-off is required to merge the pull request and trigger the environment pipeline synchronization.

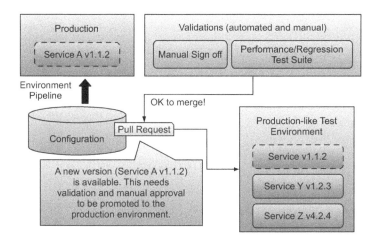

Figure 4.21   Promoting changes to the production environment

Environment pipelines are the mechanism you use to encode your organization's requirements to release and promote software to different environments. We have seen in this chapter what a tool like Argo CD can do for us. Next, we need to evaluate if a single Argo CD installation would be enough and who will manage it and keep it secure. Do you need to extend Argo CD with custom hook points? Do you need to integrate it with other tools? We will explore these questions in chapter 6, so before closing this chapter, let's look at how environment pipelines and tools like Argo CD fit into the platform engineering story.

4.4   Linking back to platform engineering

From a platform engineering perspective, providing a GitOps approach is becoming increasingly popular for teams to configure different environments. With the popularity of tools like Argo CD, more people feel comfortable storing and manipulating environment configurations on version control systems like Git. As a platform engineering team, you can enable your teams to use this approach without pushing them to learn how to install, maintain, and configure these tools.

Platforms can automate the creation of environment repositories and make sure that the right teams have access to read and write configurations to promote services.

Consumers of these platforms are expected to know how to interact with their environments, but not how the tools provided by the platform work or how they are configured. There are cases, for example, in development environments, where using a GitOps approach might not work, because some development teams will want direct access to clusters, and your platform should be flexible enough to allow this access when needed.

As discussed in section 4.3, service and environment pipelines work hand in hand to produce software artifacts and move them between environments. Both service and environment pipelines are key mechanisms to get in place to implement what is known as golden paths. The more mature your platform becomes, the coordination between environment pipelines becomes essential to automate how your new software releases go from source to production environments and are validated by your end users (customers). These golden paths are automated workflows to move the changes that our teams are producing to our production environments where customers will be able to access them. Figure 4.22 shows from a high level what a golden path looks like for our applications.

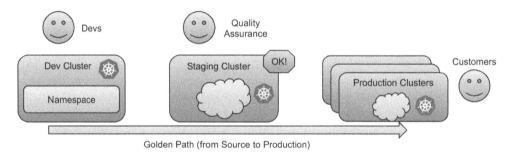

Figure 4.22   What does it take to promote new releases to our production environments?

Think about how many service and environment pipelines will need to be executed to take the software produced in our development environments to our production clusters, where customers can access the release of a single service. How are these pipelines coordinated and wired to ensure our deployments work as expected? How many manual verifications do you need in this whole process? And most importantly, what can you automate for your teams not to worry about all these complex interactions?

So far, we have covered how to install an application into a Kubernetes cluster, build and package the application services into containers, and package and distribute the configuration files needed to deploy these services into a Kubernetes cluster. This chapter adds to the picture of how to manage different environments where this application will run using a GitOps approach. Figure 4.23 shows all the pieces together.

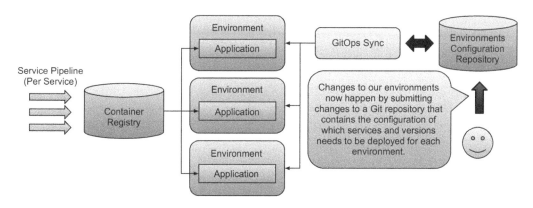

Figure 4.23   Adding GitOps to manage multiple environments

Before digging deeper into golden paths (in chapter 6), we must explore one more challenge we face when we deploy our applications to different environments: application infrastructure, in the next chapter.

Summary

- Environment pipelines are responsible for deploying software artifacts to live environments. Environment pipelines avoid teams interacting directly with the cluster where the applications run, reducing errors and misconfigurations. Environment pipelines should check that environments are fully operational after updating their configuration.
- Using tools like Argo CD, you can define the content of each environment into a Git repository that is used as the source of truth for what the environment configuration should look like. Argo CD will keep track of the state of the cluster where the environment is running and ensure no drift in the configuration applied in the cluster.
- Teams can upgrade or downgrade the versions of the services running in an environment by submitting pull/change requests to the repository where the environment configuration is stored. A team or an automated process can validate these changes, and when approved and merged, these changes will be reflected in the live environment. Changes can be rolled back if things go wrong by reverting commits to the git repository.
- If you followed the step-by-step tutorial, you got hands-on experience on how to deploy application workloads following a GitOps approach by using Argo CD.

Multi-cloud (app) infrastructure

This chapter covers

- Defining and managing the infrastructure for your cloud-native applications
- Identifying the challenges of managing infrastructure components
- Learning how Crossplane is the Kubernetes way to deal with infrastructure

In previous chapters, we installed a walking skeleton, and we learned how to build each separate component using service pipelines and then how to deploy them into different environments using environment pipelines. We now face a big challenge: dealing with our application infrastructure, meaning running and maintaining not only our application services but also the components that our services need to run. These services expect other components to work correctly, such as databases, message brokers, identity management solutions, email servers, etc. While several tools exist to automate the installation (for on-premises setups) or provisioning of these components in different cloud providers, this chapter will focus on just one that does it in a Kubernetes way. This chapter has three main sections:

- The challenges of dealing with infrastructure
- How to deal with infrastructure using Kubernetes constructs
- How to provision infrastructure for our walking skeleton using Crossplane

Let's get started. Why is it so difficult to manage our application infrastructure?

5.1 The challenges of managing infrastructure in Kubernetes

When you design applications like the walking skeleton introduced in chapter 1, you face specific challenges that are not core to achieving your business goals. Installing, configuring, and maintaining *application infrastructure* components that support our application's services is a big task that needs to be planned carefully by the right teams with the right expertise.

These components are classified as application infrastructure, which usually involves third-party components not developed in-house, such as databases, message brokers, identity management solutions, etc. A big reason behind the success of modern cloud providers is that they are great at providing and maintaining these components and allow your development teams to focus on building the core features of applications, which brings value to the business.

It is essential to distinguish between application infrastructure and hardware infrastructure, because this book is not concerned with hardware provisioning, the reminder of content focus on the application space. I assume that for public cloud offerings, the provider solves all hardware-related topics. For on-prem scenarios, you likely have a specialized team taking care of the hardware (removing, adding, and maintaining hardware as needed).

It is common to rely on cloud provider services to provision application infrastructure. There are a lot of advantages to doing so, such as pay-as-you-use services, easy provisioning at scale, and automated maintenance. But at that point, you heavily rely on provider-specific ways of doing things and their tools. The moment you create a database or a message broker in a cloud provider, you are jumping outside the realms of Kubernetes. Now you depend on their tools and automation mechanisms, and you are creating a strong dependency between your business and the cloud provider.

Let's look at the challenges associated with provisioning and maintaining application infrastructure, so your teams can plan and choose the right tool for the job:

- *Configuring components to scale:* Each component requires different expertise to be configured (database administrators for databases, message broker experts, machine learning experts, etc.) and a deep understanding of how our application's services will use it, as well as the hardware available. These configurations need to be versioned and monitored closely, so new environments can be created quickly to reproduce problems or test new versions of our application.
- *Maintaining components in the long run:* Databases and message brokers are constantly released and patched to improve performance and security. This constant

change pushes the operations teams to ensure they can upgrade to newer versions and keep all the data safe without bringing down the entire application. All this complexity requires a lot of coordination and impact analysis between the teams providing and consuming these components.

■ *Cloud provider services affect our multi-cloud strategy:* If we rely on cloud-specific application infrastructure and tools, we need to find a way to enable developers to create and provision their components for developing and testing their services. We need a way to abstract how infrastructure is provisioned to enable applications to define what infrastructure they need without relying directly on cloud-specific tools.

Interestingly, we had these challenges even before having distributed applications, and configuration and provisioning architectural components have always been hard and usually far away from developers. Cloud providers are doing a fantastic job by bringing these topics closer to developers so they can be more autonomous and iterate faster. Unfortunately, when working with Kubernetes, we have more options that we need to consider carefully to ensure we understand the tradeoffs. The following section covers how we can manage our application infrastructure inside Kubernetes. While this is usually not recommended, it can be practical and cheaper for some scenarios.

5.1.1 *Managing your application infrastructure*

Application infrastructure has become an exciting arena. With the rise of containers, every developer can bootstrap a database or message broker with a couple of commands, which is usually enough for development purposes. In the Kubernetes world, this translates to Helm Charts, which uses containers to configure and provision databases (relational and NoSQL), message brokers, identity management solutions, etc. As we saw in chapter 2, you installed the walking skeleton application containing four services, two databases (Redis and PostgreSQL), and a message broker (Kafka) with a single command.

For our walking skeleton, we are provisioning an instance of a Redis NoSQL database for the Agenda service, an instance of a PostgreSQL database for the Call for Proposals (C4P) service, and an instance of a Kafka cluster, all using Helm Charts. The number of Helm charts available today is impressive, and it is pretty easy to think that installing a Helm Chart will be the way to go. The Helm charts used in the example application can all be found in the Bitnami Helm Chart repositories at https://bitnami.com/stacks/helm.

As discussed in chapter 2, if we want to scale our services that keep state, we must provision specialized components such as databases. Application developers will define which kind of database will suit them best depending on the data they need to store and how that data will be structured. Figure 5.1 shows the dependency of the application services on some of the application infrastructure components that we have identified for our walking skeleton.

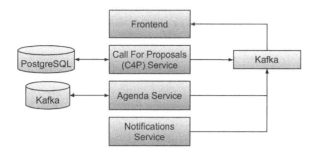

Figure 5.1   Services and their dependencies on application infrastructure components

The process of setting up these (PostgreSQL, Redis, and Kafka) components inside your Kubernetes cluster involves the following steps:

- Finding or creating a suitable Helm Chart for the component you want to boot-strap. For the walking skeleton, PostgreSQL (https://bitnami.com/stack/postgresql/helm), Redis (https://bitnami.com/stack/redis/helm), and Kafka (https://bitnami.com/stack/kafka/helm) can be found in the Bitnami Helm Chart repository. If you cannot find a Helm Chart but have a Docker container for the component you want to provision, you can create your chart after you define the basic Kubernetes constructs needed for the deployment.

- Research the chart configurations and parameters you must set up to accommodate your requirements. Each chart exposes a set of parameters that you can tune for different use cases. Check the chart website to understand what is available. Include your operations teams and DBAs to check the optimal database configurations for your use case; this is not something that a developer can do. This analysis also requires Kubernetes expertise to ensure the components can work in HA (high availability) mode inside Kubernetes.

- Install the chart into your Kubernetes cluster using `helm install`. By running `helm install`, you are downloading a set of Kubernetes manifest (YAML files) that describe how these components need to be deployed. Helm will then proceed to apply these YAML files to your cluster. For our Conference application Helm Chart that we installed in chapter 2 (section 2.1.3), all the application infrastructure components are added as a dependency to the chart.

- Configure your service to connect to the newly provisioned components. You can achieve this by giving the service the new provisioned instance URL and credentials to connect. For a database, it will be the database URL serving requests and possibly a username and password. An interesting detail to notice here is that your application will need some kind of driver to connect to the target database. More on this in chapter 8.

- Maintain these components in the long run, doing backups and ensuring the fail-over mechanisms work as expected.

Figure 5.2 shows the steps involved in installing and wiring up these application infrastructure components to our application's services.

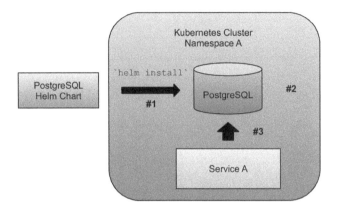

Figure 5.2   Provisioning a new PostgreSQL instance using the PostgreSQL Helm Chart. #1 Install a helm chart into a Namespace inside a Kubernetes Cluster; #2 The chart creates Kubernetes resources such as StatefulSets and Deployments to provision a PostgreSQL instance; #3 A Service needs to connect to the newly created instance, this can be done manually or by referencing a Kubernetes Secret that contains the credentials and details on how to connect.

If you are working with Helm Charts, there are a couple of caveats and tricks that you need to be aware of:

- If the chart doesn't allow you to configure a parameter that you are interested in changing, you can always use `helm template`, then modify the output to add or change the parameters that you need to finally install the components using `kubectl apply -f`. Alternatively, you can submit a pull request to the chart repository. It is a common practice not to expose all possible parameters and wait for community members to suggest more parameters to be exposed by the chart. Don't be shy and contact the maintainers if that is the case. Whatever modification you do, the chart content must be maintained and documented. By using `helm template`, you lose the Helm release management features, allowing you to upgrade a chart when a new version is available.
- Most charts have a default configuration designed to scale, meaning that the default deployment will target high-availability scenarios. This results in charts that, when installed, consume a lot of resources (CPU and memory) that might not be available if you use Kubernetes KinD or Minikube on your laptop. Once again, chart documentation usually includes special configurations for development and resource-constrained environments.
- If you are installing a database inside your Kubernetes cluster, each database container (pod) must have access to storage from the underlying Kubernetes node. For databases, you might need a special kind of storage to enable the database to scale elastically, which might require advanced configurations outside of Kubernetes.

For our walking skeleton, for example, we set up the Redis chart to use the `architecture` parameter to `standalone`, (as you can see in the environment pipeline configurations and in the Agenda service Helm Chart values.yaml file) to make it easier to run on environments where you might have limited resources, such as your laptop/workstation. This affects Redis's availability to tolerate failure, because it will only run a single replica in contrast with the default setup where a master and two slaves are created.

5.1.2 Connecting our services to the newly provisioned infrastructure

Installing the charts will not make our application services automatically connect to the Redis, PostgreSQL, or Kafka instances. We need to provide the services the configurations need to connect while also being conscious of the time needed by these components, such as databases, to start.

Figure 5.3 shows how the wiring usually happens, as most charts automatically create a Kubernetes secret hosting all the details that application's services need to connect.

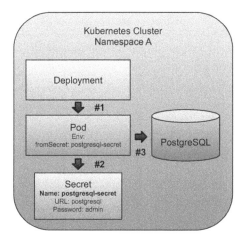

Figure 5.3 Connecting a service to a provisioned resource using secrets. #1 A Kubernetes deployment is created to run one of your services, and the pod template contains the environment variables to configure the pods that this deployment will create; #2 The pod is created using the template specified in the deployment resource, which points to a secret that contains the details to connect to the db instance; #3 The container, which is running inside the pod needs to be prepared to consume the environment variables to connect to the db instance.

A common practice is to use Kubernetes secrets to store the credentials for these application infrastructure components. The Helm Chart for Redis and PostgreSQL that we are using for our walking skeleton creates a new Kubernetes secret containing the details required to connect. These Helm Charts also create a Kubernetes service to be used as the location (URL) where the instance will run.

To connect the Call for Proposals (C4P) service to the PostgreSQL instance, you need to make sure that the Kubernetes Deployment for the C4P service (`conference -c4p-service-deployment`) has the right environment variables (listing 5.1).

Listing 5.1   Environment variables to connect to application infrastructure (PostgreSQL)

```
- name: KAFKA_URL
  value: <KAFKA SERVICE URL>
- name: POSTGRES_HOST
  valueFrom:
    secretKeyRef:
      name: <POSTGRESQL SECRET NAME>
      key: postgres-url
- name: POSTGRES_PASSWORD
  valueFrom:
    secretKeyRef:
      name: <POSTGRESQL SECRET NAME>
      key: postgres-password
```

The bold highlights how we can consume the dynamically generated password when we install the chart and the DB endpoint URL, which is the PostgreSQL Kubernetes service, also created by the chart. The DB endpoint will be different if you used a different chart release name.

A similar configuration applies to the Agenda service (`conference-agenda-service -deployment`) and Redis (listing 5.2).

Listing 5.2   Environment variables to connect to application infrastructure (Redis)

```
- name: KAFKA_URL
  value: <KAFKA SERVICE URL>
- name: REDIS_HOST
  valueFrom:
    secretKeyRef:
      name: <REDIS SECRET NAME>
      key: redis-url
- name: REDIS_PASSWORD
  valueFrom:
    secretKeyRef:
      name: <REDIS SECRET NAME>
      key: redis-password
```

As before, we extract the password from a Kubernetes secret that will be generated when installing the Redis Helm Chart. The secret name will be derived from the name of the Helm Chart release that we use. The REDIS_HOST is obtained from the name of the Kubernetes service that is created by the chart, which depends on the helm release name that you used. For all the services of the application we will need to set up the KAFKA_URL environment variable so that the services can connect to Kafka. Configuring different instances for the application infrastructure components opens the door for us to delegate the provisioning and maintenance to other teams and even cloud providers.

5.1.3   *I've heard about Kubernetes operators. Should I use them?*

Now you have four application services, two databases, and a message broker inside your Kubernetes cluster. Believe it or not, now you are in charge of seven components to maintain and scale depending on the application's needs. The team that built the services will know exactly how to maintain and upgrade each service, but they are not experts in maintaining and scaling databases or message brokers.

You might need help with these databases and message brokers depending on how demanding the services are. Imagine you have too many requests on the Agenda service, so you decide to scale up the number of replicas of the agenda deployment to 200. At that point, Redis must have enough resources to deal with 200 pods connecting to the Redis cluster. The advantage of using Redis for this scenario, where we might get a lot of reads while the conference is ongoing, is that the Redis cluster allows us to read data from the replicas so the load can be distributed.

Figure 5.4 shows a typical case of high demand, where we are tempted to increase the number of replicas of our application's services, without checking or changing the configuration of our PostgreSQL instance. In these scenarios, even if the application's services can scale, the PostgreSQL instance will be the bottleneck if not configured accordingly (to support 200+ concurrent connections).

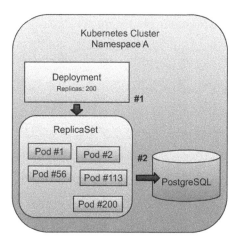

Figure 5.4   Application infrastructure needs to be configured according to how our services will be scaled. #1 If you noticed a surge in demand for one of your services, you might be tempted to increase the number of replicas, and the deployment using the ReplicaSet will not complain about it. If the cluster has enough resources, the replicas will be created; #2 If the application infrastructure is not correctly configured, you might encounter a lot of issues, such as exhausting the database connection pool or overloading the database pods, as they are not scaled when you scale up your deployments.

If you are installing your application infrastructure with Helm, notice that Helm will not check for the health of these components—it is just doing the installation. It is quite common nowadays to find another alternative to install components in a Kubernetes cluster called Operators. Usually associated with application infrastructure, you can find more active components that will install and monitor the installed components. One example of these operators is the Zalando PostgreSQL Operator, which you can find at https://github.com/zalando/postgres-operator. While these operators are focused on allowing you to provision new instances of PostgreSQL databases, they also implement other features focused on maintenance, for example:

- Rolling updates on Postgres cluster changes, including quick minor version updates
- Live volume resize without pod restarts (AWS EBS, PVC)
- Database connection pooling with PGBouncer
- Supporting fast, in-place major version upgrades

In general, Kubernetes operators try to encapsulate the operational tasks associated with a specific component, in this case, PostgreSQL. While using operators might add more features on top of installing a given component, you still need to maintain the component and the operator itself now. Each operator comes with a very opinionated flow that your teams will need to research and learn to manage. Take this into consideration when researching and deciding which operator to use.

Regarding the application infrastructure you and your teams decide to use if you plan to run these components inside your cluster, plan accordingly to have the right in-house expertise to manage, maintain, and scale these extra components.

In the following section, we will look at how we can tackle these challenges by looking at an open-source project that aims to simplify the provisioning of cloud and on-prem resources for application infrastructure components using a declarative approach.

5.2   *Declarative infrastructure using Crossplane*

Using Helm to install application infrastructure components inside Kubernetes is far from ideal for large applications and user-facing environments, because maintaining these components and their requirements, such as advanced storage configurations, might become too complex to handle for your teams.

Cloud providers do a fantastic job at allowing us to provision infrastructure, but they all rely on cloud provider-specific tools that are outside of the realm of Kubernetes.

In this section, we will look at an alternative tool—a CNCF project called Crossplane (https://crossplane.io), which uses the Kubernetes APIs and extension points to enable users to provision real infrastructure in a declarative way, using the Kubernetes APIs. Crossplane relies on the Kubernetes APIs to support multiple cloud providers; this also means that it integrates nicely with all the existing Kubernetes tooling.

By understanding how Crossplane works and how it can be extended, you can build a multi-cloud approach and run your cloud-native applications and their dependencies with different providers without worrying about getting locked in on a single vendor. Because Crossplane uses the same declarative approach as Kubernetes, you can create high-level abstractions about the applications you are trying to deploy and maintain.

To use Crossplane, you must first install its control plane in a Kubernetes cluster. You can follow the official documentation (https://docs.crossplane.io/) or the step-by-step tutorial introduced in section 5.3.

The core Crossplane components alone will not do much for you. Depending on your cloud provider(s), you will install and configure one or more *Crossplane providers*. Let's take a look at what Crossplane providers have to offer us.

5.2.1 Crossplane providers

Crossplane extends Kubernetes by installing a set of components called Crossplane providers (https://docs.crossplane.io/v1.12/concepts/providers/) in charge of understanding and interacting with cloud provider-specific services to provision cloud resources on our behalf. Figure 5.5 shows how by installing the GCP provider and the AWS provider, our Crossplane installation can provision resources on both clouds.

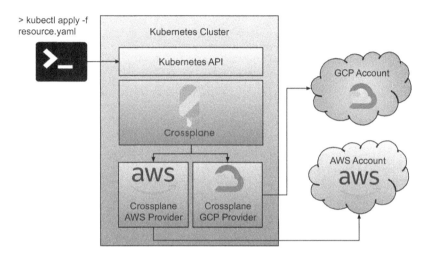

Figure 5.5   Crossplane installed with GCP and AWS providers

By installing Crossplane providers, you are extending the Kubernetes API's functionality to provision external resources such as databases, message brokers, buckets, and other cloud resources that will live outside your Kubernetes cluster but inside the cloud provider realm. There are several Crossplane providers that cover the major cloud providers such as GCP, AWS, and Azure. You can find these Crossplane providers in the Crossplane GitHub's organization: https://docs.crossplane.io/latest/concepts/providers/.

Once a Crossplane Provider is installed, you can create provider-specific resources in a declarative way, which means that you can create a Kubernetes Resource, apply it with `kubectl apply -f`, package these definitions in Helm Charts or use environment pipelines storing these resources in a Git repository.

For example, creating a bucket in Google Cloud using the Crossplane GCP provider looks like listing 5.4.

Listing 5.4   Google Cloud Platform bucket resource definition

```
cat <<EOF | kubectl create -f -
apiVersion: storage.gcp.upbound.io/v1beta1
kind: Bucket
metadata:
  generateName: crossplane-bucket-
  labels:
    docs.crossplane.io/example: provider-gcp
spec:
  forProvider:
    location: US
  providerConfigRef:
    name: default
EOF
```

Both apiVersion and kind are defined by the Crossplane GCP provider. You can find all the supported types of resources in the Crossplane provider documentation.

For each resource type, you have a set of parameters to configure the resource. In this case, we want the bucket to be in the US. Different resources will expose different configuration parameters.

By creating a bucket resource in our Kubernetes cluster where Crossplane is installed, you are creating a request for Crossplane to provision and monitor this resource on your behalf.

Provisioning cloud-specific resources relying on the Kubernetes APIs is a big step forward, but Crossplane doesn't stop there. If you look at what it takes to provision a database in any major cloud provider, you will realize that provisioning the component is just one of the tasks involved in getting the component ready to be used. You need extra network and security configurations, user credentials, and other cloud provider-specific configurations to connect to these provisioned resources. Welcome Crossplane compositions!

5.2.2   *Crossplane compositions*

Crossplane aims to serve two different personas: *platform teams* and *application teams.* While *platform* teams are cloud provider experts who understand how to provision cloud provider-specific components, *application* teams know the application requirements and understand what is required from the application infrastructure perspective. The interesting thing about this approach is that when using Crossplane, platform teams can define these complex configurations for a specific cloud provider and expose simplified interfaces for application teams.

In real-life scenarios, it is rare to create a single component. For example, if we want to provision a database instance, application teams will also require the correct network and security configurations to be able to access the newly created instance. Being able to compose and wire together several components is a very convenient feature, and to achieve these abstractions and simplified interfaces, Crossplane introduced two concepts, *Composite Resource Definitions (XRDs)* and *Composite Resources (XRs).*

Figure 5.6 shows how you can use Crossplane XRD to define abstractions for different cloud providers. The platform team might be very knowledgeable in Google Cloud or Azure, so they will be in charge of defining which Resources they want to wire up together for a specific application. The application team has a simple resource interface to request the resource they are interested in. But as usual, abstractions are complicated and good to show who is responsible for what, but let's look at a concrete example to understand the power of Crossplane compositions.

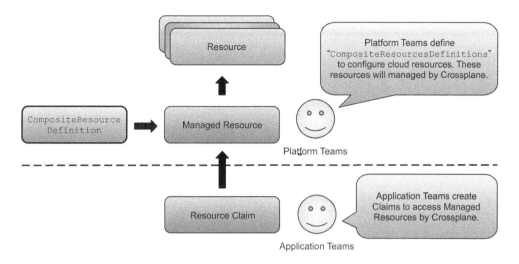

Figure 5.6 Resource composition abstractions by Crossplane composite resources

Figure 5.7 shows how the application team can create a simple PostgreSQL resource to a provision in Google Cloud a CloudSQLInstance plus a network configuration and a bucket. The application team is interested in something other than what resources are created or even in which cloud provider they were created. They are only interested in having a PostgreSQL instance to connect their applications to.

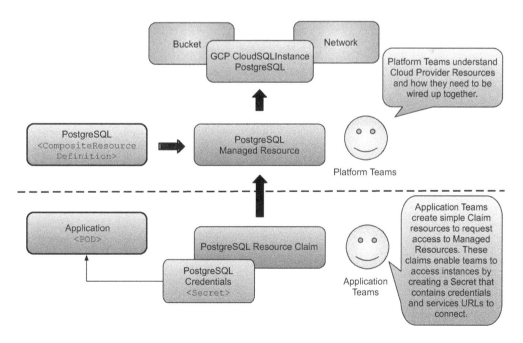

Figure 5.7 Provisioning a PostgreSQL instance in Google Cloud with Crossplane compositions

This takes us to the `Secret` box in the figure, representing a Kubernetes secret that Crossplane will create for our application/services pods to connect to the provisioned resources. Crossplane creates this Kubernetes secret with all the details our applications require to connect to the newly created resources (or just with the one relevant to the application). This secret typically contains URLs, usernames, passwords, certificates, or anything required for your applications to connect. Platform teams define what will be included in the secret when defining the CompositeResources. In the following sections, when we add real infrastructure to our Conference application, we will explore how these `CompositeResourceDefinitions` look and how they can be applied to create all the components our applications need.

5.2.3 *Crossplane components and requirements*

To work with Crossplane providers and `CompositeResourceDefinitions` we need to understand how Crossplane components will work together to provision and manage these components inside different cloud providers.

This section covers what Crossplane needs to work and how Crossplane components will manage our `CompositeResources`. First, it is important to understand that you must install Crossplane in a Kubernetes cluster. This can be the cluster where your applications run or a separate cluster where Crossplane will run. This cluster will have some Crossplane components that will understand our `CompositeResourceDefinitions` and have enough permissions on the cloud platform to provision resources on our behalf.

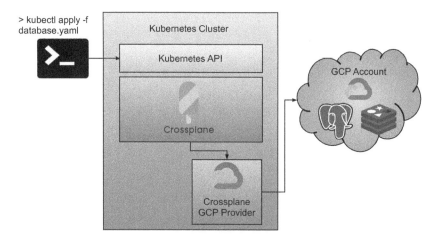

Figure 5.8   Crossplane in Google Cloud Platform

Figure 5.8 shows Crossplane installed inside a Kubernetes cluster, with the Crossplane GCP provider installed and configured to use a Google Cloud Platform account with enough rights to provision PostgreSQL and Redis instances. This means having, in some cases, admin access to create resources on the cloud provider.

For figure 5.8 to work in GCP, you need the following configurations on the cloud provider:

- For creating a Redis instance in GCP.
  - Your GCP project needs to have the `redis.googleapis.com` APIs enabled.
  - You also need to have admin rights on the Redis resources `roles/redis.admin`.
- For creating a PostgreSQL instance in GCP:
  - Your GCP project needs to have the `sqladmin.googleapis.com` APIs enabled.
  - You also need to have admin rights on the SQL resources `roles/cloudsql.admin`.

Each Crossplane provider available requires a specific security configuration to work and an account inside the cloud provider where we want to create resources. Once a Crossplane provider is installed and configured (in this case, the GCP provider) we can start creating resources managed by this provider. You can find the resources offered by each provider on the following documentation site: https://doc.crds.dev/github.com/crossplane/provider-gcp (figure 5.9).

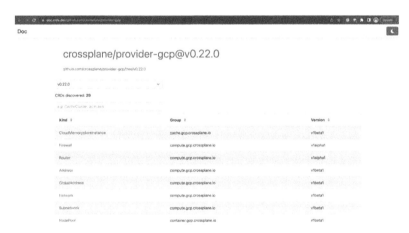

Figure 5.9 Crossplane GCP–supported resources

As you can see in the previous figure, the GCP provider version 0.22.0 supports 29 different CRDs (Custom Resource Definitions) for creating resources in the Google Cloud Platform. Crossplane defines each of these resources as managed resources. Each of these managed resources will need to be enabled for the Crossplane provider to have access to the list, create, and modify these resources.

In section 5.3, we will look at how to provision cloud or local resources for our applications using different Crossplane providers and Crossplane compositions. Before jumping into the technical aspects, let's look at Crossplane core behaviors that you should look for when working with tools in the Kubernetes space.

5.2.4   *Crossplane behaviors*

In contrast to installing Helm components in our Kubernetes clusters, we use Crossplane to interact with the cloud provider-specific APIs to provision resources inside the cloud infrastructure. This should simplify the maintenance tasks and costs related to these resources. Another important difference is that the Crossplane provider (GCP provider in this case) will observe the created managed resources for us. These managed resources offer some advantages compared with just installed resources using Helm. Managed resources have very well-defined behaviors. Here is a summary of what to expect from a Crossplane managed resource:

- *Visible as any other Kubernetes resource:* Crossplane managed resources are just Kubernetes resources. This means that we can use any Kubernetes tool to monitor and query the state of these resources.

- *Continuous reconciliation:* When a managed resource is created, the provider will continuously monitor the resource to ensure it exists and is working and report back the status to the Kubernetes resource. The parameters defined inside the managed resource are considered the desired state (source of truth) and Crossplane providers will work to apply these configurations to the cloud provider resources. Once again, we can use standard Kubernetes tools to monitor changes in state and trigger remediation flows.

- *Immutable properties* Providers are in charge of reporting back if a user manually changes properties in the cloud provider. The idea here is to avoid configuration drifts from what was defined to what is running in the cloud provider. If so, the state is reported back to the managed resource. Crossplane will not delete the cloud provider resource but will notify back so actions can be taken. Other tools like Terraform (https://www.terraform.io) will automatically delete the remote resources to recreate them.

- *Late initialization:* Some properties in the managed resources can be optional, meaning each provider will select the default values for these properties. When this happens, Crossplane creates the resource with the default values and then sets the selected values into the managed resource. This simplifies the configuration needed to create resources and reuse the sensible defaults defined by cloud providers, usually in their user interfaces.

- *Deletion:* When deleting a managed resource, the cloud provider immediately triggers the action. However, the managed resource is kept until the resource is fully removed from the cloud provider. Errors that might happen during deletion on the cloud provider will be added to the managed resource status field.

- *Importing existing resources:* Crossplane doesn't necessarily need to create the resources to manage them. You can create managed resources that start monitoring components created before Crossplane was installed. You can achieve this using a specific Crossplane annotation on the managed resource: `crossplane
.io/external-name`.

To summarize the interactions between Crossplane, the Crossplane GCP provider, and our managed resources, let's look at figure 5.10.

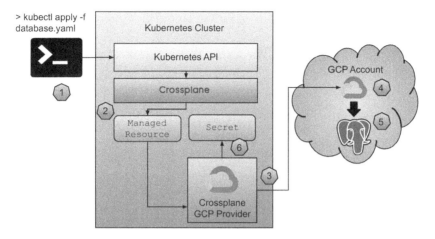

Figure 5.10   Lifecycle of managed resources with Crossplane

The following points indicate the sequence observed in figure 5.10:

1 First, we need to create a resource. We can use any tool to create Kubernetes resources; `kubectl` here is just an example.

2 If the created resource is a Crossplane managed resource, let's imagine a CloudSQLInstance resource the GCP Crossplane provider will pick up and manage.

3 The first step to execute when managing a resource will be checking if it exists in the infrastructure (that is, in the configured GCP account). If it doesn't exist, the provider will request that the resource be created in the infrastructure. The appropriate SQL database will be provisioned depending on the properties set on the resource, such as which kind of SQL database is required. Imagine that we have chosen a PostgreSQL database for the sake of the example.

4 The cloud provider, after receiving the request, if the resources are enabled, will create a new PostgreSQL instance with the configured parameters in the managed resource.

5 The status of the PostgreSQL will be reported back to the managed resource, which means that we can use `kubectl` or any other tool to monitor the status of the provisioned resources. Crossplane providers will keep these in sync.

6 When the database is up and running, the Crossplane provider will create a secret to store the credentials and properties that our applications will need to connect to the newly created instance.

Crossplane will regularly check the status of the PostgreSQL instance and update the managed resource.

By following Kubernetes design patterns, Crossplane uses the reconciliation cycle implemented by controllers to keep track of external resources. Let's see this in action! The following section will examine how we can use Crossplane with our walking skeleton application.

5.3   *Infrastructure for our walking skeleton*

In this section, we will use Crossplane to abstract away how we provision infrastructure for our Conference application. Because you might not have access to a cloud provider like GCP, AWS, or Azure, we will work with a special provider called the Crossplane Helm provider. This Crossplane Helm provider allows us to manage Helm Charts as cloud resources. The idea here is to show how using Crossplane—more specifically, using Crossplane compositions—we can enable users to request resources using a simplified Kubernetes resource to provision local or different cloud resources (hosted in different cloud providers).

For our Conference application, we need Redis, PostgreSQL, and Kafka instances. From the application perspective, as soon as these three components are available, we can connect to them, and we are good to go. How these components are configured is the responsibility of the operations teams.

The conference application helm chart that we installed in chapter 2 included the installation of Redis, PostgreSQL, and Kafka as Helm dependencies using a conditional value that can be set at installation time. Let's take a quick look at how this was wired up for our Helm Chart: https://github.com/salaboy/platforms-on-k8s/blob/main/conference-application/helm/conference-app/Chart.yaml#L13.

The Conference Helm Chart includes the Redis, PostgreSQL, and Kafka charts dependencies, as shown in listing 5.5.

Listing 5.5   Conference application with Helm Chart dependencies

> You can include any number of dependencies to your Helm Charts. This allows complex compositions.

```
apiVersion: v2
description: A Helm chart for the Conference App
name: conference-app
version: v1.0.0
type: application
icon: https://www.salaboy.com/content/images/2023/06/avatar-new.png
appVersion: v1.0.0
home: http://github.com/salaboy/platforms-on-k8s
dependencies:
- name: redis
  version: 17.11.3
  repository: https://charts.bitnami.com/bitnami
  condition: install.infrastructure
```

> Each dependency requires the chart name, the repository where it is hosted (notice that you can use oci:// references here too), and the version of the chart that you want to install.

> Custom conditions can be defined to decide if this dependency is injected when we install the chart.

```
- name: postgresql
  version: 12.5.7
  repository: https://charts.bitnami.com/bitnami
  condition: install.infrastructure
- name: kafka
  version: 22.1.5
  repository: https://charts.bitnami.com/bitnami
  condition: install.infrastructure
```

For this example, all the application infrastructure dependencies are defined at the application level (dependencies section in the Chart.yaml file), but there is nothing stopping you from having one Helm Chart per service, which internally defines its own dependencies.

This kind of chart dependency works for development teams that want to install the entire application with all the components needed with a single command. Still, we want to decouple all the application infrastructural concerns from application services for larger scenarios. Luckily, the Conference application Helm Chart allows us to turn off these component dependencies, allowing us to plug in Redis, PostgreSQL, and Kafka instances hosted and managed by different teams (figure 5.11).

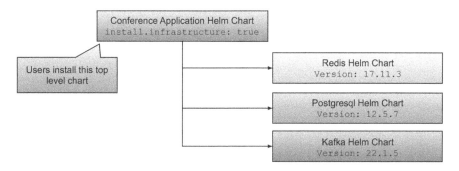

Figure 5.11   Using Helm Chart dependencies for application infrastructure

By separating who requests and who provisions the application's infrastructure components, we enable different teams to control and manage when these components are updated, backed up, or how they need to be restored in case of failure. By using Crossplane, we can enable teams to request these databases on demand, which then can be connected to our application's services. One important aspect of the mechanisms we will use in the next sections is that the components we request can be provisioned locally (using the Crossplane Helm provider) or remotely using Crossplane cloud providers. Let's see what this would look like. You can follow a step-by-step tutorial to install, configure, and create your Crossplane compositions: https://github .com/salaboy/platforms-on-k8s/tree/main/chapter-5.

In this example, we will create a KinD cluster and configure Crossplane to allow teams to request application infrastructure on demand using the Crossplane Helm provider for development purposes. In production the same requests will be satisfied via scalable cloud resources. More specifically, we enable teams to request Redis, PostgreSQL, and Kafka instances this way using a simplified interface.

For our Conference application example, the platform team decided to create two different concepts:

- *Databases:* NoSQL and SQL databases such as Redis and PostgreSQL.
- *Message brokers:* For managed and unmanaged message brokers such as Kafka.

After having Crossplane and the Crossplane Helm provider installed, the platform team needs to define two Kubernetes resources:

- *Crossplane Composite Resource Definitions (XRDs):* Defines the resources we want to expose to our teams—in this example, Database and MessageBroker. These Composite Resource Definitions define an interface that multiple Compositions can implement.
- *Crossplane composition:* The Crossplane composition allows us to define a set of resource manifests. We can link a composition to a Composite Resource Definition and implement that XRD. By doing so, when the user requests new resources from the XRD–defined resource, all the composed resource manifests in the composition will be created in the cluster. We can provide multiple compositions (for example for different cloud providers), all implementing the same XRD, and then use labels in our resources to choose which composition should kick in.

I know this might sound confusing at first, so let's see these concepts in action. Let's look at the database Crossplane Composite Resource Definition (https://github.com/salaboy/platforms-on-k8s/blob/main/chapter-5/resources/app-database-resource .yaml) in listing 5.6.

Listing 5.6   Database Composite Resource Definition

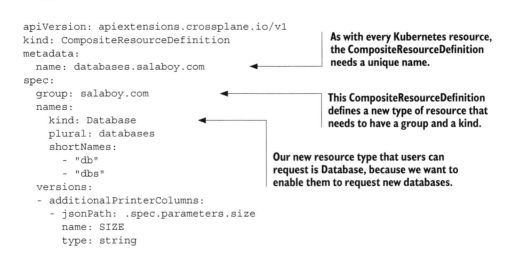

```
apiVersion: apiextensions.crossplane.io/v1
kind: CompositeResourceDefinition
metadata:
  name: databases.salaboy.com
spec:
  group: salaboy.com
  names:
    kind: Database
    plural: databases
    shortNames:
      - "db"
      - "dbs"
  versions:
  - additionalPrinterColumns:
    - jsonPath: .spec.parameters.size
      name: SIZE
      type: string
```

As with every Kubernetes resource, the CompositeResourceDefinition needs a unique name.

This CompositeResourceDefinition defines a new type of resource that needs to have a group and a kind.

Our new resource type that users can request is Database, because we want to enable them to request new databases.

```
      - jsonPath: .spec.parameters.mockData
        name: MOCKDATA
        type: boolean
      - jsonPath: .spec.compositionSelector.matchLabels.kind
        name: KIND
        type: string
    name: v1alpha1
    served: true
    referenceable: true
    schema:
      openAPIV3Schema:
        type: object
        properties:
          spec:
            type: object
            properties:
              parameters:
                type: object
                properties:
                  size:
                    type: string
                  mockData:
                    type: boolean
                required:
                - size
            required:
            - parameters
```

The new resource we are defining can also define custom parameters. For this example, and only for demonstration purposes, we are defining only two: size and mockData.

Because the Kubernetes API server can validate all resources, we can define which parameters are required and their types and other validations. The Kubernetes API server will reject our resource request if these parameters are not provided or invalid.

We have defined a new type of resource called a Database, which contains two parameters that we can set, `size` and `mockData`. Users can define how many resources are allocated for that instance by setting up the `size` parameter. Instead of worrying about how much storage they will need or how many replicas they need for the database instances, they can simply specify a size from a list of possible values (small, medium, or large). Using the `mockData` parameters, you can implement a mechanism to inject data into the instance when needed. This is just an example of what can be done, but it is up to you to define these interfaces and what parameters make sense to your teams.

Let's see what the Crossplane composition looks like that will implement this XRD, in listing 5.7.

Listing 5.7 Key/value Database Crossplane composition

```
apiVersion: apiextensions.crossplane.io/v1
kind: Composition
metadata:
  name: keyvalue.db.local.salaboy.com
  labels:
    type: dev
    provider: local
    kind: keyvalue
spec:
  writeConnectionSecretsToNamespace: crossplane-system
```

The composition resource also needs a unique name.

For each composition, we can also define labels. We will then use these to match compositions with the requested Database resources.

Using the compositeTypeRef property, we are linking
Database CompositeResourceDefinition to this composition.

Inside the resources array, we
can define all the resources this
composition will provision. It is
quite common to have more
than one resource here. For
this example, we are
configuring a single resource of
type Release defined in the
Crossplane Helm provider.

```
compositeTypeRef:
  apiVersion: salaboy.com/v1alpha1
  kind: Database
resources:
  - name: redis-helm-release
    base:
      apiVersion: helm.crossplane.io/v1beta1
      kind: Release
      metadata:
        annotations:
          crossplane.io/external-name: # patched
      spec:
        rollbackLimit: 3
        forProvider:
          namespace: default
          chart:
            name: redis
            repository: https://charts.bitnami.com/bitnami
            version: "17.8.0"
          values:
            architecture: standalone
        providerConfigRef:
          name: default
    patches:
      - fromFieldPath: metadata.name
        toFieldPath: metadata.annotations[crossplane.io/external-name]
        policy:
          fromFieldPath: Required
      - fromFieldPath: metadata.name
        toFieldPath: metadata.name
        transforms:
          - type: string
            string:
              fmt: "%s-redis"
readinessChecks:
  - type: MatchString
    fieldPath: status.atProvider.state
    matchString: deployed
```

We need to provide the values
defined for the Release
resource, in this case, the Helm
Chart details that we want to
install using the Crossplane
Helm provider. As you can see,
we are pointing to the Redis
Helm Chart hosted by Bitnami.

Because we are wiring multiple
resources, we can patch resources to
configure them to work together or to
apply the parameters of the requested
resource. Check the Crossplane
documentation for more details on what
can be achieved with these mechanisms.

For each composition, we can define a condition to flag the
resource status. For this example, we will mark the
composition as ready when the Helm Release resource status
.atProvider.state property is set to deployed. If you are
provisioning multiple resources, you, as the person defining
the composition, will need to define what this condition is.

Using the providerConfigRef,
we can target different
Crossplane Helm provider
configurations. This means
we can have different Helm
providers pointing to
different target clusters, and
this composition can select
which one to use. For the
sake of simplicity, this
composition uses the default
configuration for the local
Helm provider installation.

With this composition, we link our `Database` claim with a set of resources, in this case, installing the Redis Helm Chart using the default Helm provider we installed with Crossplane in our Kubernetes cluster. Figure 5.12 shows two user requests for the same database type.

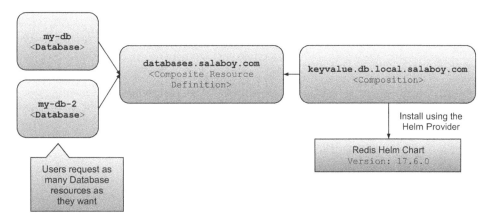

Figure 5.12 Crossplane composition and Composite Resource Definition working together

It is important to note that this Helm Chart will be installed in the same Kubernetes cluster where Crossplane is installed. Still, nothing stops us from configuring the Helm provider to have the right credentials to install charts to a completely different cluster.

In the step-by-step tutorial (https://github.com/salaboy/platforms-on-k8s/tree/main/chapter-5), you will install the three Composite Resource Definitions and three compositions. Once these are installed, as shown in figure 5.12, you can request new databases and message brokers, and for every request, all the resources defined in the composition will be provisioned. For the sake of simplicity, the key-value database composition just installs Redis, but there are no limits on how many resources you can create (except for the available hardware or quotas you have).

A `Database` resource is just another Kubernetes resource that now our cluster understands, and it looks like listing 5.8.

Listing 5.8 Teams create database resources to request new database instances

```
apiVersion: salaboy.com/v1alpha1
kind: Database
metadata:.  name: my-db-keyavalue
spec:
  compositionSelector:
    matchLabels:
      provider: local
      type: dev
      kind: keyvalue
  parameters:
    size: small
    mockData: false
```

The unique name for the resource

We use matchLabels to select the appropriate composition.

We need to set the parameters that are required by our Database resource claim.

The schema for this Database resource is defined inside the Crossplane `Composite ResourceDefinition`. Notice that the `spec.compositionSelector.matchLabels` matches with the labels used for the composition. We can use this mechanism to select a different composition for the same Database definition.

If you are following the step-by-step tutorial, try to create multiple resources and look at the Crossplane official documentation to understand how to implement parameters like `small` or `mockData` because these values are not being used yet and only serve for demonstration purposes.

The real power of these mechanisms comes when you have different compositions (implementations) for the same interface (Composite Resource Definition). For example, we can now create another composition to provision PostgreSQL instances for the Call for Proposals service, as shown in listing 5.9. The PostgreSQL composition will look similar to the one for Redis, but it will install the PostgreSQL helm chart instead.

Listing 5.9   SQL Database Crossplane Composition

```
apiVersion: apiextensions.crossplane.io/v1
kind: Composition
metadata:
  name: sql.db.local.salaboy.com          ◄────────────  We need a
  labels:                                                 unique name for
    type: dev                                             our composition,
    provider: local                                       so we can
    kind: sql             ◄────────────                   differentiate it
spec:                                      We use a different   from the
  ...                                      label to describe this   keyvalue
  compositeTypeRef:                        composition, notice   composition that
    apiVersion: salaboy.com/v1alpha1       that the provider is the   we used for
    kind: Database                         same as before.   Redis.
  resources:
  - name: postgresql-helm-release
    base:
      apiVersion: helm.crossplane.io/v1beta1
      kind: Release
      spec:                                We want to install the
        forProvider:                       PostgreSQL Helm Chart
          chart:             ◄──────────── hosted by Bitnami.
            name: postgresql
            repository: https://charts.bitnami.com/bitnami
            version: "12.2.7"
        providerConfigRef:
          name: default
      ...
```

Let's look at how to create a PostgreSQL instance using this composition. Creating a PostgreSQL instance will look pretty similar to what we did before for Redis, as shown in listing 5.10.

Listing 5.10   Database resource with kind: `sql` label to select implementation

```
apiVersion: salaboy.com/v1alpha1
kind: Database
metadata:
  name: my-db-sql
spec:
  compositionSelector:
    matchLabels:
      provider: local
      type: dev
      kind: sql
  parameters:
    size: small
    mockData: false
```

→ **The unique name used for the PostgreSQL database.**

→ **We use the "sql" label to match the previously defined composition.**

We are just using labels to select which composition will be triggered for our Database resource. Figure 5.13 shows these concepts in action. Notice how labels select the right composition based on the `kind` label value.

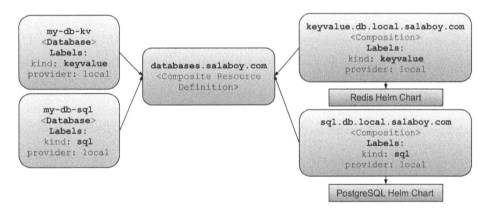

Figure 5.13   Selecting compositions using labels

Hooray! We can create databases! But of course, this doesn't stop here. If you have access to a cloud provider, you can provide compositions that create database instances inside the cloud provider, and this is where Crossplane shines.

If we use the Google Cloud Platform (GCP) as an example, for compositions that use cloud resources from GCP, you will need to install the Crossplane GCP provider and configure it accordingly, as explained in the official Crossplane documentation: https://docs.crossplane.io/latest/getting-started/provider-gcp/.

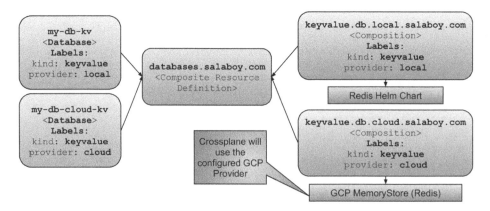

Figure 5.14   Selecting compositions using different providers, still using labels

We can still select different providers by matching labels with our desired composition. By changing a label in figure 5.14, we can use the local Helm Provider or the GCP provider to instantiate a Redis Instance.

> **NOTE**   Check the community–contributed AWS compositions for this example using the Crossplane AWS Provider at https://github.com/salaboy/platforms -on-k8s/tree/main/chapter-5/aws.

Then, creating new database resources that will be provisioned in the Google Cloud Platform will look like listing 5.11.

Listing 5.11   Requesting a new SQL database

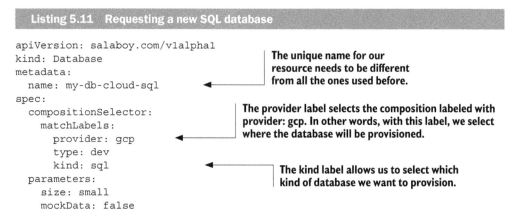

No matter where our databases or other application infrastructure components are provisioned, we can connect our application's services by following some conventions. We can use the resource name (for example, `my-db-cloud-sql`) to know which Kubernetes service will be used for service discovery. We can also use the created secret to obtain the credentials that we will need to connect.

The step-by-step tutorial also provides a `CompositeResourceDefinition` for message brokers and a composition that installs the Kafka Helm chart that you can find at https://github.com/salaboy/platforms-on-k8s/blob/main/chapter-5/resources/app-messagebroker-kafka.yaml.

One really important thing to consider for this example is that Google Cloud Platform doesn't provide a managed Kafka service. This pushes your team to decide to replace Kafka when the application is going to be deployed on Google Cloud Platform, install and manage Kafka on Google Cloud compute or hire a third-party service. In the AWS example, we have a Kafka–managed service that we can use, so there is no need to change our application code. But still, wouldn't it be nice to abstract away how we connect to these infrastructure services? More on this in chapter 7.

Figure 5.15 shows how easy it is to provide a Composite Resource Definition for key/value databases that can be provisioned locally using Helm or managed by a cloud provider. But in the case of Kafka, it gets a bit trickier because you might need to integrate with a third-party service or take the lead in having a team to manage the Kafka instance(s).

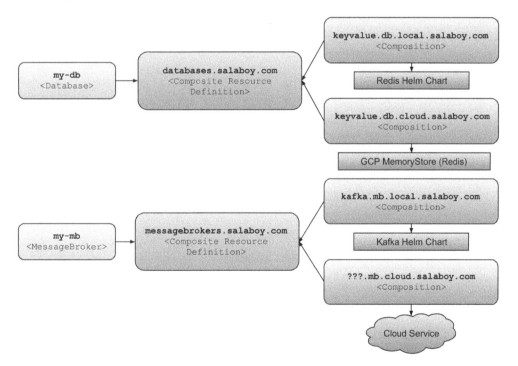

Figure 5.15 Compositions push teams to define which Cloud services are available for our applications to use.

Besides Kafka and Google Cloud Platform, your teams will need a strategy to deal with infrastructure across cloud providers, or at least make conscious choices about how to deal with situations like this. From the application's services perspective, would you maintain two copies of the same service if you decide to swap Kafka and use Google PubSub instead? One includes the Kafka dependencies, and the other includes the Google GCP SDKs to connect to Google PubSub. If you only use Google PubSub, you lose the ability to run the application outside Google Cloud.

5.3.1 Connecting our services with the new provisioned infrastructure

When we create new database or message broker resources, Crossplane will monitor the status of these Kubernetes resources against the status of the provisioned components inside the specific cloud provider, keeping them in sync and ensuring that the desired configurations are applied. This means that Crossplane will make sure that our databases and message brokers are up and running. If for some reason that changes, Crossplane will try to reapply the configurations that we requested until what we requested is up and running.

If we don't have the application deployed in our KinD cluster, we can deploy it without installing PostgreSQL, Redis, and Kafka. As we have seen in chapter 2, this can be disabled by setting one flag: `install.infrastructure=false`:

```
> helm install conference oci://docker.io/salaboy/conference-app
➥--version v1.0.0 --set install.infrastructure=false
```

I strongly recommend you check out the step-by-step tutorial that you can find at https://github.com/salaboy/platforms-on-k8s/tree/main/chapter-5 to get your hands dirty with Crossplane and the Conference application. The best way to learn is by doing!

If we just run this command, no components (Redis, PostgreSQL, or Kafka) will be provisioned by Helm. Still, the application's services will not know where to connect to the Redis, PostgreSQL, and Kafka instances we created using our Crossplane compositions. We need to add more parameters to the application chart, so the services know where to connect. First, check which databases you have available in your cluster as in listing 5.12.

Listing 5.12   Listing all database resources

```
> kubectl get dbs
NAME              SIZE     KIND       SYNCED    READY    COMPOSITION
my-db-keyavalue   small    keyvalue   True      True     keyvalue.db.local.salaboy.com
my-db-sql         small    sql        True      True     sql.db.local.salaboy.com
```

The tutorial also guides you to create a MessageBroker and checks that you have one instance of that too, as in listing 5.13.

Listing 5.13   Listing all MessageBroker resources

```
> kubectl get mbs
NAME          SIZE     KIND     SYNCED    READY    COMPOSITION
my-mb-kafka   small    kafka    True      True     kafka.mb.local.salaboy.com
```

Listing 5.14 shows the Kubernetes pods for our database instances and our message broker.

Listing 5.14 Pods for our application infrastructure

```
> kubectl get pods
NAME                              READY   STATUS    RESTARTS   AGE
my-db-keyavalue-redis-master-0    1/1     Running   0          25m
my-db-sql-postgresql-0            1/1     Running   0          25m
my-mb-kafka-0                     1/1     Running   0          25m
```

Along with the pods, four Kubernetes secrets were created: two to store the Helm releases used by our Crossplane compositions and two containing our new databases passwords that our applications will need to use to connect (see listing 5.15).

Listing 5.15 Kubernetes secrets containing credentials to connect to our Databases

```
> kubectl get secret
NAME                                   TYPE                DATA   AGE
my-db-keyavalue-redis                  Opaque              1      26m
my-db-sql-postgresql                   Opaque              1      25m
sh.helm.release.v1.my-db-keyavalue.v1  helm.sh/release.v1  1      26m
sh.helm.release.v1.my-db-sql.v1        helm.sh/release.v1  1      25m
sh.helm.release.v1.my-mb-kafka.v1      helm.sh/release.v1  1      25m
```

Take a look at the services available in the default namespace after we provisioned our databases, see Listing 5.16:

Listing 5.16 Custom values.yaml file to connect with new infrastructure

```
> kubectl get services
NAME                             TYPE        CLUSTER-IP      PORT(S)
kubernetes                       ClusterIP   10.96.0.1       443/TCP
my-db-keyavalue-redis-headless   ClusterIP   None            6379/TCP
my-db-keyavalue-redis-master     ClusterIP   10.96.49.121    6379/TCP
my-db-sql-postgresql             ClusterIP   10.96.129.115   5432/TCP
my-db-sql-postgresql-hl          ClusterIP   None            5432/TCP
my-mb-kafka                      ClusterIP   10.96.239.45    9092/TCP
my-mb-kafka-headless             ClusterIP   None            9092/TCP
```

With the database and message broker service names and secrets, we can configure our conference application chart to not only not deploy Redis, PostgreSQL, and Kafka but also to connect to the right instances by running the following command:

```
> helm install conference oci://docker.io/salaboy/conference-app
➥--version v1.0.0 -f app-values.yaml
```

Instead of setting all the parameters in the command, we are using a file for the values to be applied to the chart. For this example, the app-values.yaml file looks like listing 5.17.

Listing 5.17   Helm Chart customized values.yaml file

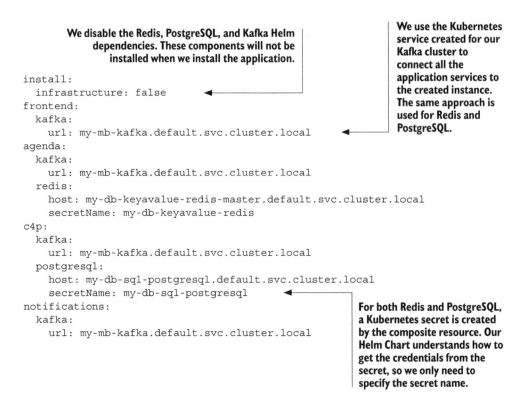

We disable the Redis, PostgreSQL, and Kafka Helm dependencies. These components will not be installed when we install the application.

We use the Kubernetes service created for our Kafka cluster to connect all the application services to the created instance. The same approach is used for Redis and PostgreSQL.

```
install:
  infrastructure: false
frontend:
  kafka:
    url: my-mb-kafka.default.svc.cluster.local
agenda:
  kafka:
    url: my-mb-kafka.default.svc.cluster.local
  redis:
    host: my-db-keyavalue-redis-master.default.svc.cluster.local
    secretName: my-db-keyavalue-redis
c4p:
  kafka:
    url: my-mb-kafka.default.svc.cluster.local
  postgresql:
    host: my-db-sql-postgresql.default.svc.cluster.local
    secretName: my-db-sql-postgresql
notifications:
  kafka:
    url: my-mb-kafka.default.svc.cluster.local
```

For both Redis and PostgreSQL, a Kubernetes secret is created by the composite resource. Our Helm Chart understands how to get the credentials from the secret, so we only need to specify the secret name.

In this app-values.yaml file, we are not only turning off the Helm dependencies for PostgreSQL, Redis, and Kafka, but we are also configuring the variables needed for the services to connect to our newly provisioned databases. Notice that if the databases were created in a different namespace or with a different name, the `kafka.url, postgresql.host` and `redis.host` should contain the appropriate namespace in the fully qualified name of the service, for example, `my-db-sql-postgresql.default.svc.cluster.local` (where `default` is the namespace).

Figure 5.16 shows the Conference application services connecting to the application infrastructure that was created with Crossplane. The boundaries between the developer realm and the platform team become more defined now, as developers interested in getting the infrastructure that they need have a set of options that are carefully selected by the platform team and exposed to developers using simpler interfaces.

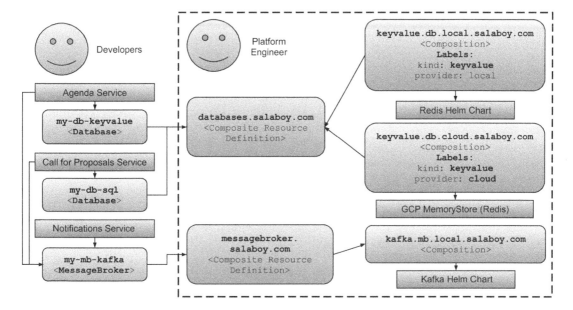

Figure 5.16 Enabling different teams to work together and focus on their tasks at hand

All this effort enables us to split the responsibility of defining, configuring, and running all the application infrastructure to another team not responsible for working on the application's services. Services can be released independently without worrying about which databases are being used or when they need to be upgraded. Developers shouldn't be worrying about cloud provider accounts or if they have access to create different resources. Hence, another team with a completely different set of skills can take care of creating Crossplane compositions and configuring Crossplane providers.

We have also enabled teams to request application infrastructure components by using Kubernetes resources. This enables them to create their setups for experimentation and testing or to set up new instances of the application quickly. This is a major shift in how we (as developers) were used to doing things, because before this, cloud providers and most companies must have access to a database and a ticketing system to request another team to provision that resource for you, which can take weeks!

To summarize what we have achieved so far, we can say that:

- We abstracted how to provision local- and cloud-specific components such as PostgreSQL and Redis databases and message brokers such as Kafka and all the configurations needed to access these new instances.
- We exposed a simplified interface for the application teams that is cloud-provider independent because it relies on the Kubernetes API.
- Finally, we connected our application service to the newly provisioned instances by relying on Kubernetes Secrets created by Crossplane, containing all the details required to connect to the newly created instances.

If you use mechanisms like Crossplane compositions to create higher-level abstractions, you will create domain-specific concepts that your teams can consume using a self-service approach. We have created our database and message broker concept by creating a Crossplane Composite Resource that uses Crossplane compositions that knows which resources to provision (and in which cloud provider).

NOTE   You can follow a step-by-step tutorial that covers all the steps described in this section at https://github.com/salaboy/platforms-on-k8s/tree/main/chapter-5.

5.4   *Linking back to platform engineering*

We need to be cautious. We cannot expect every developer to understand or be willing to use tools like the ones we have discussed (Crossplane, ArgoCD, Tekton, etc.). We need a way to reduce the complexity these tools introduce. Platforms are meant to reduce the cognitive load of their users, as described in chapter 1 when we looked at Google Cloud Platform and how it enables teams to create a Kubernetes cluster with a few clicks. For GCP and other platforms, the users interacting with the platform don't need to understand what is going on under the covers, what tools are being used, or the design of the entire platform to use it.

Crossplane was created to serve both platform teams and development teams (or consumers), which have different priorities, interests, and skills. By creating the right abstractions (XRDs) the platform team can expose simple resources that development teams can configure according to their needs, while behind the covers, a complex composition is being set up to create and wire together a group of cloud resources. We have also seen how by using labels and selectors, we can choose between different compositions, enabling the creation of infrastructure in different cloud providers but keeping the same user experience for the teams creating the requests. Crossplane, by extending the Kubernetes APIs, unifies how we manage our workloads and how we can manage application infrastructure across cloud providers. In other words, if we install Crossplane into a Kubernetes cluster, we cannot only deploy and run our clusters but also provision and manage cloud resources by using the same tooling that we use for our workloads.

With all the goodies that Crossplane brings, you must also be ready for some drawbacks and challenges. Platform teams looking into Crossplane have other more popular options available to provision cloud resources, such as Hashicorp's Terraform and Pulumi. Crossplane is much more recent than Terraform, and because Crossplane is focused on Kubernetes, it requires platform teams to be fully invested in Kubernetes. Teams not used to managing Kubernetes clusters will find tools like Crossplane challenging at first, so you need to level up your Kubernetes skills to run and maintain a tool like Crossplane.

Platform teams will be forced to make a decision about using Crossplane or tools like Terraform, and my recommendation is to think about how much you want to align the tools that you are using with the Kubernetes APIs. Being able to manage infrastructure (cloud resources) in the same way that we manage our applications makes a lot of sense in theory. Still, it also needs to make sense to the teams managing and maintaining these components up and running. In the last couple of years, there has been a huge increase in maturity around observability, security, and operations in the cloud-native space. More and more teams are feeling comfortable with managing and operating Kubernetes at scale. For those teams, Crossplane can be a great addition, because it is going to work with all their existing Kubernetes observability stacks, policy enforcers, and dashboards.

When having tools as flexible as Crossplane, you open the door to new possibilities that can span across cloud providers. Platform teams now have more options available, and that can be counterproductive, but one thing is clear. If you use the right abstractions, the platform can be flexible, as consumer interfaces will not change. At the same time, the platform team can iterate on their previous decisions and provide new implementations behind the covers.

Figure 5.17 shows how by using Crossplane, we can provide self-service abstractions for development teams to consume. They can request databases, message brokers, identity services, and any other internal or external services they might need for their applications. But what do they need from an application perspective? Think about the Kafka example provided before. What needs to change in your applications if you move from Kafka to Google PubSub?

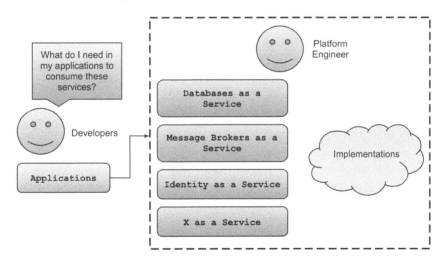

Figure 5.17   What do developers need to consume all these Platform services?

We have covered a lot of ground so far, from installing a simple application into a cluster to building services and deploying them using a GitOps approach and now provisioning application infrastructure declaratively. Figure 5.18 shows how using a GitOps approach we can define not only which services/applications should be running inside an environment, but also which cloud resources need to be provisioned and wired to our application services.

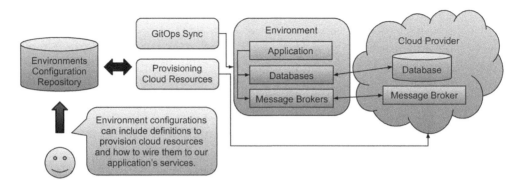

Figure 5.18   Provisioning application infrastructure using a declarative GitOps approach

It is time to put everything together into a platform, because it doesn't make too much sense to have our applications running in the same cluster where our pipelines and other tools are running. What would a platform on top of Kubernetes look like? What are the main challenges that your teams will face when trying to build one? There is only one way to find out: Let's build a platform on top of Kubernetes!

Summary

- Cloud-native applications depend on application infrastructure to run, as each service might require different persistent storages, a message broker to send messages, and other components to work.
- Creating application infrastructure inside cloud providers is easy and can save us a lot of time, but then we rely on their tools and ecosystem.
- Provisioning infrastructure in a cloud-agnostic way can be achieved by relying on the Kubernetes API and tools like Crossplane, which abstracts the underlying cloud provider and lets us define which resources must be provisioned using Crossplane compositions.
- Crossplane provides support for major cloud providers. It can be extended for other service providers, including third-party tools that might not be running on cloud providers (for example, legacy systems we want to manage using the Kubernetes APIs).
- By using Crossplane Composite Resource Definitions, we create an interface that application teams can use to request cloud resources using a self-service approach.
- If you followed the step-by-step tutorial, you got hands-on experience on how to provision application infrastructure using a multi-cloud approach using Crossplane.

Let's build a platform
on top of Kubernetes

6

This chapter covers

- Identifying features that platforms should provide on Kubernetes
- Learning the challenges with multi-cluster and multi-tenant setups
- Seeing what a platform on top of Kubernetes looks like

So far, we have looked at what platform engineering is, why we need to think about platforms in the context of Kubernetes, and how teams must choose the tools they can use from the CNCF landscape (chapter 1). Then we jumped into figuring out how our applications would run on top of Kubernetes (chapter 2), and how to build, package, and deploy (chapters 3 and 4), and connect these applications to other services that they need to work (chapter 5). This chapter puts all the pieces together to create a walking skeleton for our platform. We will use some of the open-source projects introduced in the previous chapters and new tools to solve some of the challenges we will face when creating the first iteration of our platform. This chapter is divided into three main sections:

- The importance of the platform APIs
- Kubernetes platform architecture and how we can architect a scalable platform despite multi-tenancy and multi-cluster challenges
- Introducing our platform walking skeleton and learning how to build a platform on top of Kubernetes

Let's start by considering why defining the platform APIs is the first step to platform building.

6.1 The importance of the platform APIs

In chapter 1, we looked at existing platforms, such as Google Cloud Platform, to understand what key features they offer to teams building and running cloud applications. We now need to compare this to the platforms that we are building on top of Kubernetes, because these platforms share some common goals and features with cloud providers while at the same time being closer to our organizations' domains.

Platforms are nothing other than software that we will design, create, and maintain. As with any good software, our platform will evolve to help teams with new scenarios, make our teams more efficient by providing automation, and give us the tools to make the business more successful. As with any other software, we will start by looking at the platform APIs, which will provide us with a manageable scope to start with and define the contracts and behaviors our platform will provide its users.

Figure 6.1 shows how the platform APIs are the main entry point for consumers of the platform—in this case, developers. These APIs should hide away the complexity of the tools, decisions, supported workflows, and golden paths that the platform provides to its users while at the same time offering a self-service place for teams to get what they need.

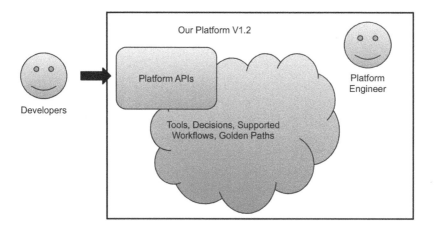

Figure 6.1 The platform engineering team is responsible for platform APIs.

Our platform APIs are important, because good APIs can simplify the life of development teams wanting to consume services from our platform. If our platform APIs are well designed, more tailored tools like CLIs, SDKs, or even user interfaces can be created to assist users in consuming our platform services.

If we build custom and more domain-specific APIs for our platform, we can start by tackling one problem at a time and then expand these APIs/interfaces to cover more and more workflows, even for different teams. Once we understand which workflows we want to cover and have an initial platform API dashboard, more tooling can be created to help teams adopt the platform.

Let's use an example to make it more concrete. I hope you can translate the example I am showing here into more concrete examples inside your organization. All the mechanisms should apply in the same way. Let's enable our development teams to request new development environments.

6.1.1   *Requesting development environments*

A common scenario where a platform can help teams get up to speed when they start working on new features is provisioning them with all they need to do their work. To achieve this task, the platform engineering team must understand what they will work on, what tools they need, and which other services must be available to succeed.

Once the platform engineering team understands what development teams require, they can define an API to provision new development environments on demand. Behind these APIs, the platform has the mechanisms to create, configure, and provide access for the requesting team to connect.

For our Conference application example, if a development team is extending the application, we (the platform engineering team) must ensure they have a running version to work against and test changes. This isolated application instance will also need its databases and other infrastructural components to work. More advanced use cases include loading the application with mock data, allowing teams to test their changes with pre-populated data, and having the right tools to verify the changes. The interactions between the application development team and the platform should look like figure 6.2.

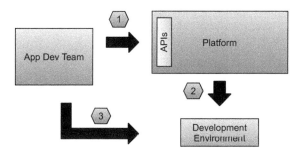

Figure 6.2   Application development team interactions with the platform . #1 App dev teams can request as many Development Environments as they need to the platform APIs; #2 The platform has encoded how to provision all the components and tools needed for the app dev team to work; #3 The platform needs to give access to the app dev team to use the newly provisioned environment.

As mentioned before, development environments are just an example. You must ask yourself what tools your teams need to do their work. A development environment might not be the best way to expose tools to a team of data scientists, for example, because they might need other tools to gather and process data or train machine learning models.

Implementing this simple flow in Kubernetes is not an easy task. To implement this scenario, we need to:

- Create new APIs that understand development environment requests.
- Have the mechanisms to encode what a development environment means for our teams.
- Have the mechanisms to provision and configure components and tools.
- Have the mechanisms to enable teams to connect to the newly provisioned environments.

There are several options for implementing this scenario, including creating custom Kubernetes extensions or using more specialized tools for development environments. But before diving into implementation details, let's define what our platform API would look like for this scenario.

As with object-oriented programming (OOP), our APIs are `Interfaces` that can be implemented by different `Classes`, which finally provide concrete behavior. For provisioning development environments, we can define a very simple interface called `Environment`. Development teams requesting a new development environment can create new requests to the platform by creating new environment resources. The `Environment` interface represents a contract between the user and the platform. This contract can include parameters to define the type of environment the team is requesting or options and parameters they need to tune for their specific request.

Figure 6.3 shows the simplest environment definition, which includes a name for the environment and the kind of environment that we want to create (we might enable teams to request different setups, and for this example, we want a new `development` environment). The environment definition also includes custom configurations that make sense for the consuming team to parameterize. In this case, because we will install the Conference application, we want to enable teams to decide if the infrastructure components need to be installed or not.

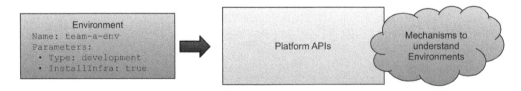

Figure 6.3 Environment resource defined by the Platform API

It is important to note that the `Environment` interface shouldn't include (or leak) any implementation details about our environments. These resources (environments in this case) serve as our abstraction layer to hide complexity from our platform users about how these environments will be created. The simpler these resources are, the better for the platform users. In this example, the platform can use the `Environment Type` parameter to decide which environment to create, and we can plug in new types as we evolve our platform mechanisms.

Once we recognize which interfaces we need, we can slowly add parameters that teams can configure. For our example, it might make sense to parameterize some features for the services we want to deploy in our environment if we also want the application infrastructure to be created or to connect our services to existing components. Figure 6.4 shows the definition of an environment that requires the platform to install the application infrastructure that the services need. We also want to enable some debug features on our Frontend service. The possibilities here are endless, depending on what makes sense for your teams to parameterize. The platform team can control what is possible and what is not. Expanding the environment interface to cover more use cases can look like figure 6.4.

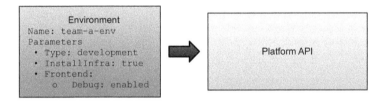

Figure 6.4   Extended environment resource to enable/disable the application's services.

Encoding this environment resource into a format like JSON or YAML to implement the platform API is straightforward, as shown in listing 6.1.

Listing 6.1   Environment definition in JSON format

```json
{
  "name": "my-dev-env",
  "parameters":{
    "type": "development",
    "installInfra": true,
    "frontend": {
      "debug": "true",
    }
  }
}
```

Once the interface is defined, the next logical step is to provide one implementation to provision these environments for our platform users. Before jumping into implementation details, we need to cover two of the main challenges you will face when deciding where the mechanisms for implementing these environments will reside.

NOTE   When building these interfaces, we are designing user experiences. From a platform engineering perspective, consider these interfaces as layers we are building to simplify how teams interact with our platform. But it is also important to recognize that we are not trying to build a black-box approach where this interface is the only way of interacting with our platform. If teams have the technical experience to interact with the underlying layers and tools, they should be able to do so.

6.2   *Platform architecture*

This section discusses how we'll architect our platform. On the technical side of building platforms, we will encounter challenges requiring the platform team to make some hard choices. In this section, we will talk about how we can architect a platform that allows us to encapsulate a set of tools behind our platform APIs and enable development teams to perform their tasks without worrying about which tools are being used by the platform to provision and wire up complex resources.

Because we are already using Kubernetes to deploy our workloads in the Conference application, it also makes sense to run the platform services on top of Kubernetes, right? But would you run the platform services and components right beside your workloads? Probably not. Let's step back a bit.

If your organization adopts Kubernetes, you will likely already deal with multiple Kubernetes clusters. As discussed in chapter 4, your organization probably has production, staging, or QA environments already in place. If you want your application development teams to work on environments that feel like the production environment, you must enable them with Kubernetes clusters.

Figure 6.5 shows a typical distribution of Kubernetes clusters inside an organization, where tons of small clusters might be created for short periods for development purposes. One or more mid-size clusters can be used for staging and testing purposes; these clusters tend to stay the same as they might be purposefully created to run performance tests or a large set of integration tests. Finally, one or more large clusters are created for running our production workloads. Depending on how many regions we want to cover, we might need multiple production clusters that are geographically distributed. The configuration of these clusters is static and does not change. In contrast with development and testing clusters, production clusters are the responsibility of Site Reliability Engineering teams, ensuring that these clusters and the applications running on them are up and running 24/7.

Development
Clusters

Staging/QA Clusters

Production Clusters

Figure 6.5
Environment
clusters, in case
you want to enable
developers to
have their own
environments.

While the production cluster(s) and staging/QA cluster(s) should be handled carefully and hardened to serve real-life traffic, development environments tend to be more ephemeral and sometimes even run on the development team laptops. Certainly, you don't want to run any platform-related tools in any of these environments. The reason is simple: tools like Crossplane, ArgoCD, or Tekton shouldn't be competing for resources with our application's workloads. Security considerations might apply too; we don't want our application's security compromised due to a vulnerability in our platform tools.

When looking at building platforms on top of Kubernetes, teams tend to create one or more special clusters to run platform-specific tools. The terms still need to be standardized, but creating a platform or management cluster to install platform-wide tools is becoming increasingly popular.

Figure 6.6 shows how by having separate platform cluster(s), you can install the tools that you need to implement your platform capabilities while at the same time building a set of management tools to control environments where your workloads run.

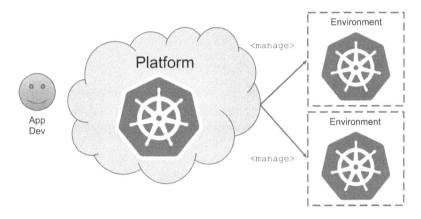

Figure 6.6   Platform cluster with platform tools managing environments

Now that you have a separate place to install these tools, you can also host the platform API on this cluster, once again, to not overload your workload clusters with platform components. Wouldn't it be great to reuse or extend the Kubernetes API to serve also as our platform API? There are pros and cons to this approach. For example, suppose we want our platform API to follow Kubernetes conventions and behaviors. In that case, our platform will use the declarative nature of Kubernetes and promote all the best practices followed by the Kubernetes APIs, such as versioning, the resource model, etc. This API might be too complex for non-Kubernetes users, or the organization might follow other standards when creating new APIs that do not match the Kubernetes style. *If we reuse the Kubernetes APIs for our platform APIs, all the CNCF tools designed to work with these APIs will automatically work with our platform.* Our platform automatically becomes part of the ecosystem. In the last couple of years, I've seen a trend around teams adopting the Kubernetes APIs as their platform APIs. How much you lean on the Kubernetes APIs is a decision that platform engineering teams will need to make, and there are always tradeoffs.

Figure 6.7 shows the relationship between having the Kubernetes APIs to use the CNCF and cloud-native ecosystem while at the same time exposing an organization-specific API that follows company standards on how APIs should be created. To make sure that the message is clear, these are not exclusive, and as we will see in section 6.3, it makes a lot of sense to have both.

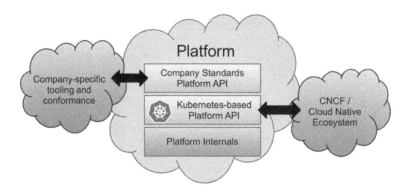

Figure 6.7
Kubernetes-based
platform APIs
complemented by
company-specific
APIs

Adopting the Kubernetes APIs for your platform API doesn't stop you from building a layer on top for other tools to consume or to follow the company's standards. By having a Kubernetes-based API layer, you can access all the amazing tools created in the CNCF and cloud-native space. On top of the Kubernetes-based APIs, another layer can follow company standards and conformance checks, enabling easier integrations with other existing systems.

Following our previous example, we can extend Kubernetes to understand our environment requests and provide the mechanisms to define how these environments will be provisioned.

Figure 6.8 shows a Kubernetes resource used to define our environments. This resource can be sent to a Kubernetes API server with an installed set of extensions to understand what to do when a new environment definition arrives.

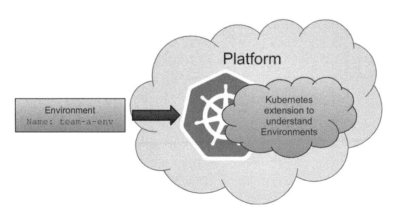

Figure 6.8
Extending
Kubernetes
to understand
environments
and serve as our
platform APIs

In principle, this looks good and doable. Still, before implementing these Kubernetes extensions to serve as our platform API and central hub of platform tooling, we need to understand the questions that our platform implementation will try to answer. Let's look at the main platform challenges that teams in these scenarios will face.

6.2.1 Platform challenges

Sooner or later, if you are dealing with multiple Kubernetes clusters, you must manage them and all the resources related to these clusters. What does it take to manage all these resources? The first step to understanding the underlying problems is to understand who the users of our platforms are. Are we building a platform for external customers or internal teams? What are their needs and the level of isolation that they need to operate autonomously without bothering their neighbors? What guardrails do they need to be successful?

While I cannot answer these questions for all use cases, one thing is clear—platform tools and workloads need to be separated. We need to encode in our platform our tenant boundaries based on each tenant's expectations. No matter if these tenants are customers or internal teams. We must set clear expectations about our tenancy model and guarantees for our platform users, so they understand the limitations of the resources the platform gives them to do their work.

The platform we will build needs to encode all these decisions. In the following two sections, we will look at the two most common decisions that platform teams will need to make early in their journey: (1) managing more than one cluster and (2) isolation and multi-tenancy.

6.2.2 Managing more than one cluster

The platform we will build needs to manage and understand which environments are available for teams. More importantly, it should enable the team to request their own environments whenever needed.

Using the Kubernetes APIs as our platform API to request environments, we can use tools like ArgoCD (covered in chapter 4) to persist and sync our environment configurations to live Kubernetes clusters. Managing our clusters and environments becomes just managing Kubernetes resources that must be synced to our platform cluster(s).

Figure 6.9 shows using two tools that we have already used (Crossplane and ArgoCD) for our Conference application but use now in the context of managing platform-wide resources.

By combining tools like ArgoCD and Crossplane inside our platform clusters, we promote the techniques we discussed in chapter 4 for environment pipelines, which sync application-level components which we now use for managing high-level platform concerns. In this case, tools like Crossplane can help us provision full-fledged environments on cloud providers.

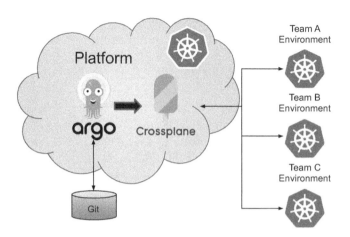

Figure 6.9 Combining GitOps and Crossplane for managing environments and clusters

As you can see in the previous figure, our platform configuration itself will become more complex, because it will need to have its source of truth (Git repository) to store the environment and resources that the platform manages. It will also need to have access to a secret store, such as HashiCorp Vault, to enable Crossplane to connect and create resources in different cloud providers. In other words, you now have two extra concerns. First, you will need to define, configure, and give access to one or more Git repositories to contain the configurations for the resources created in the platform. Second, you must manage a set of cloud provider accounts and their credentials so the platform cluster(s) can access and use these accounts.

If you can manage all the platform resources like your workloads (using a GitOps approach, managing credentials and users, and exposing the right abstractions/APIs), the platform artifacts become just an extension of your development and continuous delivery practices.

While the example in section 6.3 doesn't focus on configuring all these concerns, it provides a nice playground to build on top and experiment with more advanced setups depending on your teams' requirements.

I recommend prioritizing which configurations make sense to understand what your teams or tenants will do with the resources, expectations, and requirements. Let's dig a bit more into that space.

6.2.3 *Isolation and multi-tenancy*

Depending on your tenants' (teams, internal or external customers) requirements, you might need to create different isolation levels, so they don't disturb each other when working under the same platform roof.

Multi-tenancy is a complicated topic in the Kubernetes ecosystem. Using Kubernetes RBAC (role-based access control), Kubernetes Namespaces, and multiple Kubernetes controllers that might have been designed with different tenancy models makes it hard to define isolation levels between tenants inside the same cluster.

Companies embarking on adopting Kubernetes tend to take one of the following approaches for isolation:

- Kubernetes Namespaces:
  - Pros:
    - Creating namespaces is very easy, and it has almost zero overhead.
    - Creating namespaces is cheap, because it is just a logical boundary that Kubernetes uses to separate resources inside the cluster.
  - Cons:
    - Isolation between namespaces is very basic, and it will require RBAC roles to limit users' visibility outside the namespaces they have been assigned. Resource quotas must also be defined to ensure that a single namespace is not consuming all the cluster resources.
    - Providing access to a single namespace requires sharing access to the same Kubernetes APIs endpoints that admins and all the other tenants are using. This limits the operations clients can execute on the cluster, such as installing cluster-wide resources.
    - All the tenants will be interacting against the same Kubernetes API server, which might cause problems depending on the scale and the needs of each of the tenants.
    - Sharing the same Kubernetes API server limits the cluster-wide resources that can be installed in the cluster. For example, installing two different versions of the same extensions is not possible.
- Kubernetes clusters:
  - Pros:
    - Users interacting with different clusters can have full admin capabilities enabling them to install as many tools as they need.
    - You have full isolation between clusters, and tenants connecting to different clusters will not share the same Kubernetes API server endpoints. Each cluster can have different configurations for how scalable and resilient they are. This allows you to define different tenants' categories based on their requirements.
  - Cons:
    - This approach is expensive, as you will be paying for computing resources to run Kubernetes. The more clusters you create, the more money you will spend running Kubernetes.
    - Managing multiple Kubernetes clusters becomes complex if you enable teams to create (or request) their own. Zombie clusters (clusters nobody uses and are abandoned) start to pop up, wasting valuable resources.
    - Sharing resources, installing, and maintaining tools across a fleet of different Kubernetes clusters is challenging and a full-time job.

Based on my experience, teams will create isolated Kubernetes clusters for sensitive environments such as production environments and performance testing. These sensitive environments tend to stay the same and are only managed by operation and site reliability teams. Using a big cluster with namespaces is a common practice when you shift towards development teams and more ephemeral environments for testing or day-to-day development tasks.

Choosing between these two options is hard, but what is important is not to overcommit to just a single option. Different teams might have different requirements, so in the next section, we will look at how the platform can abstract these decisions, enabling teams to access different setups depending on their needs.

My recommendation for platform teams making these decisions is to build and have practices in place that enable you to pivot from one solution to another. Starting with simple solutions such as namespace isolation is quite common, but after a while, when having a single cluster with tons of namespaces is not enough, you need a more robust plan. To make this decision easier, ask yourself if your consumers need access to the Kubernetes APIs. If they don't, you might want to evaluate following an approach similar to Google Cloud Run (https://cloud.google.com/run), Azure Container Apps (https://azure.microsoft.com/en-us/products/container-apps), or AWS App Runner (https://aws.amazon.com/apprunner/), which enables teams to run containers without the need of accessing the orchestrator APIs.

6.3   *Our platform walking skeleton*

This section looks into creating a simple platform allowing internal teams to create development environments. Because our teams are deploying the conference application to Kubernetes clusters, we want to offer them the same developer experience.

> **NOTE**   You can follow a step-by-step tutorial, where you will install and interact with the platform walking skeleton at https://github.com/salaboy/platforms-on-k8s/tree/main/chapter-6.

To achieve this, we will use some tools that we used before, like Crossplane, to extend Kubernetes to understand development environments. Then, we will use a project called `vcluster` (https://vcluster.com) to provision small Kubernetes clusters for our teams. These clusters are isolated, allowing teams to install extra tools without worrying about what other teams are doing. Because teams will have access to the Kubernetes APIs, they can do whatever they need with the cluster without requesting complicated permissions to debug their workloads.

Figure 6.10 shows how the process works. Teams can request new environments by creating environment Kubernetes resources. The platform will take these resources and provision small Kubernetes clusters with `vcluster` for them to use. We will keep things simple for the walking skeleton, but the platforms are complicated.

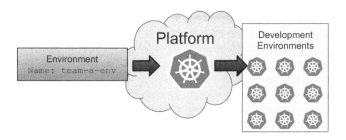

Figure 6.10 Building a platform prototype to provision development environments

I can't stress enough the importance that this example, on purpose, is using existing tools instead of creating our custom Kubernetes extensions. If you create custom controllers to manage environments, you create a complex component that will require maintenance and probably overlaps 95% with the mechanisms shown in this example. In other words, no custom Kubernetes controllers have been created while building this example.

In the same way that we started this chapter talking about our platform APIs, let's look at how we can build these APIs without creating custom Kubernetes extensions that we will need to test, maintain, and release. We will use Crossplane compositions as we did for our databases and message brokers in chapter 5, but now we will implement our environment custom Crossplane Composition Resource Definition. We can keep the environment resource simple and use Kubernetes label matches and selectors to match a resource with one of the possible compositions we can create to provision our environments.

Figure 6.11 shows how changing a property/label from our environment helps Crossplane to pick the right composition for our team.

Figure 6.11 Mapping environment resources to Crossplane compositions

Crossplane compositions offer the flexibility to use different providers to provision and configure resources together, and as we saw in chapter 5, multiple compositions (implementations) can be provided for different kinds of environments. For this example, we want each environment to be isolated from the other to avoid teams unintentionally deleting others' team resources. The two most intuitive ways of creating isolated environments would be to create a new namespace per environment or a full-blown Kubernetes cluster for each environment.

Figure 6.12 shows how another Crossplane provider (called Kubernetes provider) can be used to create Kubernetes resources such as Namespaces. This compares against using a cloud-provider Crossplane provider that enables us to create a full-blown cluster, in this case in Google Cloud Platform (GCP). Once we have a cluster, we can install our Conference application Helm Chart.

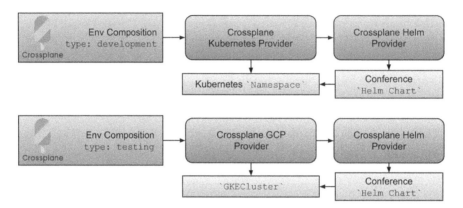

Figure 6.12   Different environment compositions, Namespace, and GKECluster

While creating a fully-fledged Kubernetes cluster might be overkill for every development team, a Kubernetes Namespace might not provide enough isolation for your use case, because all teams will interact with the same Kubernetes API server. For this reason, we will use `vcluster` in conjunction with the Crossplane Helm provider, which gives us the best of both worlds without the costs of creating new clusters. Figure 6.13 shows how we can reuse the Crossplane Helm provider to create `vclusters`.

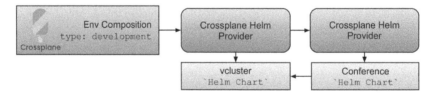

Figure 6.13   Using vcluster to create isolated environments

You might be wondering: what is a `vcluster`? And why are we using the Crossplane Helm provider to create one? While `vcluster` is just another option that you can use to build your platforms, I consider it a key tool in every platform engineer toolbox.

6.3.1 *vcluster for virtual Kubernetes clusters*

I am a big fan of the `vcluster` project. If you are discussing multi-tenancy on top of Kubernetes, `vcluster` tends to pop up in the conversation, because it offers a really nice alternative to the Kubernetes Namespaces vs. Kubernetes clusters discussions.

`vcluster` focuses on providing Kubernetes API server isolation between different tenants by creating virtual clusters inside your existing Kubernetes cluster (host cluster). Figure 6.14 shows how `vcluster` works inside an existing Kubernetes cluster (HOST).

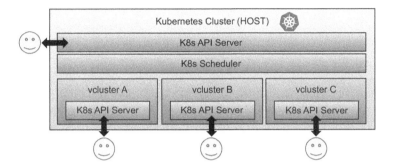

Figure 6.14   vcluster provides isolation at the Kubernetes (K8s) API server

By creating new virtual clusters, we can share an isolated API server with tenants where they can do whatever they need without worrying about what other tenants are doing or installing. For scenarios where you want each tenant to have cluster-wide access and full control of the Kubernetes API server, `vcluster` provides a simple alternative to implement this. If you don't need to provide your teams with access to the Kubernetes APIs, I recommend using the namespace approach mentioned before.

Creating a `vcluster` is easy: you can create a new `vcluster` by installing the `vcluster` Helm Chart. Alternatively, you can use the `vcluster` CLI to create one and connect to it.

Finally, a great table comparing `vcluster`, Kubernetes Namespaces and Kubernetes clusters can be found in their documentation. If you are already having these conversations with your teams, this table explains the advantages and tradeoffs in crystal clear language (figure 6.15).

	Separate Namespace For Each Tenant	vcluster	Separate Cluster For Each Tenant
Isolation	very weak	strong	very strong
Access For Tenants	very restricted	vcluster admin	cluster admin
Cost	very cheap	cheap	expensive
Resource Sharing	easy	easy	very hard
Overhead	very low	very low	very high

**Figure 6.15
Pros and cons
of Kubernetes
Namespaces
vs. vcluster vs.
Kubernetes cluster
tenants**

I strongly recommend checking their website (https://vcluster.com) and the blog post available at https://www.salaboy.com/2023/06/19/cost-effective-multi-tenancy-on -kubernetes/ to learn more about this project and how it can help your teams provision cost-effective clusters.

Next, let's see what our platform walking skeleton looks like for teams that want to create, connect, and work against new environments that use `vcluster`.

6.3.2   *The platform experience*

The platform walking skeleton implemented in the GitHub repository at https:// github.com/salaboy/platforms-on-k8s/tree/main/chapter-6 allows teams connected to the platform API to create new environment resources and submit a request for the platform to provision it for them.

Figure 6.16 shows the architecture for our platform walking skeleton. First, application development teams can create requests to the platform APIs for new development environments. The platform will provision a new environment—in this case, following a Crossplane composition that uses the Crossplane Helm provider to create a new virtual cluster (using `vcluster`)—and then install the Conference application Helm Chart for development teams to do their work. Second, application development teams can connect to this new isolated environment without fearing breaking other teams' setups.

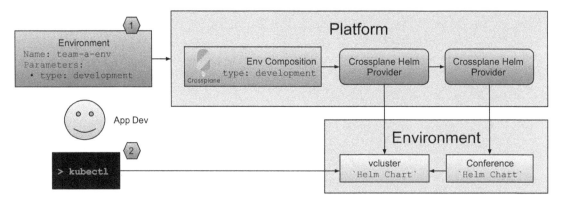

Figure 6.16   Using Crossplane and `vcluster` to create isolated environments for application development teams

> **NOTE**   It makes a lot of sense to have a large cluster to host all the ephemeral development environment clusters. The tools we used for building the platform walking skeleton can be easily configured to implement that setup, but it is quite hard to demonstrate running on a single and local KinD cluster.

The platform cluster uses Crossplane and Crossplane compositions to define how to provision the environment. To run the Crossplane composition in a local Kubernetes cluster (and not require access to a specific cloud provider), the walking skeleton uses `vcluster` to provision each environment on its own (virtual) Kubernetes cluster. Having separate Kubernetes clusters enables teams to connect to these environments and do the work they need to do with our Conference application, which is by default installed when the environment is created.

Application teams need to be connected to the platform API (Kubernetes clusters hosting the platform tools—in this case, Crossplane and the `vcluster` configurations) to request new environments using tools like `kubectl`. For the walking skeleton, sending an environment resource to the platform APIs will result in the platform provisioning a new `vcluster` that the team can connect to. See listing 6.2, which shows an environment resource definition that we can send to the Kubernetes API server.

Listing 6.2 Environment definition as a Kubernetes resource

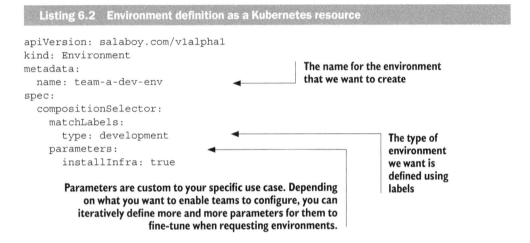

```
apiVersion: salaboy.com/v1alpha1
kind: Environment
metadata:
  name: team-a-dev-env
spec:
  compositionSelector:
    matchLabels:
      type: development
    parameters:
      installInfra: true
```

The name for the environment that we want to create

The type of environment we want is defined using labels

Parameters are custom to your specific use case. Depending on what you want to enable teams to configure, you can iteratively define more and more parameters for them to fine-tune when requesting environments.

Because these are Kubernetes resources, teams can query these resources using `kubectl`, as shown in listing 6.3.

Listing 6.3 Listing environment resources

```
> kubect get environments
NAME           CONNECT-TO          TYPE          INFRA READY
team-a-dev-env team-a-dev-env-jp7j4 development true  True
```

Once the environment is ready, teams will be able to connect to it. Because we are using `vcluster`, connecting to it is just like connecting to any other Kubernetes cluster. Luckily, `vcluster` makes our life easier, and we can use their CLI to configure the access tokens for us.

Running the following command will connect you to the `vcluster` instance that has been just created and host the Conference application installed by the Crossplane composition:

```
vcluster connect team-a-dev-env-jp7j4 --server https://localhost:8443 -- zsh
```

NOTE   When running `vcluster connect`, you are now connected to a new cluster context, meaning that if you list all the pods and Namespaces, you will only see the resources that are available in this new cluster. You shouldn't see any Crossplane resources, for example.

A natural extension to the walking skeleton would be to use Crossplane compositions to create environments spawning Kubernetes clusters on a cloud provider. Managing these environment resources inside a Git repository using ArgoCD is also a natural step forward. In such cases and in contrast to requiring application development teams to connect directly with the platform APIs, teams can request new environments by sending a pull request to a repository that can be validated and automatically merged.

The step-by-step tutorial (https://github.com/salaboy/platforms-on-k8s/tree/main/chapter-6) finishes by deploying a custom Platform Admin User Interface application. This Platform Admin application enables teams to consume the platform features without connecting to the Kubernetes platform APIs, commonly called "Click Ops," because we are trying to avoid teams writing complex YAML files or long commands like cloud providers do. This application exposes REST endpoints and the functionality provided by the user interface to reduce the cognitive load from application teams who need to know how the platform is operating behind the covers. Figure 6.17 shows the Platform Portal admin interface (this is not part of the Conference application).

Figure 6.17   Platform Admin user interface allows teams to create and manage environments without connecting to the platform's Kubernetes APIs.

This Platform Admin application also exposes REST endpoints to perform all the actions by sending REST requests, which can be used for further automation and integrations with existing systems.

To recap, the walking skeleton offers the platform users different ways of interaction. First, it extends the Kubernetes APIs to enable platform workflows such as creating development environments using Crossplane. Then it provides a user interface and simplified REST endpoints for teams that don't want or can't use the extended Kubernetes APIs. These simplified REST APIs, SDKs, and CLIs can be created for teams to manage their environments.

There is value in having both options always available. It's good to use the power of the Kubernetes APIs and the cloud-native ecosystem, when possible, but it's also important to have a simplified option for reducing the cognitive load and following company API standards when needed.

Before closing this chapter, let's bring back all the topics and projects we have seen together. How are all these tools and configurations related to platform engineering? Who is responsible for which component? And what comes next?

6.4 *Linking back to platform engineering*

So far, we have explored open-source projects that tackle different challenges we face when building distributed applications. Most of these tools are not focused on application developers, requiring skills and knowledge that are usually not needed to build business applications and features. The common denominator across all tools has been Kubernetes, and in most cases, projects have extended Kubernetes to perform tasks besides running our workloads. In this short section, I want to recap how all these projects fit together to delineate responsibilities, contracts, and expectations.

If we look at all these examples from a distance, there are two kinds of teams: platform and application development teams. These two teams have different responsibilities and require different tools to do their job. From what we have seen so far:

- Platform teams are responsible for the following:
  - Understanding the needs of different teams related to IT services, cloud resources, and tools.
  - Facilitating access to credentials and to different resources.
  - Creating automation for other teams to get what they need.
- Application development teams are responsible for the following:
  - Defining the customer-facing architecture and tech stack.
  - Creating customer-facing features.
  - Releasing new versions to continuously improve how the business operates.

These responsibilities materialize in software artifacts that can be managed similarly. Figure 6.18 shows the artifacts we have used for the platform walking skeleton. The tools not included in the step-by-step tutorial are drawn with dashed lines.

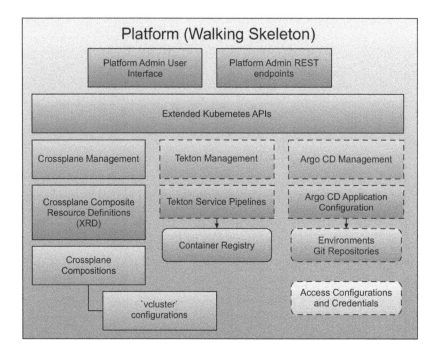

Figure 6.18   Platform walking skeleton tools, configurations, and services

As you can see, even for a very simple platform, the platform team is managing and administrating different tools that need to be highly available for our application development teams to consume. I haven't focused on managing credentials or secrets, but this is something that the platform team will face early on in their journey. Using tools like the external-secrets project (https://github.com/external-secrets/external-secrets) and/or tools like Vault by HashiCorp (https://www.vaultproject.io/) would make managing and storing credentials much easier and more centralized. This level of complexity has historically led to two implementation scenarios:

1   Purchase a solution that provides fantastic application developer experience but limited platform engineering customization or operability (e.g., Heroku, CloudFoundry)
2   Build a solution from a set of primitives, including scripting languages (BASH, Python, etc.), declarative infrastructure languages (Crossplane, Terraform, Chef, Ansible), and workflow engines (ArgoCD Workflows, CircleCI, GitHub Actions).

Recently there has been an explosion of new tools that enable the first scenario (e.g., Vercel, Fly.io). However, for many organizations, these solutions have needed help managing their business process and compliance requirements fully. To address this challenge, there is more focus on lowering the cost of building bespoke internal offerings. For example, a project called Kratix (https://kratix.io/), which is a framework that optimizes the definition and implementation of experiences as a service to other internal teams.

Kratix is centered around the platform-building experience instead of the application user experience. A framework like Kratix can enable an internal marketplace where specialists can offer capabilities as a service while maintaining consistency across offerings, similar to what we explored with Crossplane compositions.

Whether you use an external tool or build your own, the platform engineering team must build a knowledge base about the projects they are using to build the platform and have a release process to manage changes when the tools are online for other teams to use.

Similar to this book's examples repository at https://github.com/salaboy/platforms -on-k8s/, the platform engineering team will need to manage all the configuration files to install and recreate all the tools and resources the platform needs to work.

> **NOTE**   Ideally, as with Kubernetes, if the control plane (tools we installed) is down, our teams should be able to keep working. We (as platform engineering teams) need to build resilient platforms and ensure that if something goes wrong, we don't block teams and the important work they are doing. While the platform we build should speed up software delivery, it shouldn't be on the critical path for the teams' success. In other words, there should always be a way around the platform, meaning that if teams want to directly access some of the tools that the platform is using, they should be able to do so.

The walking skeleton we built in this chapter offers different layers for different users to work and integrate with. If your team understands the platform's tools, they can access the Kubernetes APIs of the platform cluster for full flexibility and control. If they choose, they can also use the provided user interface and REST endpoints to integrate with other systems. Figure 6.19 shows our platform walking skeleton, how it provides teams with predefined workflows exposed by the platform APIs, and the tools and behaviors implemented under the hood by the platform team.

I strongly recommend platform teams document their journey with each of the tools that they are planning to use as part of their platform initiatives, because bringing team members up to speed on these decisions is usually the most challenging aspect of maintaining a platform like the one described here.

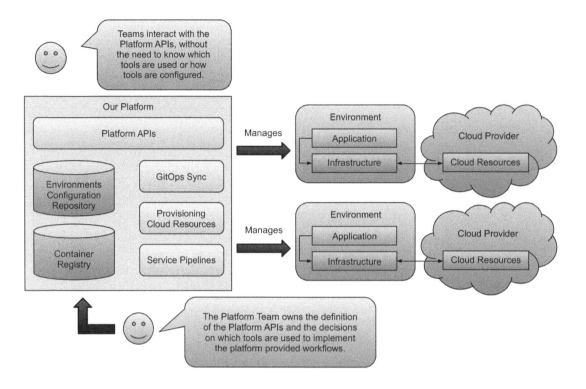

Figure 6.19   Platform responsibilities and boundaries

In the next couple of chapters, we will explore some core capabilities the platform should provide when creating environments for teams. Which functionalities can be provided to the application development teams so they can be more efficient when delivering software? Chapter 7 covers release strategies and why they are important to enable teams to experiment and release more software. Chapter 8 covers shared concerns that you will need to provide to all services of your applications and different approaches to facilitate these mechanisms to your developers.

Summary

- Building platforms on top of Kubernetes is a complex task that involves combining different tools to serve teams with different requirements.
- Platforms are software projects as your business applications. Starting by understanding who the main users will be and defining clear APIs is the key to prioritizing tasks on how to build your platform.
- Managing multiple Kubernetes clusters and dealing with tenant isolations are two main challenges that platform teams face early on in their platform-building journey.

- Having a platform walking skeleton can help you to demonstrate to internal teams what can be built to speed up their cloud-native journey.
- Using tools like Crossplane, ArgoCD, `vcluster`, and others can help you promote cloud-native best practices at the platform level but, most importantly, avoid the urge to create your custom tools and ways to provision and maintain complex configurations of cloud-native resources.
- If you followed the step-by-step tutorial, you got hands-on experience using tools like Crossplane and `vcluster` to provision on-demand development environments. You also interacted with a simplified API that reduces the cognitive load for teams that don't want or can't interact with a full-blown Kubernetes API server.

Platform capabilities I: Shared application concerns

This chapter covers

- Learning requirements of 95% of cloud-native applications
- Reducing friction between application and infrastructure
- Addressing shared concerns with standard APIs and components

In chapter 5 we created abstractions such as databases and message brokers to provision and configure all the components required by our application's services. In chapter 6, we extended these mechanisms to build our platform walking skeleton. This platform enables teams to request new development environments that not only create isolated environments but also install an instance of the Conference application (and all the components required by the application) so teams can do their work. By going through the process of building a platform, we defined the responsibilities of a platform team and where each tool belongs and why. We ended chapter 6 with clear guidelines for where tools like Crossplane, Argo CD, and Tekton would run to manage and enable different environments with capabilities that teams will need to deliver more software in front of customers.

So far, we have given developers Kubernetes clusters with an instance of their application running. This chapter looks at mechanisms to provide developers with capabilities closer to their application needs. Most of these capabilities will be accessed by APIs that abstract away the application's infrastructure needs, allowing the platform team to evolve (update, reconfigure, change) infrastructural components without updating any application code. At the same time, developers will interact with these platform capabilities without knowing how they are implemented and without bloating their applications with a load of dependencies. This chapter is divided into three sections:

- What are most applications doing 95% of the time?
- Standard APIs and abstractions to separate application code from infrastructure.
- Updating our Conference application with Dapr (Distributed Application Runtime), a CNCF and open-source project created to provide solutions to distributed application challenges.

Let's start by analyzing what most applications are doing. Don't worry; we will also cover edge cases.

7.1   *What are most applications doing 95% of the time?*

We have worked with our walking skeleton Conference applications for seven chapters. We have learned how to run it on top of Kubernetes and how to connect the services to databases, key-value stores, and message brokers. There was a good reason to go over those steps and include those behaviors in the walking skeleton. Most applications, like the Conference application, will need the following functionality:

- *Call other services to send or receive information:* Application services don't exist on their own. They need to call and be called by other services. Services can be local or remote, and you can use different protocols, most commonly HTTP and GRPC. We use HTTP calls between services for the conference application walking skeleton.
- *Store and read data from persistent storage:* This can be a database, a key-value store, a blob store like S3 buckets, or even writing and reading from files. For the conference application, we are using Redis and PostgreSQL.
- *Emit and consume events or messages asynchronously:* Using asynchronous messaging for communicating systems implementing an event-driven architecture is a common practice in distributed systems. Using tools like Kafka, RabbitMQ, or even cloud-provider messaging systems is common. Each service in the Conference application is emitting or consuming events using Kafka.
- *Accessing credentials to connect to services:* When connecting to an application's infrastructure components, whether local or remote, most services will need credentials to authenticate to other systems. In this book I've only mentioned tools like external-secrets (https://github.com/external-secrets/external-secrets) or HashiCorp's Vault (https://www.vaultproject.io/), but we haven't dug deeper into it.

Whether we are building business applications or machine learning tools, most applications will benefit from having these capabilities easily available to consume. And while complex applications require much more than that, there is always a way to separate the complex part from the generic parts.

Figure 7.1 shows several example service interactions with each other and available infrastructure. Service A is calling Service B using HTTP (for this topic, GRPC would fit similarly). Service B stores and reads data from a database and will need the right credentials to connect. Service A also connects to a message broker and places messages into it. Service C can pick messages from the message broker and, using some credentials, connect to a Bucket to store some calculations based on the messages it receives.

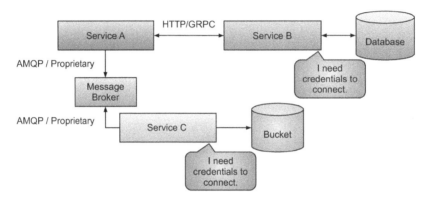

Figure 7.1   Common communication patterns in distributed applications

No matter what logic these services are implementing, we can extract some constant behaviors and enable development teams to consume without the hassle of dealing with the low-level details or pushing them to make decisions around cross-cutting concerns that can be solved at the platform level.

To understand how this can work, we must look closely at what is happening inside these services. As you might know already, the devil is in the details. While from a high-level perspective, we are used to dealing with services doing what is described in figure 7.1, if we want to unlock an increased velocity in our software delivery pipelines, we need to go one level down to understand the intricate relationships between the components of our applications. Let's take a quick look at the challenges the application teams face when trying to change different services and infrastructure that our services require.

7.1.1   The challenges of coupling application and infrastructure

Fortunately, this is not a programming language competition, independent of your programming language of choice. If you want to connect to a database or message broker, you must add some dependencies to your application code. While this is a common practice in the software development industry, it is also one of the reasons why delivery speed is slower than it should be.

Coordination between different teams is the reason behind most blockers when releasing software. We have created architectures and adopted Kubernetes because we want to go faster. By using containers, we have adopted an easier and more standard way to run our applications. No matter in which language the application is written or which tech stack is used, if you give me a container with the application inside, I can run it. We have removed the application dependencies on the operating system and the software that we need to have installed in a machine (or virtual machine) to run your application, which is now encapsulated inside a container.

Unfortunately, we haven't tackled the relationships and integration points between containers (our application's services). We also haven't solved how these containers will interact with application infrastructure components that can be local (self-hosted) or managed by a cloud provider.

Let's take a closer look at where these applications heavily rely on other services and can block teams from making changes, pushing them for complicated coordination that can end up causing downtime to our users. We will start by splitting up the previous example into the specifics of each interaction.

7.1.2 Service-to-service interaction challenges

To send data from one service to another, you must know where the other service is running and which protocol it uses to receive information. Because we are dealing with distributed systems, we also need to ensure that the requests between services arrive at the other service and have mechanisms to deal with unexpected network problems or situations where the other services might fail. In other words, we need to build resilience in our services. We cannot always trust the network or other services to behave as expected.

Let's use Service A and Service B as examples to go deeper into the details. In figure 7.2, Service A needs to send a request to Service B.

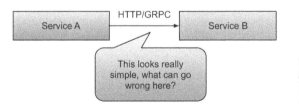

Figure 7.2
Service-to-service
interaction
challenges

But let's dig deeper into the mechanisms services can use internally. Suppose we leave the fact that Service A depends on the Service B contract (API) to be stable and not change for this to work on the side. What else can go wrong here? As mentioned, development teams should add a resiliency layer inside their services to ensure that Service A requests reach Service B. One way to do this is to use a framework to retry the request if it fails automatically. Frameworks implementing this functionality are available for all programming languages. Tools like `go-retryablehttp` (https://github.com/hashicorp/go-retryablehttp) or Spring Retry for Spring Boot (https://github.com/spring-projects/spring-retry) add resiliency to your service-to-service interactions.

Some of these mechanisms also include exponential backoff functionality to avoid overloading services and the network when things are going wrong.

Unfortunately, there is no standard library shared across tech stacks that can provide the same behavior and functionality for all your applications, so even if you configure both Spring Retry and `go-retryablehttp` with similar parameters, it is quite hard to guarantee that they will behave in the same way when services start failing.

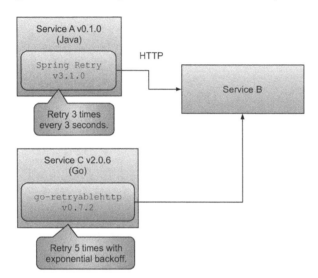

Figure 7.3
Service-to-service
interactions retry
mechanisms

Figure 7.3 shows Service A written in Java using the Spring Retry library to retry three times with a wait time of 3 seconds between each request when the request fails to be acknowledged by Service B. Service C, written in Go using the `go-retryable http` library, is configured to retry five times but using an exponential backoff (the retry period between requests is not fixed; this can provide time for the other service to recover and not be flooded with retries) mechanism when things go wrong.

Even if the applications are written in the same language and using the same frameworks, both services (A and B) must have compatible versions of their dependencies and configurations. If we push both Service A and Service B to have the versions of the frameworks, we are coupling them together, meaning we will need to coordinate the update of the other service whenever any of these internal dependency versions change. This can cause even more slowdowns and increase the complexity of coordination efforts.

> **NOTE** In this section, I've used retrying mechanisms as an example, but think about other cross-cutting concerns that you might want to include for these service-to-service interactions, like circuit breakers (also for resiliency) rate limiting and observability. Consider the frameworks and libraries you will need to add to instrument your application code to get metrics from it.

On the other hand, using different frameworks (and versions) for each service will complicate troubleshooting these services for our operations teams. Wouldn't it be great to have a way to add resiliency to our applications without modifying them? Before answering this question, what else can go wrong?

Something that developers often overlook relates to the security aspect of these communications. Service A and Service B don't live in a vacuum, meaning other services surround them. If any of these services is compromised by a bad actor, having a free-for-all service-to-service invocation between all the services makes our entire system insecure. This is where having service identity and the right security mechanisms to ensure that, for this example, Service A can only call Service B is extremely important, as shown in figure 7.4.

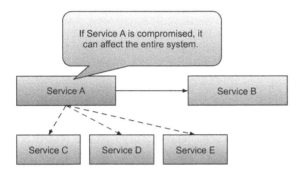

Figure 7.4
If a service is
compromised,
it can affect the
entire system.

Having a mechanism that allows us to define our service's identity, we can define which service-to-service invocations are allowed and which protocols and ports are allowed for the communications to happen. Figure 7.5 shows how we can reduce the blast radius (how many services are affected if a security breach happens) by defining rules that enforce which services are allowed in our system and how they are supposed to interact.

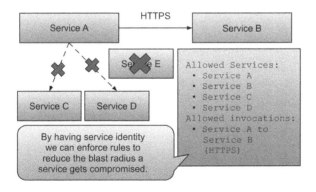

Figure 7.5
Reducing the
blast radius by
defining system-
level rules

Having the right mechanisms to define and validate these rules cannot be easily built inside each service. Hence developers tend to assume that an external mechanism will be in charge of performing these checks.

As we will see in the following sections, service identity is something that we need across the board and not only for service-to-service interactions. Wouldn't it be great to have a simple way to add service identity to our system without changing our application's services?

Before answering this question, let's look at other challenges teams face when architecting distributed applications. Let's talk about storing and reading state, which most applications do.

7.1.3   *Storing/reading state challenges*

Our application needs to store or read state from persistent storage. That is quite a common requirement, right? You need data to do some calculations, then store the results somewhere so they don't get lost if your application goes down. In our example, figure 7.6, Service B needed to connect to a database or persistent storage to read and write data.

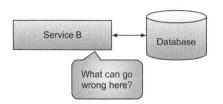

Figure 7.6
Storing/reading
state challenges

What can go wrong here? Developers are used to connecting to different kinds of databases (relational, NoSQL, files, buckets) and interacting with them. But two main friction points slow teams from moving their services forward: dependencies and credentials.

Let's start by looking at dependencies. What kind of dependencies does Service B need to connect to a database? Figure 7.7 shows Service B connecting to both a relational database and a NoSQL database. To achieve these connections, Service B needs to include a driver and a client library, plus the configuration needed to fine-tune how the application will connect to these two databases. These configurations define the size of the connection pool (how many application threads can connect concurrently to the database), buffers, health checks, and other important details that can change how the application behaves.

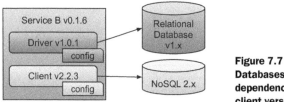

Figure 7.7
Databases
dependencies and
client versions

Besides the configuration of the driver and the client, their versions need to be compatible with the version of the databases we are running, and this is where the challenges begin.

NOTE It is important to notice that each driver/client is specific to the database (relational or NoSQL) that you are connecting to. This section assumes you used a specific database because it meets your application's requirements. Each database vendor has unique features optimized for different use cases. In this chapter, we are more interested in 95% of the cases that do not use vendor-specific features.

Once the application's service is connected to the database using the client APIs, it should be fairly easy to interact with it. Whether by sending SQL queries or commands to fetch data or using a key-value API to read keys and values from the database instance, developers should know the basics to start reading and writing data.

Do you have more than one service interacting with the same database instance? Are they both using the same library and the same version? Are these services written using the same programming language and frameworks? Even if you manage to control all these dependencies, there is still a coupling that will slow you down. Whenever the operations teams decide to upgrade the database version, each service connecting to this instance might or might not need to upgrade its dependencies and configuration parameters. Would you upgrade the database first or the dependencies?

For credentials, we face a similar problem. It is quite common to consume credentials from a credential store like HashiCorp's Vault (https://www.vaultproject.io/). If not provided by the platform and not managed in Kubernetes, application services can include a dependency to consume credentials from their application's code easily. Figure 7.8 shows Service B connecting to a credential store, using a specific client library, to get a token to connect to a database.

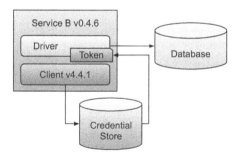

**Figure 7.8
Credentials store
dependencies**

In chapters 2 and 5, we connected the Conference services to different components using Kubernetes Secrets. By using Kubernetes Secrets, we were removing the need for application developers to worry about where to get these credentials from.

Otherwise, if your service connects to other services or components that might require dependencies in this way, the service will need to be upgraded for any change in any of the components. This coupling between the service code and dependencies creates the need for complex coordination between application development teams, the platform team, and the operations teams in charge of keeping these components up and running.

Can we get rid of some of these dependencies? Can we push some of these concerns down to the platform team, so we remove the hassle of keeping them updated from developers? If we decouple these services with a clean interface, then the infrastructure and applications can be updated independently.

Before jumping into the next topic, I wanted to briefly talk about why having service identity at this level can also help reduce security problems when interacting with application infrastructure components. Figure 7.9 shows how similar service identity rules can be applied to validate who can interact with infrastructure components. Once again, the system will limit the blast radius if a service is compromised.

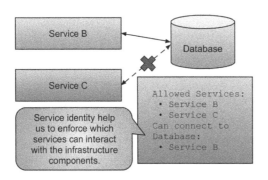

**Figure 7.9
Enforcing rules
based on service
identity**

But what about asynchronous interactions? Let's look at how these challenges relate to asynchronous messaging before jumping into the solutions space.

7.1.4 *Asynchronous messaging challenges*

With asynchronous messaging, you want to decouple the producer from the consumer. When using HTTP or GRPC, Service A needs to know about Service B, and both services need to be up to exchange information. When using asynchronous messaging, Service A doesn't know anything about Service C. You can take it even further, where Service C might not even be running when Service A places a message into the message broker. Figure 7.10 shows Service A placing a message into the message broker; at a later point in time, Service C can connect to the message broker and fetch messages from it.

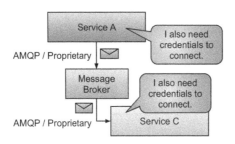

Figure 7.10   Asynchronous messaging interactions

Similar to HTTP/GRPC service-to-service interactions, when using a message broker, we need to know where the message broker is to send messages to or to subscribe to get messages from. Message brokers also provide isolation to enable applications to group messages together using the concept of topics. Services can be connected to the same message broker instance but send and consume messages from different topics.

When using message brokers, we face the same problems described with databases. We need to add a dependency to our applications depending on which message broker we decide to use, its version, and the programming language that we have chosen. Message brokers will use different protocols to receive and send information. A standard increasingly adopted in this space is the CloudEvent specification (https://cloudevents.io/) from the CNCF. While CloudEvents is a great step forward, it doesn't save your application developers from adding dependencies to connect and interact with your message brokers.

Figure 7.11 shows Service A, which includes the Kafka client library to connect to Kafka and send messages. Besides the URL, port, and credentials to connect to the Kafka instance, the Kafka client also receives configurations on how the client will behave when connecting to the broker, similar to databases. Service C uses the same client, but with different versions, to connect to the same broker.

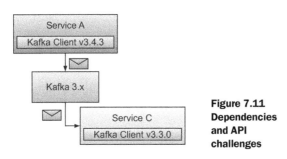

**Figure 7.11
Dependencies
and API
challenges**

Message brokers face the same problem as with databases and persistent storage. But unfortunately, with message brokers, developers will need to learn specific APIs that might not be that easy initially. Sending and consuming messages using different programming languages present more challenges and cognitive load on teams without experience with the specifics of the message broker at hand.

Same as with databases, if you have chosen Kafka, for example, it means that Kafka fits your application requirements. You might want to use advanced Kafka features that other message brokers don't provide. However, let me repeat it here: we are interested in 95% of the cases where application services want to exchange messages to externalize the state and let other interested parties know. For those cases, we want to remove the cognitive load from our application teams and let them emit and consume messages without the hassle of learning all the specifics of the selected message broker. By reducing the cognitive load required on developers to learn specific technologies, you can onboard less experienced developers and let experts take care of the details. Similar to databases, we can use service identity to control which services can connect, read, and write messages from a message broker. The same principles apply.

7.1.5   *Dealing with edge cases (the remaining 5%)*

There is always more than one good reason to add libraries to your application's services. Sometimes these libraries will give you the ultimate control over how to connect to vendor-specific components and functionalities. Other times, we add libraries because it is the easiest way to get started or because we are instructed to do so. Someone in the organization decided to use PostgreSQL, and the fastest way to connect and use it is to add the PostgreSQL driver to our application code. We usually don't realize that we are coupling our application to that specific PostgreSQL version. For edge cases, or to be more specific, scenarios where you need to use some vendor-specific functionality, consider wrapping up that specific functionality as a separate unit from all the generic functionality you might consume from a database or message broker.

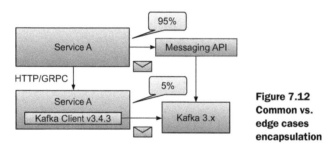

**Figure 7.12
Common vs.
edge cases
encapsulation**

I've chosen to use async messaging as an example in figure 7.12, but the same applies to databases and credential stores. If we can decouple 95% of our services to use generic capabilities to do their work and encapsulate edge cases as separate units, we reduce the coupling and the cognitive load on new team members tasked to modify these services. Service A in figure 7.12 is consuming a message API provided by the platform team to consume and emit messages asynchronously. We will look deeper into this approach in the next section. But more importantly, the edge cases, where we need to use some Kafka-specific features, for example, are extracted into a separate service that Service A can still interact with using HTTP or GRPC. Notice that the messaging API also uses Kafka to move information around. Still, for Service A, that is no longer relevant, because a simplified API is exposed as a platform capability.

When we need to change these services, 95% of the time, we don't need team members to worry about Kafka. The messaging API removes that concern from our application development teams. For modifying Service Y, you will need Kafka experts, and the Service Y code will need to be upgraded if Kafka is upgraded because it directly depends on the Kafka client. For this book, platform engineering teams should focus on trying to reduce the cognitive load on teams for the most common cases while at the same time allowing teams to choose the appropriate tool for edge cases and specific scenarios that don't fit the common solutions.

The following section will look at some approaches to address some of the challenges we have been discussing. However, keep in mind that these are generic solutions, and further steps may be required within your own specific context.

7.2   *Standard APIs to separate applications from infrastructure*

What about if we encapsulate all these common functionalities (storing and reading data, messaging, credential stores, resiliency policies) into APIs that developers can use from within their applications to solve common challenges while, at the same time, enabling the platform team to wire infrastructure in a way that doesn't require the application's code to change? In figure 7.13 we can see the same services, but instead of adding dependencies to interact with infrastructure, they use HTTP/GRPC requests.

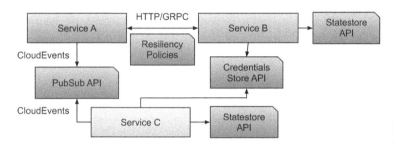

Figure 7.13   Platform capabilities as APIs

Suppose we expose a set of HTTP/GRPC APIs that our applications services can consume. In that case, we can remove vendor-specific dependencies from our application code and consume these services using standard HTTP or GRPC calls.

This separation between application services and platform capabilities enables separate teams to handle different responsibilities. The platform can evolve independently from applications, and application code will now only depend on the platform capabilities interfaces but not the version of the components running under the hood. Figure 7.14 shows the separation between application code (our three services) managed by application development teams and platform capabilities that are managed by the platform team.

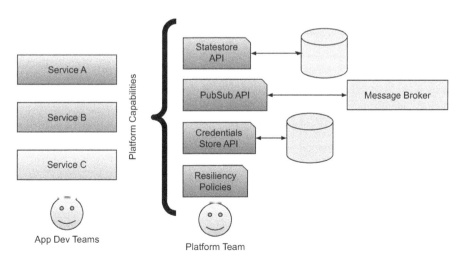

Figure 7.14   Decoupling responsibilities from app dev teams and platform capabilities

When using an approach like the one suggested here, the platform team can expand the platform capabilities, introducing new services for application development teams. More importantly, they can do so without affecting the existing applications or forcing them to release new versions. This enables teams to decide when to release new versions of their services based on their features and the capabilities that they want to consume.

By following this approach, the platform team can make new capabilities available for services to use and promote best practices. Because these platform capabilities are accessible to all services, they can promote standardization and implement best practices behind the covers. Each team can decide which capabilities are needed to solve their specific problems based on the available ones. If capabilities are correctly versioned, teams can decide how and when to upgrade to the latest version, allowing teams to move at their own pace without the platform pushing every team to upgrade whenever a new version is available.

For the sake of argument, imagine that the platform team decides to expose a consistent feature flagging capability to all the services. Using this capability, all services can consistently define and use feature flags without adding anything to their code except the feature flag conditional checks. Teams then can manage, visualize, and toggle on and off all their flags consistently. A capability like feature flags introduced and managed by the platform team directly affects developers' performance, because they don't need to worry about defining how feature flags will be handled under the hood (persistence, refresh, consistency, etc.), and they know for sure that they are doing things aligned with other services.

Figure 7.15 shows how the platform team can add extra capabilities, like, for example, feature flags, directly enabling teams to use this new capability uniformly in all the services. No new dependencies are needed.

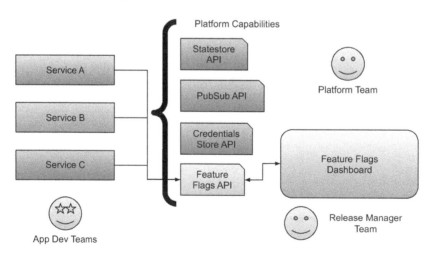

Figure 7.15   Enabling teams by providing consistent and unified capabilities such as feature flags

Before moving forward, here's a word of caution. Let's look at some challenges that you will face when externalizing capabilities like APIs, as suggested in the previous figure.

7.2.1 Exposing platform capabilities challenges

Externalizing APIs for teams to use will require, first of all, stable (and versioned) contracts that application teams can trust. When these APIs change, all applications consuming those APIs will break and must be updated. Platform teams can adopt a non-breaking changes policy that guarantees backward compatibility to teams and their applications. Adopting such policies makes your platform easier to consume, because the platform APIs and contracts are reliable for teams to use.

One of the main advantages of adding dependencies to your application code and, for example, using containers is that for local development, you can always start a PostgreSQL instance using Docker or Docker Compose and connect your application locally to it. If you move toward platform-provided capabilities, you must ensure that you can provide a local development experience for your teams unless your organization is mature enough to always work against remote services.

Another big difference is that the connection between your services and the platform provided APIs will introduce latency and require security by default. Before, calling the PostgreSQL driver APIs was a local call in the same process as your application. HTTPS, or a secure protocol, established the connection to the database itself, but setting that secure channel between your application and the database was the responsibility of the operations team.

It is also essential to recognize all the edge cases we can find when applying this approach to real-life projects. If you want to build these platform capabilities and push for your teams to consume them, you need to make sure that there is always a door open for edge cases so that teams (or even the platform team) aren't forced to make common cases more complex to account for an obscure feature that will be used only 1% of the time. Figure 7.16 shows Services A, B, and C using the capabilities exposed by the platform via the capabilities APIs. Service Y, on the other hand, has very specific requirements for how to connect to the database, and the team maintaining the service has decided to bypass the platform capabilities APIs to connect directly to the database using the database client.

Treating edge cases separately allows Services A, B, and C to evolve separately from the platform components (database, message brokers, credential stores), while Service Y is now heavily dependent on the database that is connecting to and requires a specific version of the client. While this sounds bad, in practice, it is acceptable and should be considered a platform feature. Teams that cannot solve their business problems with the exposed APIs will hate the platform and silently find workarounds. Good platforms (and platform teams) will promote APIs that cover a wide range of use cases, solving and facilitating the implementation of common functionality for application developers. If these APIs are not enough for all teams, documenting and deeply understanding the edge cases leads to new APIs and platform features that the platform team can implement in future versions.

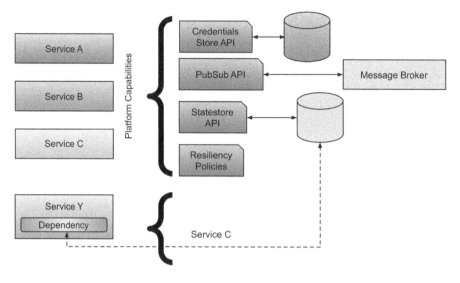

Figure 7.16   Handling edge cases; do not ignore them

The following section will examine a couple of CNCF initiatives that took these ideas forward and helped us implement the platform capabilities that most of our applications require.

7.3   *Providing application-level platform capabilities*

In this section, we will look at two projects that can save development teams time in standardizing these generic APIs that most of our applications will need. We will start by looking at the Dapr project (https://dapr.io/), what it is, how it works, and what it can do for our development and platform teams. Then we will look into OpenFeature (https://openfeature.dev/), a CNCF initiative that provides our applications with the right abstractions to define and use feature flags without being tied to a specific feature flag provider.

Once we get a bit of an understanding of how these two projects work and complement each other by helping us to provide application-level platform capabilities, we will look into how these projects can be applied to our Conference application, what changes are needed, the advantages of following this approach, and some examples showing edge cases. Let's start with Dapr, our Distributed Application Runtime.

7.3.1   *Dapr in action*

Dapr provides a set of consistent APIs to solve common and recurrent distributed application challenges. The Dapr project has spent the last four years implementing a set of APIs (called Building Block APIs) to abstract away common challenges and best practices that distributed applications will need 95% of the time. Created by Microsoft in 2019 and donated to the CNCF in 2021, the Dapr project has a large community contributing with extensions and improvements to the project APIs, making it the 10th fastest-growing project in the CNCF of 2023.

Dapr defines a set of building blocks that provide concrete APIs to solve distributed application challenges and swappable implementations that the platform team can configure. If you visit the https://dapr.io website, you will see the list of Building Block APIs, including Service Invocation, State Management, Publish & Subscribe, Secrets Store, Input/Output Bindings, Actors, Configurations Management, and, more recently Workflows. Figure 7.17 shows the Dapr official website describing the current Dapr Building Block APIs that teams can use to build their distributed applications. Check the Dapr Overview page at https://docs.dapr.io/concepts/overview/ for more information about the Dapr project.

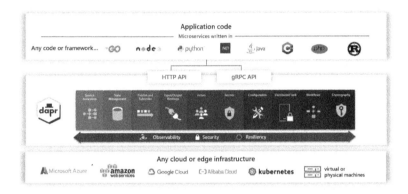

Figure 7.17   **Dapr components for building distributed applications**

While Dapr does much more than just expose APIs, in this chapter, I wanted to focus on the APIs provided by the project and the mechanisms used by the project to enable applications/services to consume these APIs.

Because this is a Kubernetes book, we will look at Dapr in the context of Kubernetes, but the project can also be used outside of Kubernetes clusters, making Dapr a generic tool to build distributed applications no matter where you are running them. As a side note, Dapr is currently part of Azure Container Apps service (https://azure.microsoft .com/en-us/products/container-apps), where it is configured with another CNCF project KEDA (https://keda.sh/) for autoscaling your distributed applications.

7.3.2   *Dapr in Kubernetes*

Dapr works as a Kubernetes extension or add-on. You must install a set of Dapr controllers (a Dapr control plane) on your Kubernetes clusters. Figure 7.15 shows Service A deployed in a Kubernetes cluster with Dapr installed. Service A needs to be annotated with two annotations: `dapr.io/enabled: "true"` for the Dapr control plane to be aware of the application and `dapr.io/appid: "service-a"` to use Dapr service identity features.

Once Dapr is installed in your clusters, your applications deployed in the cluster can start using the Dapr APIs by adding a set of annotations to your deployments. This enables the Dapr control plane services to understand that your application wants to use the Dapr APIs, as shown in figure 7.18.

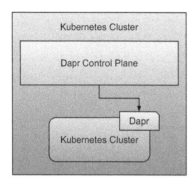

**Figure 7.18
The Dapr
control plane
monitor for
applications
with Dapr
annotations**

By default, Dapr will make all the Dapr APIs available to your applications/services as a sidecar (`daprd` is the container that will run beside your applications/services) that runs beside your application's containers. Using the sidecar pattern, we enable our application to interact with a co-located (localhost) API that runs very close to the application's container and avoids network round trips. Figure 7.19 shows how the Dapr control plane injects the `daprd` sidecar into the application annotated with the Dapr annotations. This enables the application to access the configured Dapr components.

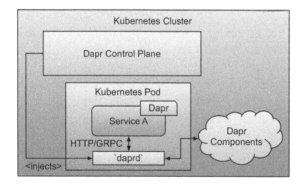

**Figure 7.19
Dapr sidecars
(daprd) give your
applications local
access to Dapr
components.**

Once the Dapr sidecar is running beside your applications/service container, it can use the Dapr APIs by sending requests (using HTTP or GRPC) to `localhost`, because the `daprd` sidecar runs inside the same pod as the application, sharing the same networking space.

Now for the Dapr APIs to be of some use, the platform team needs to configure the implementation (or backing mechanisms named Dapr components) for these APIs to work. For example, if you want to use the Statestore Dapr APIs (https://docs.dapr .io/operations/components/setup-state-store/) from your applications/services, you must define and configure a Statestore component.

When working with Dapr on Kubernetes, you configure a Dapr component specification using a Kubernetes resource. For example, you can configure a Statestore Dapr component to use Redis. See listing 7.1 for an example Dapr component resource definition.

Listing 7.1 Dapr Statestore component definition

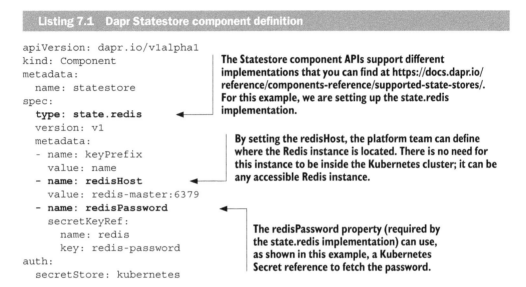

```
apiVersion: dapr.io/v1alpha1
kind: Component
metadata:
  name: statestore
spec:
  type: state.redis
  version: v1
  metadata:
  - name: keyPrefix
    value: name
  - name: redisHost
    value: redis-master:6379
  - name: redisPassword
    secretKeyRef:
      name: redis
      key: redis-password
auth:
  secretStore: kubernetes
```

The Statestore component APIs support different implementations that you can find at https://docs.dapr.io/reference/components-reference/supported-state-stores/. For this example, we are setting up the state.redis implementation.

By setting the redisHost, the platform team can define where the Redis instance is located. There is no need for this instance to be inside the Kubernetes cluster; it can be any accessible Redis instance.

The redisPassword property (required by the state.redis implementation) can use, as shown in this example, a Kubernetes Secret reference to fetch the password.

If the component resource is available in the Kubernetes cluster, the `daprd` sidecar can read its configurations and connect to the Redis instance for this example. From the application perspective, there is no need to know if Redis is being used or if any other implementation for the Statestore component. Figure 7.20 shows how Dapr components are wired so Service A can use the Statestore component APIs. For this example, by calling a local API, Service A will be able to store and read data from the Redis instance.

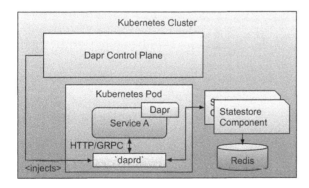

Figure 7.20
Dapr sidecars
use component
configurations
to connect to
the component's
infrastructure.

Dapr makes it easy to build your application using a local/self-hosted Redis instance but then move it to the cloud where a managed Redis service can be used. No code or dependencies changes are needed, just a different Dapr component configuration.

Do you want to emit and consume messages between different applications? You just need to configure a Dapr PubSub component (https://docs.dapr.io/operations/components/setup-pubsub/) and its implementation. Now your service can use a local API to emit asynchronous messages. Do you want to make all service interactions (including infrastructure) calls resilient? You can use Dapr resiliency policies (https://docs.dapr.io/operations/resiliency/policies/) to avoid writing custom logic inside your application code.

Figure 7.21 shows how Service A and Service B can send requests to each other using the Service Invocation APIs, in contrast to calling the other service directly. Using these APIs (that send traffic through the `daprd` sidecar) enables the platform team to configure resiliency policies at the platform level, uniformly without adding any dependencies or changing the application code.

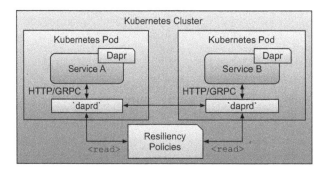

Figure 7.21 Dapr-enabled services can use service-to-service communications and resiliency policies.

OK, so the Dapr control plane will inject the Dapr sidecars (`daprd`) to the applications that are interested in using Dapr components. But how does this look from the application point of view?

7.3.3   *Dapr and your applications*

If we go back to the example introduced in the previous section where Service A wants to use the Statestore component to store/read some data from persistent storage like Redis, the application code is straightforward. No matter which programming language you use, as soon as you know how to create HTTP or GRPC requests, you have all you need to work with Dapr.

For example, to store data using the Statestore APIs your application code needs to send an HTTP/GRPC request to the following endpoint:

```
http://localhost:<DAPR_HTTP_PORT>/v1.0/state/<STATESTORE_NAME>
```

Using `curl`, the request will look like this, where `-d` shows the data we want to persist and `3500` is the default `DAPR_HTTP_PORT` and our Statestore component is called `statestore`:

```
> curl -X POST -H "Content-Type: application/json"
➥-d '[{ "key": "name", "value": "Bruce Wayne"}]'
➥http://localhost:3500/v1.0/state/statestore
```

To read the data that we have persisted, instead of sending a POST request, we just write a GET request. With `curl`, it would look like this:

```
curl http://localhost:3500/v1.0/state/statestore/name
```

Usually, you will not be using `curl` from inside your applications. You will use your programming language tools to write these requests. So, if you use Python, Go, Java, .NET, or JavaScript, you can find tutorials online on using popular libraries or built-in mechanisms to write these requests.

Another option is to use one of the Dapr SDKs (Software Development Kits) available for different programming languages. Adding the Dapr SDK to your application as a dependency allows you to make your developers' lives easier, so they don't need to craft HTTP or GRCP requests manually. It is crucial to notice that while you are now adding a new dependency to your application, this dependency is optional and only used as a helper to speed things up, because this dependency is not tied to any of the infrastructural components that the Dapr APIs are interacting with.

Check the Dapr website for examples of how your code will look if you use the Dapr SDK. For example, for a multi-programming language example on how to use the Statestore component using the SDKs, you can visit https://docs.dapr.io/getting-started/quickstarts/statemanagement-quickstart/.

While I decided to focus on Dapr for API abstractions, Dapr offers much more. By allowing platform teams to swap Dapr components implementations, applications can be moved across cloud providers without needing to change any application code. By default, the entire system is observable (https://docs.dapr.io/operations/observability/), secure (https://docs.dapr.io/operations/security/), and resilient (https://docs.dapr.io/operations/resiliency/), as Dapr sidecars will enforce service identity and the rules specified by the platform team, while at the same time extracting metrics from all the Dapr-enabled applications and components. I recommend platform teams familiarize themselves with the Dapr Project, as the project was built to solve common challenges that teams will face when working with distributed applications. Check section 7.3.5 of this chapter to see how we can make our Conference application Dapr-enabled. Now let's talk a bit about feature flags.

7.3.4 *Feature flags in action*

Feature flags enable teams to release software that includes new features without making those features available immediately. New features can be hidden behind feature flags that can be enabled later. In other words, feature flags allow teams to keep deploying new versions of their services or applications, and once these applications are running, features can be turned on or off based on the company's needs.

Compared to application-level APIs, which directly enabled developers with out-of-the-box behaviors to implement complex features, feature flags can enable other teams that make business-related decisions on when features should be enabled to customers.

While most companies might build mechanisms to implement feature flags, it is a well-recognized pattern to be encapsulated into a specialized service or library. In the Kubernetes world, you can consider using `ConfigMaps` as the simplest way to parameterize your containers. As soon as your container can read environment variables to turn on and off features, you are ready to go. We used this approach in chapter 2 with the `FEATURE_DEBUG_ENABLED=true` environment variable.

Unfortunately, this approach is too simplistic and doesn't work for real-world scenarios. First, one of the main reasons is that your containers will need to be restarted to reread the content of the ConfigMap if it changes. Second, you might need many flags for your different services, so you might need multiple ConfigMaps to manage your feature flags. Third, if you use environment variables, you will need to develop a convention to define each flag's status, default values, and type, because you cannot get away with just defining variables as plain strings.

Because this is a well-understood problem, several companies have come up with tools and managed services like LaunchDarkly (https://launchdarkly.com/) and Split (https://www.split.io/product/feature-flags/), among others, which enable teams to host their feature flags in a remote service that offers simplified access to view and modify feature flags without the need for technical knowledge. For each of these services, to fetch and evaluate complex feature flags, you will need to download and add a dependency to your applications. As each feature flag provider will offer different functionalities, switching between providers would require many changes.

OpenFeature (https://openfeature.dev/) is a CNCF initiative to unify how feature flags can be consumed and evaluated in cloud-native applications. In the same way that Dapr is abstracting how to interact with Statestores (storing and reading state) or Pub-Sub (async message brokers) components, OpenFeature provides a consistent API to consume and evaluate feature flags no matter which features flag provider we use.

In this short section, we will look at a simple example using a ConfigMap to hold a set of feature flag definitions. We will also be using the `flagd` implementation provided by OpenFeature, but the beauty of this approach is that you can then swap the provider where the feature flags are stored without changing any single line of code in your application.

Figure 7.22 shows a simple application including the OpenFeature SDK that is configured to connect to an OpenFeature provider—in this case, `flagd`, which is in charge of hosting our feature flag definitions.

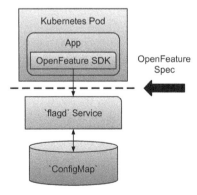

**Figure 7.22
Consuming and
evaluating feature
flags from our
application services**

For this simple example, our app is written in Go and uses the OpenFeature Go SDK to fetch feature flags from the flagd service. The flagd service for this example is configured to watch a Kubernetes ConfigMap that contains some complex feature flags definitions.

While this is a simple example, it allows us to see how a service like flagd can allow us to abstract away all the complexities of the storage and implementation of the mechanisms needed to provide a feature flag capability as part of our platform.

In contrast with Dapr, the OpenFeature SDK is needed because we are not only fetching the feature flag definitions but also performing evaluations that can involve complex feature flags.

You can hook every service in your application to connect to an OpenFeature provider to perform feature flag evaluations. An important difference with just using plain ConfigMaps is that by using OpenFeature, containers don't need to be restarted to fetch values if they change; that is now the responsibility of the OpenFeature flag provider.

In the next section, we look at how to apply both Dapr and OpenFeature to the Conference application walking skeleton.

7.3.5 *Updating our Conference application to consume application-level platform capabilities*

Conceptually and from a platform perspective, it will be great to consume all these capabilities without the platform leaking which tools are used to implement different behaviors. This would enable the platform team to change/swap implementations and reduce the cognitive load from teams using these capabilities. But as we discussed with Kubernetes, understanding how these tools work, their behaviors, and how their functionalities were designed influences how we architect our applications and services. In this last section of the chapter, I wanted to show how tools like Dapr and OpenFeature can influence your application architecture and, at the same time, show how these tools offer building blocks to create higher-level abstractions to reduce consumers' cognitive load.

For our Conference application, we can use the following Dapr components, so let's focus on these:

- *Dapr Statestore component:* Using the Statestore component APIs enables us to remove the Redis dependency from the Agenda service included in the Conference application. If, for some reason, we want to swap Redis for another persistent store, we will be able to do so without changing any of the application code.
- *Dapr PubSub component:* For emitting events, we can replace the Kafka client from all the services to use the PubSub component APIs, allowing us to test different

implementations, such as RabbitMQ or a cloud provider service to exchange asynchronous messages between applications.

- *Dapr service-to-service invocations and Dapr resiliency policies:* If we use the service-to-service invocation APIs, we can configure resiliency policies between the services without adding a library or custom code to our services code. By default, all services have resiliency policies defined if no custom configuration is provided.

While we can choose to use the Statestore component APIs also to remove the PostgreSQL dependency in our Call for Proposals service, I have chosen not to do so to support the use of SQL and PostgreSQL features that the team needed for this service. When adopting Dapr, you must avoid pushing for an "all or nothing" approach.

Let's look at how the application will change if we decide to use Dapr. Figure 7.23 shows the application services using Dapr components, because all the services are annotated to use Dapr, and the `daprd` sidecar has been injected all services. Once the PubSub and Statestore components have been configured, they can be accessed by the Call for Proposals service, Agenda service, and Notifications service. Finally, a Dapr Subscription pushes events to the Frontend application.

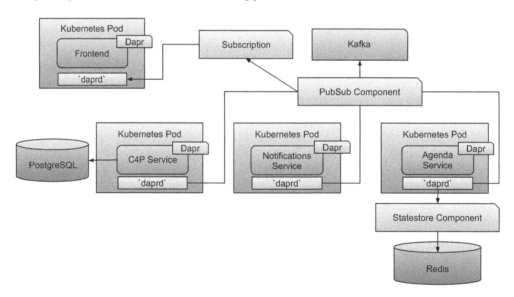

Figure 7.23   Using Dapr components for our walking skeleton / Conference application

Resiliency policies can also be configured and defined for the Call for Proposals service to interact with the agenda and notifications services, as shown in figure 7.24.

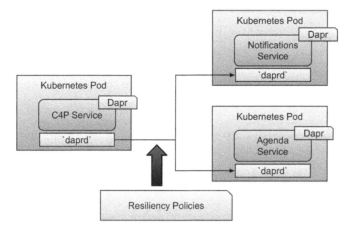

Figure 7.24 Service-to-service interactions can be handled by the `daprd` **sidecar, allowing platform teams to define different resiliency policies.**

Dapr applies default resiliency policies if we don't configure any. These resiliency policies also apply to, for our example, contacting the `statestore` and `pubsub` components. This means that not only our service-to-service invocations are resilient, but every time our application code wants to interact with infrastructure components such as databases, caches and message brokers, the resiliency policies will kick in.

The application code needs to change slightly, because when services want to talk to each other, they need to use the Dapr API to use resiliency policies.

Finally, because we wanted to enable all the services to use feature flags, each service now includes the OpenFeature SDK, which allows the platform team to define which feature flag implementation all services will use.

In figure 7.25 each service has included the OpenFeature SDK library and is configured to point to the `flagd` service that enables the platform team to configure the mechanism used to store, fetch, and manage all the feature flags used by all the services.

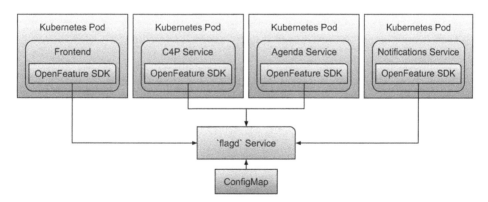

Figure 7.25 Services using the `flagd` **feature flag provider.**

Using the OpenFeature SDK, we can change the feature flag provider without changing our application code. The OpenFeature SDK now standardizes all the feature flag consumption and evaluation of our service code.

While in Dapr, using the SDK is optional (because you can always craft your HTTP or GRPC requests by hand), in OpenFeature, the scenario is a bit more complicated. because the SDKs provide some of the evaluation logic to understand which type each flag is and if it is on or off.

The step-by-step tutorial (https://github.com/salaboy/platforms-on-k8s/tree/v2.0.0/chapter-7) deploys version v2.0.0 of the conference application that uses Dapr and OpenFeature flags to enable application teams to keep evolving the application services. Version v2.0.0 of the application services doesn't include the Kafka or Redis client to interact with infrastructure. These services can be deployed in different environments (including cloud providers) and wired against different implementations of these standard APIs. Figure 7.26 shows the dependencies that we managed to remove for version v2.0.0 of the application using the Dapr component APIs.

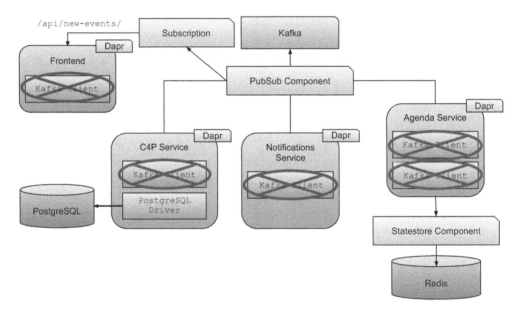

Figure 7.26   Kafka and Redis client removed from services' dependencies.

From a platform perspective, three Kubernetes resources are defined by the Dapr Statestore component, the Dapr PubSub component, and the Dapr Subscription.

We've already seen in section 7.3.1 how a Dapr Statestore component is defined. In listing 7.2, we can see how a PubSub component is defined, in this case selecting the type to be pubsub.kafka, which uses the Kafka instance installed using Helm.

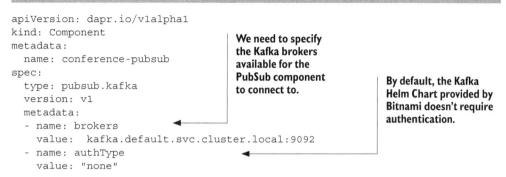

Listing 7.2 Dapr PubSub component definition

```
apiVersion: dapr.io/v1alpha1
kind: Component
metadata:
  name: conference-pubsub
spec:
  type: pubsub.kafka
  version: v1
  metadata:
  - name: brokers
    value:  kafka.default.svc.cluster.local:9092
  - name: authType
    value: "none"
```

We need to specify the Kafka brokers available for the PubSub component to connect to.

By default, the Kafka Helm Chart provided by Bitnami doesn't require authentication.

You can find all the supported PubSub implementations on the official Dapr website (https://docs.dapr.io/reference/components-reference/supported-pubsub/). Finally, the Dapr Subscription resources allow us to declaratively configure subscriptions to PubSub components and route events to the application's endpoints, as shown in listing 7.3.

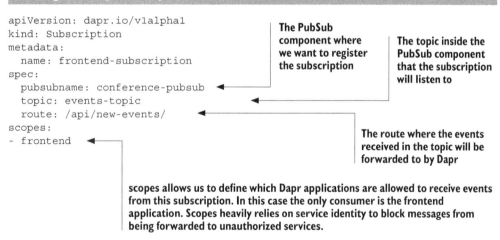

Listing 7.3 Dapr Subscription definition

```
apiVersion: dapr.io/v1alpha1
kind: Subscription
metadata:
  name: frontend-subscription
spec:
  pubsubname: conference-pubsub
  topic: events-topic
  route: /api/new-events/
scopes:
- frontend
```

The PubSub component where we want to register the subscription

The topic inside the PubSub component that the subscription will listen to

The route where the events received in the topic will be forwarded to by Dapr

scopes allows us to define which Dapr applications are allowed to receive events from this subscription. In this case the only consumer is the frontend application. Scopes heavily relies on service identity to block messages from being forwarded to unauthorized services.

From an application developer perspective, the changes in v2.0.0 use the Dapr Go SDK to call the Dapr components API. For example, to read the state from the Statestore component, the Agenda service performs the call shown in listing 7.4.

Listing 7.4 Getting state from a Statestore using the Dapr SDK

To store state, you only need to provide the Statestore component name configured in Dapr.

```
s.APIClient.GetState(ctx,
STATESTORE_NAME,
KEY,
nil)
```

You also need to provide the key that you want to retrieve from the Statestore.

The APIClient instance here is just a Dapr client that provides helpers to interact with the DAPR HTTP and GRPC APIs. Similarly, to store state, you can use the `SaveState` method; see listing 7.5.

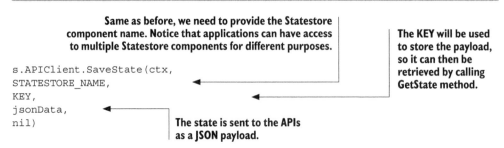

Listing 7.5   Saving state from a Statestore using the Dapr SDK

Same as before, we need to provide the Statestore component name. Notice that applications can have access to multiple Statestore components for different purposes.

The KEY will be used to store the payload, so it can then be retrieved by calling GetState method.

```
s.APIClient.SaveState(ctx,
STATESTORE_NAME,
KEY,
jsonData,
nil)
```

The state is sent to the APIs as a JSON payload.

Finally, and following exactly the same approach, applications can publish events to the PubSub component by using the API shown in listing 7.6.

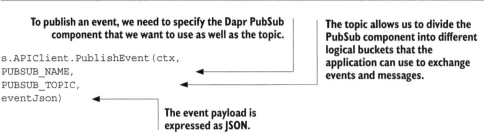

Listing 7.6   Publishing an event using the Dapr SDK

To publish an event, we need to specify the Dapr PubSub component that we want to use as well as the topic.

The topic allows us to divide the PubSub component into different logical buckets that the application can use to exchange events and messages.

```
s.APIClient.PublishEvent(ctx,
PUBSUB_NAME,
PUBSUB_TOPIC,
eventJson)
```

The event payload is expressed as JSON.

On the OpenFeature side, the feature flag configurations are defined inside a ConfigMap (https://github.com/salaboy/platforms-on-k8s/blob/v2.0.0/conference-application /helm/conference-app/templates/openfeature.yaml#L49). The tutorial shows three different feature flags added to the Conference application to control frontend and backend features. By modifying the ConfigMap that contains the flag definitions, we can change the application behavior without the need to restart any container. The `eventsEnabled` feature flag in listing 7.7 shows a feature flag of type Object that contains properties for each of the services. By defining different variants, we can codify profiles, allowing us to define complex scenarios.

Listing 7.7   Feature flag definitions, including variants

```
"eventsEnabled": {
"state": "ENABLED",
"variants": {
  "all": {
    "agenda-service": true,
    "notifications-service": true,
    "c4p-service": true
```

```
  },
  "decisions-only": {
    "agenda-service": false,
    "notifications-service": false,
    "c4p-service": true
  },
  "none": {
    "agenda-service": false,
    "notifications-service": false,
    "c4p-service": false
  }
},
"defaultVariant": "all"
```

Listing 7.7 shows an Object feature flag that defines three variants: `all`, `decisions-only`, and `none`. By changing the `defaultVariant` property, we can change which profile is selected, in this case to enable and disable which services will emit events. Inside the Agenda service source code, we use the OpenFeature GO SDK to fetch and evaluate the flag, as shown in the following listing.

Listing 7.8   Feature flag evaluation using OpenFeature SDK

```
s.FeatureClient.ObjectValue(ctx, "eventsEnabled",
EventsEnabled{},
openfeature.EvaluationContext{})
```

Listing 7.8 shows using the OpenFeature client to fetch the `eventsEnabled` feature. The `EventsEnabled{}` struct is the default value that should return in case there is a problem fetching the feature flag. Finally, the `EvaluationContext` struct allows you to add extra parameters for OpenFeature to evaluate the flag for more complex scenarios.

You can find the differences between `v1.0.0` and `v2.0.0` by comparing the `main` branch and the `v2.0.0` branch in the application repository at https://github.com/salaboy/platforms-on-k8s/compare/v2.0.0. At the same time, the platform team is free to configure and wire up application infrastructure and define all the backing mechanisms and implementations for feature flags, storage, messaging, configuration, managing credentials, resiliency, and other common challenges they don't want to expose directly to developers.

7.4   *Linking back to platform engineering*

In this chapter, we have seen how to enable teams with platform-wide capabilities in the form of APIs. We aim to speed up their process of writing and delivering complex software by providing teams with common and standard APIs to solve everyday challenges when creating distributed applications and mechanisms such as feature flags.

By separating application infrastructure from the application's code, we not only remove dependencies from our services, but we also enable the platform team to decide how to configure application infrastructure components and how the services will connect to them. If different environments require different implementations, the platform team can work behind the APIs to provide different configurations for different scenarios.

Figure 7.27 shows how we can reduce friction and dependencies related to the application infrastructure. This allows our application's services to work in various environments the platform team can control. Using projects like Dapr, you also gain portability of your applications across cloud providers, consistent APIs that can be used from any programming language, and you enable teams to bring their applications from a local development environment to production environments, allowing the platform team to wire up the infrastructure that your application needs to work. With feature flags, we enable developers to keep releasing software by masking features behind feature flags that can be turned on and off, enabling other teams closer to customers (like product teams) to decide when these features should be exposed.

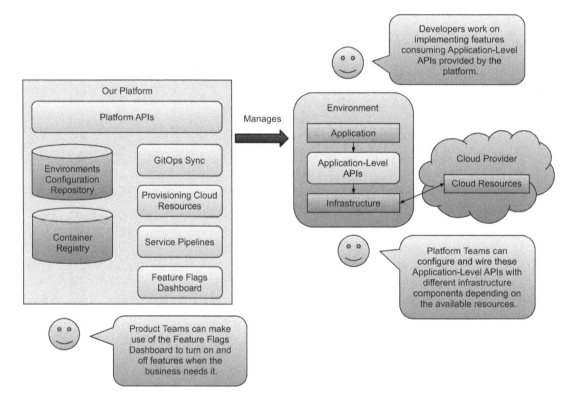

Figure 7.27   Consistent capabilities across environments enable smoother paths to production.

By providing consistent capabilities across environments, we enable easier paths to production, because we can control which features are exposed to customers after releasing the new version to production. Developers can keep building features relying on platform-provided application-level APIs without knowing where the available infrastructure is or which versions of databases and message brokers are used in the production environment.

For the sake of space, topics such as observability, metrics, and logs, service meshes haven't been covered in these sections, because these capabilities are currently more mature and more operations-focused. I've decided to focus on capabilities that build on top of the operation and infrastructure teams to speed up development teams and solve everyday challenges. Platform teams will define which observability stack they will use across environments early and how this data can be available to developers troubleshooting problems. Service meshes and certificate rotation tools for mutual TLS (encryption between services) are often discussed in these conversations because these are topics that development teams will not want to spend time on and should be provided at the platform level. Figure 7.28 shows how our platform is responsible for defining, fetching, and aggregating data from the tools available inside each environment. Our platform should provide a single entry point to understand what is happening in different environments and provide teams with enough information to troubleshoot problems and access the tools the organization needs to deliver software to customers.

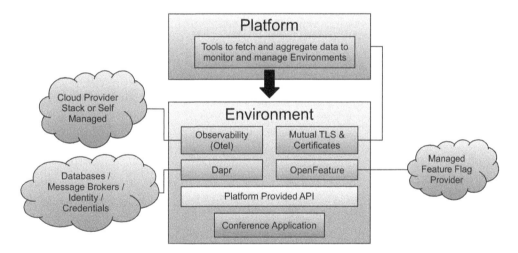

Figure 7.28 The platform that we build needs to define, manage, and monitor the tools available in each environment.

The next chapter will explore tools to enable teams to experiment while releasing software. Along the same lines of using feature flags, we will dig deeper into how to use different release strategies to catch problems earlier in the release process and enable stakeholders to try different approaches simultaneously.

Summary

- Moving dependencies to application infrastructure enables application code to stay agnostic to platform-wide upgrades. Separating the lifecycle of the applications and the infrastructure enables teams to rely on stable APIs instead of dealing with provider-specific clients and drivers for everyday use cases.

- Treating edge cases separately allows experts to make more conscious cases based on their application requirements. This also allows common scenarios to be handled by less experienced team members, who don't need to understand the specifics of tools like vendor-specific database features or low-level message broker configurations when they only want to store or read data or emit events from their application's code.

- Dapr solves common and shared concerns when building distributed applications. Developers that can write HTTP/GRPC requests can interact with infrastructure that the platform team will wire up.

- Feature flags enable developers to keep releasing software by masking new features behind feature flags that can be turned on and off.

- OpenFeature standardizes the way applications consume and evaluate feature flags. Relying on OpenFeature abstractions allows platform teams to decide where feature flags are stored and how they are managed. Different providers can offer non-technical people dashboards where they can see and manipulate flags.

- If you followed the step-by-step tutorial, you gained hands-on experience in using tools like Dapr and OpenFeature in the context of a cloud-native application composed of four services that interact with SQL and NoSQL databases and a message broker like Kafka. You also modified feature flags on a running application to change its behavior without restarting any of its components.

Platform capabilities II: Enabling teams to experiment

This chapter covers

- Enabling teams by providing release strategies capabilities
- Identifying the challenges of using Kubernetes built-in mechanisms to implement release strategies
- Using Knative Serving advanced traffic management to release our cloud-native applications
- Leveraging Argo Rollouts out-of-the-box release strategies

In chapter 7, we looked at how enabling development teams with application-level APIs can reduce the cognitive load on developers to solve common distributed application challenges while at the same time enabling platform teams to wire and configure these components to be accessible for applications to consume. We also evaluated using feature flags to enable developers to keep releasing new features and enable other teams closer to the business to decide when these new features are exposed to customers.

In this chapter, we will look at how introducing different release strategies can help the organization catch errors earlier in the process, validate assumptions, and enable teams to experiment with different versions of the same application running simultaneously.

We want to avoid teams being worried about deploying a new version of your services, as this slows down your release cadence and causes stress to everyone involved in the release process. Reducing risk and having the proper mechanisms to deploy new versions drastically improves confidence in the system. It also reduces the time from a requested change until it is live in front of your users. New releases with fixes and new features directly correlate to business value, because software is not valuable unless it serves our company's users.

While Kubernetes built-in resources such as deployments, services, and ingresses provide us with the basic building blocks to deploy and expose our services to our users, a lot of manual and error-prone work must happen to implement well-known release strategies. For these reasons, the cloud-native communities have created specialized tools to help teams be more productive by providing mechanisms to implement the most common release strategy patterns we will discuss in this chapter. This chapter is divided into three main sections:

- Release strategies fundamentals:
  - Canary releases, blue/green deployments, and A/B testing
  - Limitations and complexities of using Kubernetes built-in mechanisms
- Knative Serving: Autoscaling, advanced traffic management, and release strategies
  - Introduction to Knative Serving
  - Release strategies in action with Knative Serving and the Conference application
- Argo Rollouts: Release strategies automated with GitOps
  - Introducing Argo Rollouts
  - Argo Rollouts and progressive delivery

The first section of this chapter covers the most common and well-documented release strategies from a high level, and we'll quickly look at why implementing these release strategies with Kubernetes building blocks can be challenging. Section 8.2 looks at Knative Serving, which provides higher-level building blocks that highly simplify how to implement these release strategies while at the same time providing advanced traffic management and dynamic autoscaling for our workloads. Section 8.3 introduces Argo Rollouts, another project from the Argo family that focuses on enabling teams with out-of-the-box release strategies and progressive delivery. Let's start covering the fundamentals of release strategies.

8.1 Release strategies fundamentals

If you look for the most common release strategies teams implement to promote services to sensitive environments, you will find canary releases, blue/green deployments, and A/B testing. Each release strategy has a different purpose and can be applied to various scenarios. In the following short sections, we will look at what is expected for each release strategy, the expected benefits of having these mechanisms in place, and how they relate to Kubernetes. Let's start by looking into canary releases.

8.1.1 Canary releases

With canary releases, we want to enable teams to deploy a new version of a service and have full control over how much live traffic is routed to this new version. This allows teams to slowly route traffic to the new version to validate that no problems were introduced before routing all the production traffic to it.

Figure 8.1 shows users accessing our software, where 95% of the requests are forwarded to the service that we know is stable and only 5% are forwarded to the new version of the service.

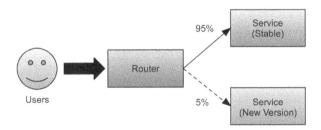

Figure 8.1 Releasing a new version (canary) of the service with 5% traffic routed to it

The term *canary release* comes from coal miners who used canary birds to alert them when toxic gasses reached dangerous levels. In this case, our canary release can help us identify problems or regressions introduced by the new version early on, where rolling back 100% of the traffic to the stable version doesn't include a full deployment.

In the context of Kubernetes, and as shown in figure 8.2, you can implement a sort of canary release by using two Kubernetes deployments resources (one with the stable version and one with the new version) and a single Kubernetes service that matches these two deployments. If each deployment has a single replica, there will be a 50% and 50% traffic split. Adding more replicas to each version creates a different percentage traffic split (for example, three replicas for the stable version and only one replica for the new version will give you a 75% to 25% traffic split ratio), as the Kubernetes service route requests using a round-robin fashion to all pods matching the service label.

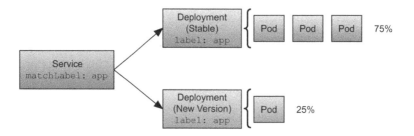

Figure 8.2   Canary release in Kubernetes using two deployments and one service.

Tools like Istio (https://istio.io/) or Linkerd (https://linkerd.io/) service meshes can give you finer-grained control of how traffic gets routed to each service. I strongly recommend you check Martin Fowler's website, which explains this release strategy in more detail at https://martinfowler.com/bliki/CanaryRelease.html.

8.1.2   Blue/green deployments

With blue/green deployments, we aim to enable teams to switch between two versions of their services or applications that are running parallel. This parallel version can act as a staging instance for testing, and when the team is confident enough, they can switch traffic to this parallel instance. This approach gives the team the safety of having another instance ready if the new version starts experiencing problems. This approach requires having enough resources to run both versions simultaneously, which can be expensive, but it gives your teams the freedom to experiment with an instance that is running with the same resources as your production workloads.

Figure 8.3 shows internal teams testing a production-like setup of the service's new version. Whenever this new version is ready, the team can decide to switch production traffic to the new version while still having the stable version to rollback if things go wrong.

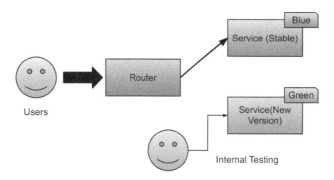

Figure 8.3   Blue/green deployments run in parallel with production-grade setups, allowing teams to switch traffic when they feel confident in the new version.

In the Kubernetes context, you can implement blue/green deployments by using two Kubernetes deployment resources and a Kubernetes service, but in this case, the service should only match the pods of a single deployment. Updating the service configuration to match the green deployment label(s) will automatically switch the traffic to the new version.

Figure 8.4 shows how by changing the `matchLabel` of the service to "green," the traffic will be automatically routed to the new version of the service. In the meantime, for testing, internal teams can use a different service to match the new version's deployment.

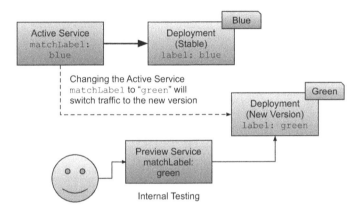

Figure 8.4   Blue/green deployments run in parallel. The service matchLabel is used to define where to route requests.

Once again, I strongly recommend you check Martin Fowler's website (https://martinfowler.com/bliki/BlueGreenDeployment.html) on blue/green deployments, because there are links and more context that you might find useful.

8.1.3   A/B testing

A/B testing is different from canary releases and blue/green deployments because it focuses more on end users than internal teams. With A/B testing, we want to enable other teams closer to the business to try different approaches to solve a business problem. Examples are having two different page layouts to see which one works better for the users or having different registration flows to validate which one takes users less time and causes less frustration. As discussed in chapter 7 with feature flags, we want to enable other teams and not only developers to experiment, in this case by providing different groups of users access to different versions of the application. These teams can then validate how effective each feature is and then decide which one to keep.

Figure 8.5 shows two different service implementations providing alternative registration flows for users. Using A/B testing, we can run both in parallel and collect data to enable business teams to decide which option works better.

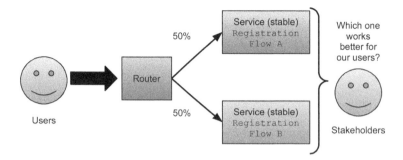

Figure 8.5   A/B testing enables teams closer to the business to evaluate different approaches and gather data to make decisions to improve business outcomes.

Because A/B testing is not a technical release strategy, it can be implemented in different ways depending on the application's requirements. Having two separate Kubernetes services and deployments would make sense to run and access two different versions of the same application. Figure 8.6 shows the use of two Kubernetes services and two deployments to route users to different versions of the same functionality. It also shows that an application-level router will be needed to define the rules on how users are routed to each of the alternatives.

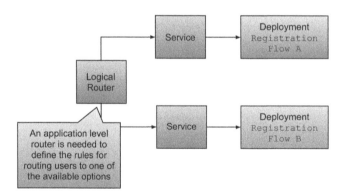

Figure 8.6   A/B testing requires some business and application-level rules to define how to route users to different options.

A/B testing can be implemented using similar mechanisms as canary releases, and we will look at several options in the following sections. *Continuous Delivery* by Jez Humble and David Farley (Addison-Wesley Professional, 2010) covers these release strategies in detail, so I strongly recommend you check that book.

8.1.4 *Limitations and complexities of using built-in Kubernetes building blocks*

Canary releases, blue/green deployments, and A/B testing can be implemented using built-in Kubernetes resources. But as you have seen, this requires creating different deployments, changing labels, and calculating the number of replicas needed to achieve percentage-based distribution of the requests is quite a major and error-prone task. Even if you use a GitOps approach, as shown with ArgoCD or other similar tools in chapter 4, creating the required resources with the right configurations is quite hard and takes a lot of effort.

We can summarize the drawbacks of implementing these patterns using Kubernetes building blocks as follows:

- Manual creation of more Kubernetes resources, such as deployments, services, and ingress rules, to implement these different strategies can be error-prone and cumbersome. The team implementing the release strategies must understand how Kubernetes behaves to achieve the desired output.

- No automated mechanisms are provided out of the box to coordinate and implement the resources required by each release strategy.

- They can be error-prone, because multiple changes need to be applied at the same time in different resources for everything to work as expected.

- Suppose we notice a demand increase or decrease in our services. In that case, we need to manually change the number of replicas for our deployments or install and configure a custom auto scaler (more on this later in this chapter). Unfortunately, if you set the number of replicas to 0, there will not be any instance to answer requests, requiring you to have at least one replica running all the time.

Out of the box, Kubernetes doesn't include any mechanism to automate or facilitate these release strategies, which becomes a problem quite quickly if you are dealing with many services that depend on each other.

> **NOTE** One thing is clear: your teams need to be aware of the implicit contracts imposed by Kubernetes regarding 12-factor apps and how their services APIs evolve to avoid downtime. Your developers need to know how Kubernetes' built-in mechanisms work to have more control over how your applications are upgraded.

If we want to reduce the risk of releasing new versions, we want to empower our developers to have these release strategies available for their daily experimentation.

In the next sections, we will look at Knative Serving and Argo Rollouts, tools and mechanisms built on top of Kubernetes to simplify all the manual work and limitations that we will find when trying to set up Kubernetes building blocks to enable teams with different release mechanisms. Let's start first with Knative Serving, which extends our Kubernetes clusters with a set of building blocks that simplifies the implementation of the release strategies described before.

8.2   Knative Serving: Advanced traffic management and release strategies

Knative is one of these technologies that are hard not to use when you learn what it can do for you. After working with the project for almost three years and observing the evolution of some of its components, every Kubernetes cluster should have Knative Serving installed; your teams will appreciate it. Knative Serving is a Kubernetes extension that provides higher-level abstractions on top of Kubernetes built-in resources to implement good practices and common patterns that enable your teams to go faster and have more control over their services.

While this chapter focuses on release strategies, you should look into Knative Serving if you are interested in the following topics:

- Providing a containers-as-a-service approach for your teams to use.
- Dynamic autoscaling for your workloads to provide a functions-as-a-service approach for your teams. Knative Serving installs its own autoscaler, which is automatically available for all Knative Services.
- Advanced and fine-grained traffic management for your services.

As the title of this section specifies, the following sections focus on a subset of the functionality provided by Knative, called Knative Serving. Knative Serving allows you to define *Knative Services*, which dramatically simplifies implementing the release strategies exemplified in the previous sections. Knative Services will create Kubernetes built-in resources for you and keep track of their changes and versions, enabling scenarios that require multiple versions to be present simultaneously. Knative Services also provides advanced traffic handling and autoscaling to scale down to zero replicas for a serverless approach.

> **NOTE**   A step-by-step tutorial on how to use Knative Serving with the Conference application to implement different release strategies can be found at https://github.com/salaboy/platforms-on-k8s/blob/main/chapter-8/knative/README.md.

It is outside of the scope of this book to explain how Knative Serving components and resources work; my recommendation is that if I manage to get your attention with the examples in the following sections, you should check out *Knative in Action* by Jacques Chester (Manning Publications, 2021).

8.2.1   Knative Services: Containers-as-a-Service

Once you have Knative Serving installed, you can create Knative Services. I can hear you thinking: "But we already have Kubernetes services. Why do we need Knative Services?" Believe me, I had the same feeling when I saw the same name, but follow along—it does make sense.

When we deployed our walking skeleton in chapter 2 (the Conference application), we created at least two Kubernetes resources: a Kubernetes deployment and a Kubernetes service. As we discussed in chapter 2, by using ReplicaSets, a deployment can perform rolling updates by keeping track of the configuration changes in the deployment resources. We also discussed in chapter 2 the need for creating an ingress resource to route traffic from outside the cluster. Usually, you only create an ingress resource to map the publicly available services, such as the Frontend of the Conference application or the Conference Admin Portal.

> **NOTE**   The Ingress resource that we created routes all the traffic straight to the in-cluster Kubernetes service, and the ingress controller used in the tutorials works as a simple reverse proxy. It doesn't have any advanced capability to split traffic, rate limit, or inspect the request headers to make dynamic decisions about it.

You can follow a step-by-step tutorial to create a cluster, install Knative Serving, and deploy the application services at https://github.com/salaboy/platforms-on-k8s/blob/main/chapter-8/knative/README.md#installation.

Knative Services are built on top of these resources (services, deployments, ReplicaSets) to simplify how we define and manage the lifecycle of our application's services. While it simplifies the task and reduces the amount of YAML that we need to maintain, it also adds some exciting features. Before jumping into the features, let's look at how a Knative Service looks in action.

Knative Services expose a simplified contract to its users that resembles a *container-as-a-service* interface such as AWS App Runner and Azure Container Apps. In fact, Knative Services share the interface used by Google Cloud Run to enable users to run containers on-demand without the need to understand Kubernetes.

Because Knative Serving installs its own autoscaler, Knative Services are automatically configured to scale based on demand. This makes Knative Serving a very good way to implement a *function-as-a-service* platform, because workloads that are not being used will be automatically downscaled to zero.

Let's see these features in action, beginning with the Knative Service Kubernetes resource. We will start simple and use the notification service from the Conference application to demonstrate how Knative Services work. Check the notifications-service.yaml resource definition (available at https://github.com/salaboy/platforms-on-k8s/blob/main/chapter-8/knative/notifications-service.yaml), as shown in the following listing.

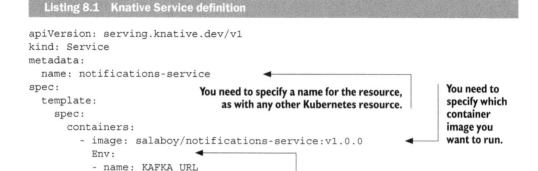

Listing 8.1   **Knative Service definition**

```
apiVersion: serving.knative.dev/v1
kind: Service
metadata:
  name: notifications-service
spec:
  template:
    spec:
      containers:
        - image: salaboy/notifications-service:v1.0.0
          Env:
          - name: KAFKA_URL
            value: <URL>
```

You need to specify a name for the resource, as with any other Kubernetes resource.

You need to specify which container image you want to run.

You can parameterize your containers using environment variables.

In the same way as a deployment will pick the `spec.template.spec` field to cookie-cut pods, a Knative Service defines the configuration for creating other resources using the same field.

Nothing too strange so far, but how is this different from a Kubernetes Service? If you create this resource using `kubectl apply -f`, you can start exploring the differences.

NOTE   All the examples in this section are based on running the step-by-step tutorial on a KinD cluster. Outputs will be different if you run in a cloud provider. See https://github.com/salaboy/platforms-on-k8s/blob/main/chapter-8/knative/README.md#knative-services-quick-intro.

You can also list all Knative Services using `kubectl get ksvc` (`ksvc` stands for Knative Service), and you should see your newly created Knative Service there:

```
NAME                    URL                                    LATEST CREATED                  READY
notifications-service   http://notifications1-service...notifications-service-00001   True
```

There are a couple of details to notice right here; first, there is a URL that you can copy into your browser and access the service. If you were running in a cloud provider and configured DNS while installing Knative, this URL should be accessible immediately. The `LASTCREATED` column shows the name of the latest Knative Revision of the Service. Knative Revisions are pointers to the specific configuration of our service, meaning that we can route traffic to them.

You can go ahead and test the Knative Service URL by using `curl` or by pointing your browser to http://notifications-service.default.127.0.0.1.sslip.io/service/info. Notice that we are using jq (https://jqlang.github.io/jq/download/), a very popular JSON utility, to pretty-print the output. You should see the output in listing 8.2.

Listing 8.2   Interacting with our newly created Knative Service

```
curl http://notifications-service.default.127.0.0.1.sslip.io/service/info

{
    "name" : "NOTIFICATIONS",
    "podIp" : "10.244.0.18",
    "podName" : "notifications-service-00001-deployment-74cf6f5f7f-h8kct",
    "podNamespace" : "default",
    "podNodeName" : "dev-control-plane",
    "podServiceAccount" : "default",
    "source" : "https://github.com/salaboy/platforms-on-k8s/tree/main/
      conference-application/notifications-service",
    "version" : "1.0.0"
}
```

As with any other Kubernetes resource, you can also use `kubectl describe ksvc notifications-service` to get a more detailed description of the resource. If you list other well-known resources such as deployment, services, and pods, you will find out that Knative Serving is creating them for you and managing them. Because these are managed resources now, it is usually not recommended to change them manually. If you want to change your application configurations, you should edit the Knative Service resource.

A Knative Service, as we applied it before to our cluster, by default behaves differently from creating a service, a deployment, and an ingress manually. A Knative Service by default:

- *Is accessible:* It exposes itself under a public URL so you can access it from outside the cluster. It doesn't create an ingress resource, because it uses the available Knative Networking stack that you installed previously. Because Knative has more control over the network stack and manages deployments and services, it knows when the service is ready to serve requests, reducing configuration errors between services and deployments.
- *Manages Kubernetes resources:* It creates two services and a deployment. Knative Serving allows us to run multiple versions of the same service simultaneously. Hence, it will create a new Kubernetes service for each version (which in Knative Serving is called a revision).
- *Collects service usage:* It creates a pod with the specified `user-container` and a sidecar container called `queue-proxy`.
- *Scales-up and down based on demand:* It automatically downscales itself to zero if no requests are hitting the service (by default after 90 seconds):
  - It achieves this by downscaling the Deployment replicas to 0 using the data collected by the `queue-proxy`.
  - If a request arrives and there is no replica available, it scales up while queuing the request, so it doesn't get lost.

– Our notification service has set a minimum number of replicas to 1 to be kept running at all times.

▪ *Configuration changes history is managed by Knative Serving*: If you change the Knative Service configuration, a new *Revision* will be created. By default, all traffic will be routed to the latest revision.

Of course, these are the defaults, but you can fine-tune each of your Knative Services to serve your purpose and, for example, implement the previously described release strategies.

In the next section, we will look at how Knative Serving advanced traffic-handling features can be used to implement canary releases, blue/green deployments, A/B testing, and header-based routing.

8.2.2 Advanced traffic-splitting features

Let's start by looking at how you can implement a canary release for one of our application's services with a Knative Service. This section starts by looking into doing canary releases using percentage-based traffic splitting. Then it goes into A/B testing by using tag-based and header-based traffic splitting.

CANARY RELEASES USING PERCENTAGE-BASED TRAFFIC SPLITTING

If you get the Knative Service resource (with `kubectl get ksvc notifications -service -oyaml`), you will notice that the `spec` section now also contains a `spec.traffic` section (as shown in listing 8.3) that was created by default, because we didn't specify anything. By default, 100% of the traffic is being routed to the latest Knative Revision of the service.

> **Listing 8.3   The Knative Service allows us to set traffic rules**

```
traffic:
 - latestRevision: true
   percent: 100
```

Now imagine that you made a change in your service to improve how emails are sent, but your team is not sure how well it will be received by people, and we want to avoid having any backlash from people not wanting to sign into our conference because of the website. Hence, we can run both versions side-by-side and control how much of the traffic is being routed to each version (Revision in Knative terms).

Let's edit (`kubectl edit ksvc notifications-service`) the Knative Service and apply the changes, as shown in listing 8.4.

> **Listing 8.4   Changing our Knative Service**

```
apiVersion: serving.knative.dev/v1
kind: Service
metadata:
  name: notifications-service
spec:
```

```
template:
  spec:
    containers:
      - image: salaboy/image: salaboy/notifications-service-0e27884e01429ab7
e350cb5dff61b525:v1.1.0
        env:
name: KAFKA_URL
value: <URL>
  traffic:
  - percent: 50
    revisionName: notifications-service-00001
  - latestRevision: true
    percent: 50
```

You have updated the container image that the service will use from "notifications-service-0e27884e0142 9ab7e350cb5dff6lb525:vl.0.0" to "notifications-service-0e27884e0142 9ab7e350cb5dff6lb525:vl.l.0".

You have created a 50% / 50% traffic split where 50% of the traffic will keep going to your stable version and 50% to the newest version that you just updated.

If you try now with `curl`, you should be able to see the traffic split in action.

Listing 8.5   New requests hitting different versions that are running parallel

```
curl http://notifications-service.default.127.0.0.1.sslip.io/service/info
{
  "name":"NOTIFICATIONS-IMPROVED",
  "version":"1.1.0",
  ...
}
```

One in five requests will go to the new "NOTIFICATIONS-IMPROVED" version. Notice that this can take a while until the new Knative Revision is running.

```
curl http://notifications-service.default.127.0.0.1.sslip.io/service/info
{
  "name":"NOTIFICATIONS",
  "version":"1.0.0",
  ...
}

curl http://notifications-service.default.127.0.0.1.sslip.io/service/info
{
  "name":"NOTIFICATIONS-IMPROVED",
  "version":"1.1.0",
  ...
}

curl http://notifications-service.default.127.0.0.1.sslip.io/service/info
{
  "name":"NOTIFICATIONS",
  "version":"1.0.0",
  ...
}
```

Once you have validated that the new version of your service is working correctly, you can start sending more traffic until you feel confident to move 100% of the traffic to it. If things go wrong, you can revert the traffic split to the stable version.

Notice that you are not limited to just two service revisions; you can create as many as you want as long as the traffic percentage sum of all the revisions is 100%. Knative will follow these rules and scale up the required revisions of your services to serve requests. You don't need to create any new Kubernetes resources, as Knative will create those for you, reducing the likelihood of errors that come with modifying multiple resources simultaneously.

Figure 8.7 shows some challenges that you will face when using this feature. By using percentages, you don't have control over where subsequent requests will land. Knative will just make sure to maintain a fair distribution based on the percentages that you have specified. This can become a problem if, for example, you have a user interface instead of a simple REST endpoint.

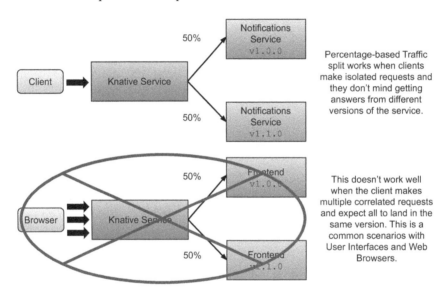

Figure 8.7   Percentage-based traffic split scenarios and challenges

User interfaces are complex because a browser will perform several correlated GET requests to render the page HTML, CSS, images, and so forth. You can quickly end up in a situation where each request hits a different version of your application. Let's look at a different approach that might be better suited for testing user interfaces or scenarios when we need to ensure that several requests end up in the correct version of our application.

A/B TESTING WITH TAG-BASED ROUTING

If you want to perform A/B testing of different versions of the user interface included with the Conference application, you will need to give Knative some way to differentiate where to send the requests. You have two options. First, you can point to a special URL for the service you want to try out, and the second is to use a request header to differentiate where to send the request. Let's look at these two alternatives in action.

The step-by-step tutorial (https://github.com/salaboy/platforms-on-k8s/tree/main/chapter-8/knative#run-the-conference-application-with-knative-services) defines all the Conference application services to be Knative Services and deploys them to the cluster. The Frontend Knative Services looks like listing 8.6.

Listing 8.6 Knative Service definition for the Frontend application

```
apiVersion: serving.knative.dev/v1
kind: Service
metadata:
  name: frontend
spec:
  template:
    metadata:
      annotations:
        autoscaling.knative.dev/min-scale: "1"
    spec:
      containers:
      - image: salaboy/frontend-go-1739aa83b5e69d4ccb8a5615830ae66c:v1.0.0
        env:
        - name: KAFKA_URL
          value: kafka.default.svc.cluster.local
        ...
```

> You need to specify a name for this service.

> We don't want Knative Serving to downscale the Frontend service if nobody is using it. We want to keep at least one instance running all the time.

> You now define the Frontend container image, because we are going to test multiple requests going to the same version.

Once again, we have just created a Knative Service, but we cannot specify percentage-based routing rules because this container image contains a web application composed of HTML, CSS, images, and JavaScript files. Knative will not stop you from doing so. Still, you will notice requests going to different versions and errors popping up because a given image is not in one of the versions, or you end up with the wrong stylesheet (CSS) coming from the wrong version of the application.

Let's start by defining a Tag that you can use to test a new stylesheet and also include the Debug tab in the Back Office section. You can do that by modifying the Knative Service resource as we did before. First, change the image to `salaboy/frontend-go-1739aa83b5e69d4ccb8a5615830ae66c:v1.1.0`, add the `FEATURE_DEBUG_ENABLED` environment variable with value `true` and then create some new traffic rules using the `traffic.tag` property:

```
traffic:
- percent: 100
  revisionName: frontend-00001
- latestRevision: true
  tag: version110
```

> 100% of the traffic will go to our stable version, and no request will be sent to our newly updated revision with version v1.1.0.

> We created a new tag called "color"; you can find the URL for this new tag by describing the Knative Service resource.

As shown in listing 8.7, if you describe the Knative Service (`kubectl describe ksvc frontend`) you will find the URL for the tag that we just created, as shown in the following listing.

Listing 8.7   Traffic rules when using tags

```
Traffic:
    Latest Revision:    false
    Percent:            100
    Revision Name:      frontend-00001
    Latest Revision:    true
    Percent:            0
    Revision Name:      frontend-00001
    Tag:                version110
    URL:                http://version110-frontend.default.127.0.0.1.sslip.io  ◄─┐
```
                                                                          You can find the tag and its generated
                                                                          URL in the ksvc traffic section.

Figure 8.8 shows how the Knative Service will route 100% of the traffic to version v1.0.0 when no tags are specified. If the tag "version110" is specified, the Knative Service will route traffic to the version v1.1.0.

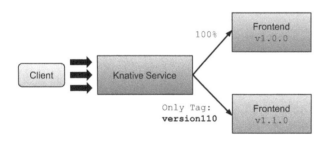

Figure 8.8   Knative Serving tag-based routing for version v1.1.0.

Using a web browser, check that you can consistently access version v1.1.0 by using the following URL (http://version110-frontend.default.127.0.0.1.sslip.io) and version v.1.0.0 using the original service URL (http://frontend.default.127.0.0.1.sslip.io). Figure 8.9 shows both side by side using a different color palette.

v1.0.0 - 100% traffic   v1.1.0 - Tag based traffic

Figure 8.9   A/B testing with tag-based routing

Using tags guarantees that all requests are hitting the URL to the correct version of your service. One more option avoids you pointing to a different URL for doing A/B testing, and it might be useful for debugging purposes. The next section looks at tag-based routing using HTTP headers instead of different URLs.

A/B TESTING WITH HEADER-BASED ROUTING

Finally, let's look at a Knative Serving feature (https://knative.dev/docs/serving/configuration/feature-flags/#tag-header-based-routing) that allows you to use HTTP headers to route requests. This feature also uses tags to know where to route traffic, but instead of using a different URL to access a specific revision, you can add an HTTP header that will do the trick.

Imagine that you want to enable developers to access a debugging version of the application. Application developers can set a special header in their browsers and then access a specific revision.

To enable this experimental feature, you or the administrator that installs Knative needs to patch a ConfigMap inside the `knative-serving` namespace:

```
kubectl patch cm config-features -n knative-serving
➥-p `{"data":{"tag-header-based-routing":"Enabled"}}'
```

Once the feature is enabled, you can test this by using the tag `version110` that we created before. Listing 8.8 shows the traffic rules that we have defined. The tag name that we want to target using HTTP header-based routing is highlighted.

> **Listing 8.8   HTTP headers-based routing using the name of the tag**

```
traffic:
- percent: 100
  revisionName: frontend-00001
- latestRevision: true
  tag: version110
```

If you point your browser to the Knative Service URL (`kubectl get ksvc`), you will see the same application as always, as shown in figure 8.10, but if you use a tool like ModHeader extension (https://chrome.google.com/webstore/detail/modheader/idgpnmonknjnojddfkpgkljpfnnfcklj?hl=en) for Chrome, you can set your custom HTTP headers that will be included in every request that the browser produces. For this example, and because the tag that you created is called `version110`, you need to set the following HTTP header: `Knative-Serving-Tag: version110`. As soon as the HTTP header is present, Knative Serving will route the incoming request to the `version110` tag.

Figure 8.10 shows how Knative Serving routes the request to our `version110` tag by using an HTTP header set using ModHeader. Notice that we are using the default service URL http://frontend.default.127.0.0.1.sslip.io.

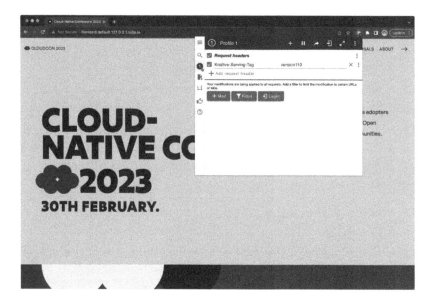

Figure 8.10   Using ModHeader Chrome extension to set custom HTTP headers for header-based routing.

Both tag and header-based routing are designed to ensure that all requests will be routed to the same revision if you hit a specific URL (created for the tag) or if one particular header is present. Finally, let's look at how to do blue/green deployments with Knative Serving.

BLUE/GREEN DEPLOYMENTS

For situations where we need to change from one version to the next at a very specific point in time, because there is no backward compatibility, we can still use tag-based routing with percentages. Instead of going gradually from one version to the next, we use percentages as a switch from 0 to 100 on the new version and from 100 to 0 on the old version.

Most blue/green deployment scenarios require coordination between different teams and services to make sure that both the service and the clients are updated at the same time. Knative Serving allows you to declaratively define when to switch from one version to the next in a controller way. Figure 8.11 shows the scenario where we want to deploy a new version of the notifications service `v2.0.0` that is not backward compatible with `v1.x` versions. This means that this upgrade will require changes to the clients. By using Knative Serving traffic rules and tags, we can decide when the switch happens. Teams responsible for the clients and the upgrade of the notification service `v2.0.0` will need to coordinate the upgrade.

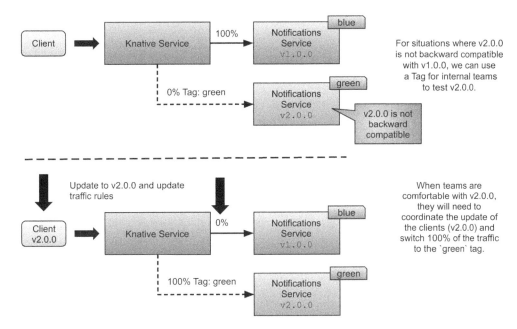

Figure 8.11 **Blue/green deployments using Knative Serving tag-based routing**

To achieve the scenario described in figure 8.11, we can create the "green" tag for the new version inside our Knative Service, as shown in listing 8.9.

Listing 8.9   Using tags to define blue and green revisions

```
...
traffic:
    - revisionName: <blue-revision-name>
      percent: 100 # All traffic is still being routed to the first revision
    - revisionName: <green-revision-name>
      percent: 0 # 0% of traffic routed to the second revision
      tag: green # A named route
```

By creating a new tag (called "green"), we will now have a new URL to access the new version for testing. This is particularly useful for testing new versions of the clients, because if the Service API is changing with a non-backward compatible change, clients might need to be updated as well. Once all tests are performed, we can safely switch all traffic to the "green" revision of our service, as shown in listing 8.10. Notice that we removed the tag from the "green" revision and created a new tag for the "blue" revision.

Listing 8.10   Switching traffic using the Knative declarative approach

```
...
traffic:
    - revisionName: <first-revision-name>
      percent: 0 # All traffic is still being routed to the first revision
```

```
tag: blue # A named route
- revisionName: <second-revision-name>
  percent: 100 # 100% of traffic routed to the second revision
```

Notice that the "blue" original version before the update is now accessible using header–or tag–based routing and is receiving all the traffic sent to the service.

Generally, we cannot progressively move traffic from one version to the next, because the client consuming the service will need to understand that requests might land in different (and non-compatible) versions of the service.

In the previous sections, we have been looking into how Knative Serving simplifies the implementation of different release strategies for your teams to deliver features and new versions of your services continuously. Knative Serving reduces the need to create several Kubernetes built-in resources to manually implement the release strategies described in this chapter. It provides high-level abstractions such as Knative Services, which creates and manages Kubernetes built-in resources and a network stack for advanced traffic management.

Let's switch to another alternative for managing release strategies in Kubernetes with Argo Rollouts.

8.3   *Argo Rollouts: Release strategies automated with GitOps*

In most cases you will see Argo Rollouts working hand in hand with ArgoCD. This makes sense because we want to enable a delivery pipeline that removes the need to interact with our environments to apply configuration changes manually. For the examples in the following sections, we will focus only on Argo Rollouts, but in real-life scenarios, you shouldn't apply resources to the environments using `kubectl`, because Argo CD will do it for you.

As defined on the website, Argo Rollouts is "a Kubernetes controller and set of CRDs which provide advanced deployment capabilities such as blue-green, canary, canary analysis, experimentation, and progressive delivery features to Kubernetes." As we have seen with other projects, Argo Rollouts extend Kubernetes with the concepts of `Rollouts`, `Analysis`, and `Experimentations` to enable progressive delivery features. The main idea with Argo Rollouts is to use the Kubernetes built-in blocks without the need to manually modify and keep track of deployment and services resources.

Argo Rollouts is composed of two big parts: the Kubernetes controller that implements the logic to deal with our rollouts, definitions (also analysis and experimentations) and a `kubectl` plugin that allows you to control how these rollouts progress, enabling manual promotions and rollbacks. Using the `kubectl` Argo Rollouts plugin, you can also install the Argo Rollouts Dashboard and run it locally.

> **NOTE**   You can follow a tutorial on how to install Argo Rollouts on a local Kubernetes KinD cluster at https://github.com/salaboy/platforms-on-k8s/blob/main/chapter-8/argo-rollouts/README.md. Notice that this tutorial requires creating a different KinD cluster than the one we used for Knative Serving.

Let's start by looking at how we can implement canary releases with Argo Rollouts to see how it compares with using plain Kubernetes resources or Knative Services.

8.3.1 *Argo Rollouts canary rollouts*

We'll begin by creating our first `Rollout` resource. With Argo Rollouts, we will be not defining deployments, because we will delegate this responsibility to the Argo Rollouts controller. Instead, we define an Argo Rollouts resource that also provides our pod specification (`PodSpec` in the same way that a Deployment defines how pods need to be created).

For these examples, we will use only the notifications service from the Conference platform application, and we will not use Helm. When using Argo Rollouts, we need to deal with a different resource type currently not included in the Conference application Helm charts. Argo Rollouts can work perfectly fine with Helm, but we will create files to test how Argo Rollouts behave for these examples. You can take a look at an Argo Rollouts example using Helm at https://argoproj.github.io/argo-rollouts/features/helm/. Let's start by creating an Argo Rollouts resource for the notifications service in listing 8.11.

Listing 8.11 Argo Rollouts resource definition

```
apiVersion: argoproj.io/v1alpha1
kind: Rollout          ◄──────────    The Rollouts resource definition
metadata:                              allows us to configure our workloads
  name: notifications-service-canary   to use different releases.
spec:
  replicas: 3          ◄──────────    Notice that as
  strategy:                            with
    canary:            ◄──────────    deployments, we
      steps:           ◄──────────    can set up the
      - setWeight: 25                  number of
      - pause: {}                      replicas that we
      - setWeight: 75                  want for our
      - pause: {duration: 10}          notification
  revisionHistoryLimit: 2              service.
  selector:
    matchLabels:
      app: notifications-service
  template:
    metadata:
      labels:
        app: notifications-service
    spec:
      containers:
      - name: notifications-service
        image: salaboy/notifications-service-<HASH>:v1.0.0
        env:
          - name: KAFKA_URL
            value: kafka.default.svc.cluster.local
        ...
```

This example sets the spec.strategy property to canary, which requires a set of specific steps to configure how the canary release will behave for this specific service.

The steps defined will be executed in sequence when we make any update on our service. For this example, the canary will start with 25% of the traffic and wait for manual promotion and then switch to 75%, wait for 10 seconds, and finally move to 100%.

NOTE You can find the full file at https://github.com/salaboy/platforms-on -k8s/blob/main/chapter-8/argo-rollouts/canary-release/rollout.yaml.

This Rollout resource manages the creation of Pods using what we define inside the `spec.template` and `spec.replicas` fields. But it adds the `spec.strategy` section, which for this case is set to `canary` and defines the steps (amount traffic (weight) that will be sent to the canary) in which the rollout will happen. As you can see, you can also define a pause between each step. The `duration` is expressed in seconds and allows us to have a fine-grain control of how the traffic is shifted to the canary version. If you don't specify the `duration` parameter, the rollout will wait there until manual intervention happens. Let's see how this rollout works in action.

Let's apply the Rollout resource to our Kubernetes cluster (check the step-by-step tutorial available at https://github.com/salaboy/platforms-on-k8s/tree/main/chapter-8/ argo-rollouts#canary-releases for all the steps):

```
> kubectl apply -f argo-rollouts/canary-release/
```

NOTE This command will also create a Kubernetes service and a Kubernetes ingress resource.

Remember, if you are using ArgoCD, instead of manually applying the resource, you will push this resource to your Git repository that Argo CD is monitoring. Once the resource is applied, we can see that a new Rollout resource is available by using `kubectl`, as shown in listing 8.12.

Listing 8.12   Getting all Argo Rollouts resources

```
> kubectl get rollouts.argoproj.io
NAME                            DESIRED    CURRENT    UP-TO-DATE    AVAILABLE
notifications-service-canary    3          3          3             3
```

This looks pretty much like a normal Kubernetes deployment, but it is not. If you use `kubectl get deployments`, you shouldn't see any deployment resource available for our `email-service`. Argo Rollouts replace the use of Kubernetes deployments by using Rollouts resources, which are in charge of creating and manipulating replica sets, we can check using `kubectl get rs` that our Rollout has created a new Replica-Set. See listing 8.13.

Listing 8.13   Getting the ReplicaSet created by our Rollout

```
> kubectl get rs
NAME                                    DESIRED    CURRENT    READY
notifications-service-canary-7f6b88b5fb 3          3          3
```

Argo Rollouts will create and manage these replica sets that we used to manage with deployment resources, but in a way that enables us to smoothly perform canary releases.

If you have installed the Argo Rollouts Dashboard, you should see our Rollout on the main page (see figure 8.12).

Figure 8.12
Argo Rollouts
Dashboard

As with deployments, we still need a service and an ingress to route traffic to our service from outside the cluster; these resources are included in the step-by-step tutorial (https://github.com/salaboy/platforms-on-k8s/tree/main/chapter-8/argo-rollouts/canary-release). If you create the following resources, you can start interacting with the stable service and with the canary, as shown in figure 8.13.

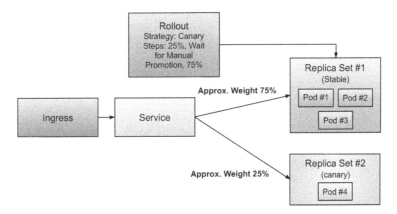

Figure 8.13   Argo Rollouts canary release Kubernetes resources. The Rollout controls the ReplicaSets and manage the approximate weights based on the number of pods in each ReplicaSet.

If you create a service and an ingress, you should be able to query the notifications service `service/info` endpoint by using the following `curl` command:

```
> curl localhost/service/info | jq
```

The output should look like listing 8.14.

Listing 8.14   Interacting with version v1.0.0 of the notification service

```
{
  "name": "NOTIFICATIONS",
  "version": "1.0.0",
  "source": "https://github.com/salaboy/platforms-on-k8s/tree/main/
➥conference-application/notifications-service",
  "podName": "notifications-service-canary-7f6b88b5fb-fq8mm",
  "podNamespace": "default",
  "podNodeName": "dev-worker2",
  "podIp": "10.244.1.5",
  "podServiceAccount": "default"
}
```

The request shows the output of the `service/info` endpoint of our notifications service. Because we have just created this Rollout resource, the Rollout canary strategy mechanism didn't kick in just yet. Now if we want to update the Rollout `spec` `.template` section with a new container image reference or change environment variables, a new revision will be created, and the canary strategy will kick in.

In a new terminal, we can watch the Rollout status before doing any modification, so we can see the Rollout mechanism in action when we change the Rollout specification. If we want to watch how the rollout progresses after we make some changes, you can run the following command in a separate terminal:

```
> kubectl argo rollouts get rollout notifications-service-canary --watch
```

You should see something like figure 8.14.

Figure 8.14   Rollout details using the `argo` plugin for `kubectl`

Let's modify our `notification-service-canary` rollout by running the following command:

```
> kubectl argo rollouts set image notifications-service-canary notifications-
service=salaboy/notifications-service-0e27884e01429ab7e350cb5dff61b525:v1.1.0
```

As soon as we replace the container image used by the Rollout, the rollout strategy will kick in. If you go back to the terminal where you are watching the rollout, you should see that a new `# revision: 2` was created; see figure 8.15.

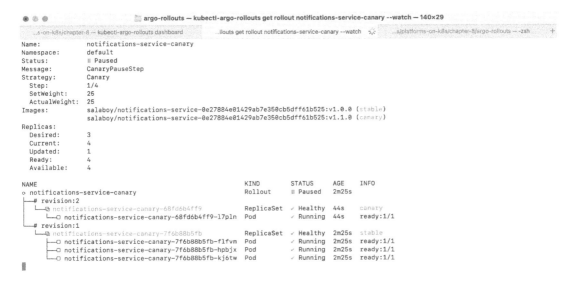

Figure 8.15 Rollout progress after updating the service

You can see that revision 2 is labeled as the "canary" and the status of the rollout is "‖ Paused" and only one pod is created for the canary. So far, the rollout has only executed the first step, as in listing 8.15.

Listing 8.15 Steps definition in our Rollout

```
strategy:
  canary:
    steps:
    - setWeight: 25
    - pause: {}
```

You can also check the status of the canary Rollout in the dashboard, as shown in figure 8.16.

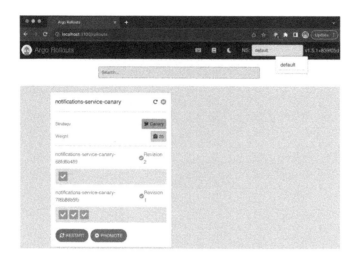

**Figure 8.16
A canary release
has been created
with approximately
20% of the traffic
being routed to it.**

The Rollout is currently paused waiting for manual intervention. We can now test that our canary is receiving traffic to see if we are happy with how the canary is working before continuing the rollout process. To do that, we can query the "service/info" endpoint again to see that approximately 25% of the time we hit the canary, as in listing 8.16.

Listing 8.16   Example output hitting version v1.1.10 from our notification service

```
> curl localhost/service/info | jq

{
  "name":"NOTIFICATIONS-IMPROVED",
  "version":"1.1.0",
  ...
}
```

We can see that one request hit our stable version and one went to the canary.

Argo Rollouts is not dealing with traffic management; in this case, the Rollout resource is only dealing with the underlying ReplicaSet objects and their replicas. You can check the `ReplicaSets` by running `kubectl get rs`, as in listing 8.17.

Listing 8.17   Checking the ReplicaSets associated to our Rollout

```
> kubectl get rs
NAME                                          DESIRED   CURRENT   READY   AGE
notifications-service-canary-68fd6b4ff9       1         1         1       12s
notifications-service-canary-7f6b88b5fb       3         3         3       17m
```

The traffic management between these different pods (canary and stable pods) is being managed by the Kubernetes Service resource, so to see our request hitting both the canary and the stable version pods, we need to go through the Kubernetes service. I am only mentioning this because if you use `kubectl port-forward svc/ notifications-service 8080:80`, for example, you might be tempted to think that traffic is being forwarded to the Kubernetes service (because we are using `svc/notifications-service`), but `kubectl port-forward` resolves to a pod instance and connects to a single pod, allowing you only to hit the canary or a stable pod. For this reason, we have used an ingress, which will use the service to load balance traffic and hit all the pods that are matching to the service selector.

If we are happy with the results, we can continue the rollout process by executing the following command, which promotes the canary to be the stable version:

```
> kubectl argo rollouts promote notifications-service-canary
```

Although we have just manually promoted the rollout, the best practice would be utilizing Argo Rollouts automated analysis steps, which we will dig into in section 8.3.2.

If you look at the Argo Rollouts Dashboard, you will notice that you can also promote the rollout to move forward using the Button Promote in the Rollout. Promotion in this context only means that the rollout can continue to execute the next steps defined in the `spec.strategy` section, as shown in listing 8.18.

Listing 8.18 Rollouts steps definition with 10 seconds pause

```
strategy:
  canary:
    steps:
    - setWeight: 25
    - pause: {}
    - setWeight: 75
    - pause: {duration: 10}
```

After the manual promotion, the weight is going to be set to 75%, followed by a pause of 10 seconds, to finally set the wait to 100%. At that point, you should see that revision 1 is being downscaled while progressively revision 2 is being upscaled to take all the traffic. See figure 8.17, which shows the final state of the rollout.

```
argo-rollouts — kubectl-argo-rollouts get rollout notifications-service-canary --watch — 140×29
...s-on-k8s/chapter-8 — kubectl-argo-rollouts dashboard   ...llouts get rollout notifications-service-canary --watch   ...s/platforms-on-k8s/chapter-8/argo-rollouts — -zsh
Name:            notifications-service-canary
Namespace:       default
Status:          ✓ Healthy
Strategy:        Canary
  Step:          4/4
  SetWeight:     100
  ActualWeight:  100
Images:          salaboy/notifications-service-0e27884e01429ab7e350cb5dff61b525:v1.1.0 (stable)
Replicas:
  Desired:       3
  Current:       3
  Updated:       3
  Ready:         3
  Available:     3

NAME                                                  KIND        STATUS        AGE    INFO
⟳ notifications-service-canary                        Rollout     ✓ Healthy     4m10s
├──# revision:2
│  └──⧉ notifications-service-canary-68fd6b4ff9       ReplicaSet  ✓ Healthy     2m29s  stable
│     ├──□ notifications-service-canary-68fd6b4ff9-17pln  Pod     ✓ Running     2m29s  ready:1/1
│     ├──□ notifications-service-canary-68fd6b4ff9-zrqn5  Pod     ✓ Running     29s    ready:1/1
│     └──□ notifications-service-canary-68fd6b4ff9-znnvn  Pod     ✓ Running     21s    ready:1/1
└──# revision:1
   └──⧉ notifications-service-canary-7f6b88b5fb       ReplicaSet  • ScaledDown  4m10s
```

Figure 8.17 Rollout finished with all the traffic shifted to revision 2

You can see this rollout progression live in the dashboard as well in figure 8.18.

**Figure 8.18
The canary
revision is
promoted to
be the stable
version.**

As you can see, revision 1 was downscaled to have zero pods, and revision 2 is now marked as the stable version. If you check the ReplicaSets, you will see the same output, as shown in listing 8.19.

Listing 8.19   The ReplicaSet responsible for revision 1 is downscaled to 0

```
> kubectl get rs
NAME                                          DESIRED   CURRENT   READY
notifications-service-canary-68fd6b4ff9       3         3         3
notifications-service-canary-7f6b88b5fb       0         0         0
```

We have successfully created, tested, and promoted a canary release with Argo Rollouts!

Compared to what we have seen in section 8.1 for canary releases, using two deployment resources to implement the same pattern with Argo Rollouts, you have full control over how your canary release is promoted, how much time you want to wait before shifting more traffic to the canary and how many manual interventions steps do you want to add. Let's now see how a blue/green deployment works with Argo Rollouts.

8.3.2   Argo Rollouts blue/green deployments

In section 8.1 we covered the advantages and the reasons why you would be interested in doing blue/green deployments using Kubernetes basic building blocks. We have also seen how manual the process is and how these manual steps can open the door for silly mistakes that can bring our services down. In this section, we will look at how Argo Rollouts allows us to implement blue/green deployments following the same approach we previously used for canary deployments. Check the step-by-step tutorial for Argo Rollouts blue/green deployments at https://github.com/salaboy/platforms-on-k8s/tree/main/chapter-8/argo-rollouts#bluegreen-deployments. Let's look at what our Rollout with a BlueGreen strategy looks like in listing 8.20.

Listing 8.20   Rollout defining a BlueGreen strategy

```
apiVersion: argoproj.io/v1alpha1
kind: Rollout
metadata:
  name: notifications-service-bluegreen
spec:
  replicas: 2
  revisionHistoryLimit: 2
  selector:
    matchLabels:
      app: notifications-service
  template:
    metadata:
      labels:
        app: notifications-service
    spec:
      containers:
      - name: notifications-service
        image: salaboy/notifications-service-<HASH>:v1.0.0
        env:
          - name: KAFKA_URL
            value: kafka.default.svc.cluster.local
          ..
  strategy:
    blueGreen:
      activeService: notifications-service-blue
      previewService: notifications-service-green
      autoPromotionEnabled: false
```

NOTE   You can find the full file at https://github.com/salaboy/platforms-on
-k8s/blob/main/chapter-8/argo-rollouts/blue-green/rollout.yaml.

Let's apply the resources for this Rollout resource to work (two Kubernetes services
and an ingress):

```
> kubectl apply -f argo-rollouts/blue-green/
```

We are using the same `spec.template` as before, but now we are setting the strategy of
the rollout to be `blueGreen`, and because of that, we need to configure the reference
to two Kubernetes services. One service will be the Active service (Blue), which is serving production traffic, and the other one is the Green service that we want to preview
but without routing production traffic to it. The `autoPromotionEnabled: false` is
required to allow for manual intervention for the promotion to happen. By default,
the rollout will be automatically promoted as soon as the new ReplicaSet is ready/
available. You can watch the rollout running the following command or in the Argo
Rollouts Dashboard:

```
> kubectl argo rollouts get rollout notifications-service-bluegreen --watch
```

In the following figure, you should see output similar to the output we saw for the
canary release.

Figure 8.19 Checking the state of our BlueGreen Rollout

And in the dashboard, see figure 8.20.

**Figure 8.20
Blue/green
deployment in
the Argo Rollouts
Dashboard.**

We can interact with revision #1 using an ingress to the service and then send a request like listing 8.21.

Listing 8.21   Hitting revision 1 of our service

```
> curl localhost/service/info
{
  "name":"NOTIFICATIONS",
  "version":"1.0.0",
  …
}
```

If we now make changes to our Rollout `spec.template` the blueGreen strategy will kick in. For this example, the expected result that we want to see is that the preview Service is now routing traffic to the second revision that is created when we make changes to the rollout:

```
> kubectl argo rollouts set image notifications-service-bluegreen
➥notifications-service=salaboy/notifications-service-<HASH>:v1.1.0
```

The rollout mechanism will kick in, and it will automatically create a new ReplicaSet with revision 2 that includes our changes. Argo Rollouts for blue/green deployments will use selectors to route traffic to our new revision by modifying the `previewService` that we referenced in our Rollout definition.

If you describe the `notifications-service-green` Kubernetes service, you will notice that a new selector was added, as in listing 8.22.

Listing 8.22 Kubernetes service selectors managed by Argo Rollouts

```
> kubectl describe svc notifications-service-green

Name:              notifications-service-green
Namespace:         default
Labels:            <none>
Annotations:       argo-rollouts.argoproj.io/managed-by-rollouts:
notifications-service-bluegreen
Selector:          app=notifications-service,rollouts-pod-template-
hash=645d484596
Type:              ClusterIP
IP Family Policy:  SingleStack
IP Families:       IPv4
IP:                10.96.198.251
IPs:               10.96.198.251
Port:              http  80/TCP
TargetPort:        http/TCP
Endpoints:         10.244.2.5:8080,10.244.3.6:8080
Session Affinity:  None
Events:            <none>
```

This selector matches with the revision 2 ReplicaSet that was created when we made the changes, as shown in listing 8.23.

Listing 8.23 The ReplicaSet uses the same labels to match the service definition

```
> kubectl describe rs notifications-service-bluegreen-645d484596

Name:           notifications-service-bluegreen-645d484596
Namespace:      default
Selector:       app=notifications-service,rollouts-pod-template-
hash=645d484596
Labels:         app=notifications-service
                rollouts-pod-template-hash=645d484596
Annotations:    rollout.argoproj.io/desired-replicas: 2
                rollout.argoproj.io/revision: 2
Controlled By:  Rollout/notifications-service-bluegreen
Replicas:       2 current / 2 desired
Pods Status:    2 Running / 0 Waiting / 0 Succeeded / 0 Failed
Pod Template:
  Labels:   app=notifications-service
            rollouts-pod-template-hash=645d484596
```

By using the selector and labels, the Rollout with the `blueGreen` strategy is handling these links automatically for us. This avoids the need to create these labels manually and makes sure they match. As shown in figure 8.21, you can check now that there are two revisions (and ReplicaSets) with two pods each.

Figure 8.21   Both Blue and Green services have the same amount of replicas running

In the Argo Rollouts Dashboard you should see the same information as in figure 8.22.

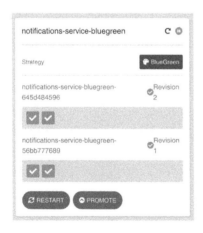

**Figure 8.22
Argo Rollouts
Dashboard
Blue and Green
revisions are up**

We can now interact with the Green service (revision #2) using a different path in our Ingress in the following listing.

Listing 8.24   Interacting with revision 2 (our Green service)

```
> curl localhost/green/service/info | jq

{
  "name": "NOTIFICATIONS-IMPROVED",
  "version": "1.1.0",
  "source": "https://github.com/salaboy/platforms-on-k8s/tree/v1.1.0/
➥conference-application/notifications-service",
  "podName": "notifications-service-bluegreen-645d484596-rsj6z",
  "podNamespace": "default",
  "podNodeName": "dev-worker",
  "podIp": "10.244.2.5",
  "podServiceAccount": "default"
}
```

Once we have the Green service running, the Rollout is in a Paused state until we decide to promote it to be the stable service. Figure 8.23 shows how the Rollout resource will orchestrate the many replicas the Green and Blue services will have depending on the progress of the rollout.

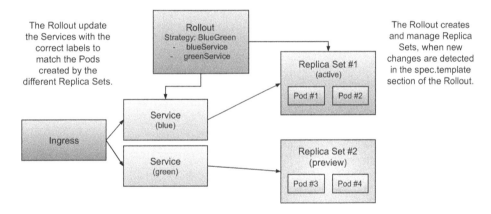

Figure 8.23   Blue/green deployment with Kubernetes resources

Because we now have two services, we can access both at the same time and make sure that our Green (green-service) is working as expected before promoting it to be our main (blue) service. While the service is in preview, other services in the cluster can start routing traffic to it for testing purposes, but to route all the traffic and replace our Blue service with our Green service, we can use once again the Argo Rollouts promotion mechanism from the terminal using the CLI or from the Argo Rollouts Dashboard. Try to promote the Rollout using the Dashboard now instead of using `kubectl`. Remember that the command for promoting the rollout from the terminal looks like this:

```
>kubectl argo rollouts promote notifications-service-bluegreen
```

Notice that a 30-second delay is added by default before the scaling down of our revision #1 (this can be controlled using the property called `scaleDownDelaySeconds`), but the promotion (switching labels to the services) happens the moment we hit the `PROMOTE` button, as shown in figure 8.24.

**Figure 8.24
Green service
promotion using
the Argo Rollouts
Dashboard**

This promotion only switches labels to the services' resources, which automatically changes the routing tables to now forward all the traffic from the Active service to our Green service. If we make more changes to our Rollout, the process will start again, and the preview service will point to a new revision which will include these changes. Now that we have seen the basics of canary releases and blue/green deployments with Argo Rollouts, let's take a look at more advanced mechanisms provided by Argo Rollouts.

8.3.3   *Argo Rollouts analysis for progressive delivery*

So far, we have managed to have more control over our different release strategies, but Argo Rollouts shine by providing the AnalysisTemplate CRD, which lets us ensure that our canary and Green services are working as expected when progressing through our rollouts. These analyses are automated and serve as gates for our Rollouts not to progress unless the analysis probes are successful.

These analyses can use different providers to run the probes, ranging from Prometheus, Datadog (https://www.datadoghq.com/), New Relic (https://newrelic .com/), and Dynatrace (https://www.dynatrace.com/), among others, providing maximum flexibility to define these automated tests against the new revisions of our services.

Figure 8.25 shows how AnalysisTemplates allows Argo Rollouts to create AnalysisRuns to validate that the new version that is rolled out is behaving as expected by looking at service metrics. `AnalysisRuns` will probe the service for metrics and only proceed with the `Rollout` steps if the metrics match the success conditions defined in the `AnalysisTemplate`.

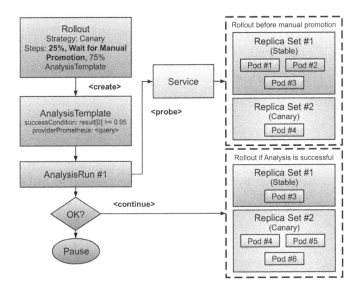

Figure 8.25 Argo Rollouts and analysis working together to make sure that our new revisions are sound before shifting more traffic to them. When receiving the signal to move forward to the next step of the Rollout, an `AnalysisRun` **is created to probe the service by running a query defined in the** `AnalysisTemplate`**. The** `AnalysisRun` **result affect if the** `Rollout`**'s update will continue, abort, or pause.**

For canary release, the analysis can be triggered as part of the step definitions, meaning between arbitrary steps, to start at a predefined step or for every step defined in the Rollout. An `AnalysisTemplate` using the Prometheus provider definition looks like listing 8.25.

Listing 8.25 AnalysisTemplate resource provided by Argo Rollouts

```
apiVersion: argoproj.io/v1alpha1
kind: AnalysisTemplate
metadata:
  name: success-rate
spec:
  args:
  - name: service-name
  metrics:
  - name: success-rate
    interval: 5m
    # NOTE: prometheus queries return results in the form of a vector.
    # It is common to access the index 0 to obtain the value
    successCondition: result[0] >= 0.95
    failureLimit: 3
    provider:
      prometheus:
        address: http://prometheus.example.com:9090
        query: <Prometheus Query here>
```

Then in our Rollout, we can refer to this template and define when a new AnalysisRun will be created, for example, if we want to run the first analysis after step 2 (listing 8.26).

Listing 8.26   Selecting analysis template when defining canary release

```
strategy:
    canary:
      analysis:
        templates:
        - templateName: success-rate
        startingStep: 2 # delay starting analysis run until setWeight: 40%
        args:
        - name: service-name
          value: notifications-service-canary.default.svc.cluster.local
```

As mentioned before, the analysis can also be defined as part of the steps. In that case, our steps definition will look like listing 8.27.

Listing 8.27   Using AnalysisTemplate reference as a step in the rollout

```
strategy:
    canary:
      steps:
      - setWeight: 20
      - pause: {duration: 5m}
      - analysis:
          templates:
          - templateName: success-rate
          args:
          - name: service-name
            value: notifications-service-canary.default.svc.cluster.local
```

For rollouts using a BlueGreen strategy, we can trigger Analysis runs pre- and post-promotion. Figure 8.26 shows the PrePromotionAnalysis step by running the SmokeTestTemplate. This will gate the rollout to switch traffic to the Green service if the AnalysisRun fails.

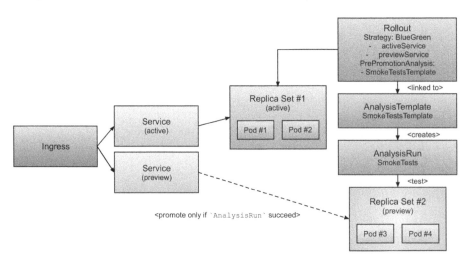

Figure 8.26   Argo Rollouts with blueGreen deployments and PrePromotionAnalysis in action. When the promotion is triggered on the Rollout it will create a new `AnalysisRun` using the `SmokeTestsTemplate` before switching the labels to route traffic to the Preview Service. Only if the `AnalysisRun` is successful the preview service becomes the new Active Service.

Here is an example of PrePromotionAnalysis configured in our Rollout in listing 8.28.

Listing 8.28   Defining a PrePromotionAnalysis as part of a BlueGreen rollout

```
apiVersion: argoproj.io/v1alpha1
kind: Rollout
metadata:
  name: notifications-service-rollout
spec:
...
  strategy:
    blueGreen:
      activeService: notifications-service-blue
      previewService: notifications-service-green
      prePromotionAnalysis:
        templates:
        - templateName: smoke-tests
        args:
        - name: service-name
          value: notifications-service-preview.default.svc.cluster.local
```

For PrePromotion tests, run a new AnalysisRun test before switching traffic to the Green service, and only if the test is successful will the labels be updated. For Post-Promotion, the test will run after the labels were switched to the Green service, and if the AnalysisRun fails, the rollout can automatically revert the labels to the previous version. This is possible because the Blue service will not be downscaled until the AnalysisRun finishes.

I recommend you check the Analysis section of the official documentation as it contains a detailed explanation of all the providers and knobs that you can use to make sure that your Rollouts go smoothly: https://argoproj.github.io/argo-rollouts/features/analysis/.

8.3.4   *Argo Rollouts and traffic management*

Finally, it is worth mentioning that Rollouts used the number of pods available to approximate the weights we define for canary releases. While this is a good start and a simple mechanism, sometimes we need more control over how traffic is routed to different revisions. We can use the power of service meshes and load balancers to write more precise rules about which traffic is routed to our canary releases.

Argo Rollouts can be configured with different `trafficRouting` rules, depending on which traffic management tool we have available in our Kubernetes cluster. Argo Rollouts today supports: Istio, AWS ALB Ingress Controller, Ambassador Edge Stack, Nginx Ingress Controller, Service Mesh Interface (SMI), and Traefik Proxy, among others. As described in the documentation, if we have more advanced traffic management capabilities, we can implement techniques like:

- Raw percentages (i.e., 5% of traffic should go to the new version while the rest goes to the stable version)
- Header-based routing (i.e., send requests with a specific header to the new version)
- Mirrored traffic where all the traffic is copied and sent to the new version in parallel (but the response is ignored)

By using tools like Istio in conjunction with Argo Rollouts, we can enable developers to test features that are only available by setting specific headers or to forward copies of the production traffic to the canaries to validate that they are behaving as they should.

Here is an example of configuring a Rollout to mirror 35% of the traffic to the canary release, which has a 25% weight. This means that 35% of the traffic routed to the stable service will be copied and forwarded to the canary. By using this technique, we don't risk any of the production traffic, because Istio is copying requests for testing purposes, as shown in listing 8.29.

Listing 8.29   Using Istio for advanced (weight-based) traffic split

```
apiVersion: argoproj.io/v1alpha1
kind: Rollout
spec:
  ...
  strategy:
    canary:
      canaryService: notifications-service-canary
      stableService: notifications-service-stable
      trafficRouting:
        managedRoutes:
          - name: mirror-route
        istio:
          virtualService:
            name: notifications-service-vsvc
      steps:
        - setCanaryScale:
            weight: 25
        - setMirrorRoute:
            name: mirror-route
            percentage: 35
            match:
              - method:
                  exact: GET
                path:
                  prefix: /
        - pause:
            duration: 10m
        - setMirrorRoute:
            name: "mirror-route" # removes mirror based traffic route
```

As you can see, this simple example already requires knowledge of Istio Virtual Services and a more advanced configuration that is out of the scope of this section. I strongly recommend checking *Istio in Action* by Christian Posta and Rinor Maloku (Manning Publications, 2022) if you want to learn about Istio. Figure 8.27 shows Rollouts configured to use Istio traffic management capabilities to do weight-based routing.

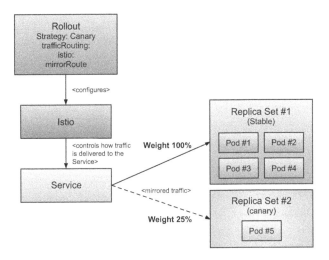

Figure 8.27 Traffic mirroring to canary release using Istio. Using tools like Istio to set `trafficRouting` **enables our canary workloads to experience real life traffic that the stable service is receiving. The Rollout Controller is in charge of configuring Istio Virtual Services to do the work for us and has a fine-grained control about which traffic is delivered to the Service.**

When using "trafficManagement" features, the Rollout canary strategy will behave differently than when we are not using any rules. More specifically, the Stable version of the service will not be downscaled when going through a canary release rollout. This ensures that the Stable service can handle 100% of the traffic. The usual calculations apply to the canary replica count.

I strongly recommend checking the official documentation (https://argoproj .github.io/argo-rollouts/features/traffic-management/) and following the examples there, because the rollouts need to be configured differently depending on the service mesh that you have available.

8.4 Linking back to platform engineering

In this chapter, we have seen what can be achieved with basic Kubernetes building blocks and how tools like Argo Rollouts or Knative Serving simplify the life of teams by releasing new versions of their applications to Kubernetes.

It is unfortunate that as of today, in 2023, Argo Rollouts and Knative Serving haven't been integrated yet (https://github.com/argoproj/argo-rollouts/issues/2186), because both communities would benefit from a consolidated way of defining release strategies instead of duplicating functionality. I like the Knative Serving building blocks that facilitate implementing these release strategies. On the other hand, I like how Argo Rollouts takes things to the next level with the concepts of `AnalysisTemplates` to ensure we can automatically test and validate new releases. The future is promising, because both projects are looking for further integrations with the Gateway API standard (https://gateway-api.sigs.k8s.io/) to unify how advanced traffic routing capabilities are managed in Kubernetes. Tools like Istio, Knative Serving, and Argo Rollouts have active initiatives to support this new standard.

I firmly believe that you will face delivery challenges sooner or later in your Kubernetes journey, and having these mechanisms available inside your clusters will increase your confidence to release more software faster. Hence, I don't take the evaluation of these tools lightly. Make sure you plan time for your teams to research and choose which tools they will use to implement these release strategies; many software vendors can assist you and provide recommendations too.

From a platform engineering perspective, we have looked into how to enable developers to be more efficient by providing them application-level APIs that they can consume no matter their language. We have enabled other teams, like product managers or more business-focused teams, to decide when certain features are enabled and how to perform different release strategies depending on their needs. We enabled operations teams to define the rules safely to validate that new Rollouts are safe and working as expected.

While the focus of this chapter wasn't analyzing tools like Knative Serving in detail, it is important to mention containers-as-a-service and function-as-a-service features when building platforms, because these represent common traits that platform teams might want to expose to their users. I would also recommend checking Knative Functions (https://knative.dev/docs/functions/), now an official Knative module, because the project highlights the importance of building a function-based development workflow based on Knative and leveraging the polyglot approach of Kubernetes.

Figure 8.28 shows tools like Knative Serving provide basic building blocks for platform teams to expose different ways to deploy and run different teams' workloads. By adding advanced traffic management, teams can implement more complex release strategies. Argo Rollouts and Knative Serving work with Istio Service Mesh, which will cover other important aspects, such as mTLS for encryption and observability. Tools like Dapr and OpenFeature fit perfectly in this picture by providing standard interfaces for teams to use while at the same time enabling platform teams to define the backing implementations without committing to a single solution.

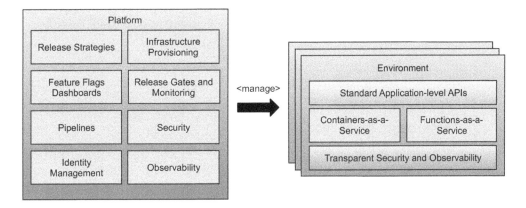

Figure 8.28 Platform capabilities defined to manage environments.

I do see tools like Knative, Argo Rollouts, Dapr, Istio, and OpenFeature leading the way in this space, and still, even if teams need to figure out all the details of each of these tools, patterns are emerging. These tools have been around for over three years, and you can notice the maturity of their features, roadmaps, and the people involved. With some of these projects graduating from the incubation process at the CNCF, I expect more integrations to help users with common workflows that most companies are implementing by hand today.

Finally, to recap our journey so far, figure 8.29 shows how release strategies fit into our platform walking skeleton and how teams closer to the business (product teams, stakeholders) can use these mechanisms to validate new versions before fully moving all customers to the latest version.

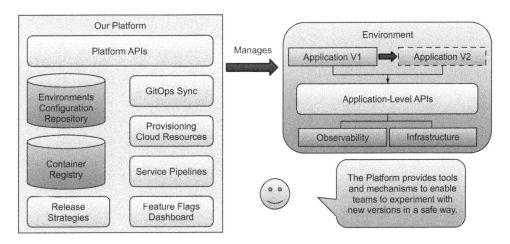

Figure 8.29 Environments that enable teams to experiment with new versions

In the next chapter, to close the book, I've decided to talk about how we can measure the platforms we are building on top of Kubernetes. The platform capabilities described in these last two chapters and the combinations of tools described in this book are good because we are improving our team's velocity for delivering software. Therefore, using metrics that focus on how efficient our teams are in delivering software directly correlates with the tools offered by the platform for these teams to use.

Summary

- Implementing common release strategies such as canary releases, blue/green deployments, and A/B testing can be challenging using Kubernetes built-in resources.
- Knative Serving introduces an advanced networking layer that gives us fine-grain control over how traffic is routed to different versions of our services that can be deployed simultaneously. This feature is implemented on top of Knative Services and reduces the manual work of creating several Kubernetes resources for implementing canary releases, blue/green deployments, and A/B testing release strategies. Knative Serving simplifies the operational burden of moving traffic to new versions and, with the help of the Knative autoscaler, can scale up and down based on demand.
- Argo Rollouts integrates with ArgoCD (discussed in chapter 4) and provides an alternative to implement release strategies using the concept of Rollouts. Argo Rollouts also include features to automate testing new releases to ensure we move safely between versions (AnalysisTemplates and AnalysisRuns).
- Platform teams must enable stakeholders (business, product managers, operations) to experiment by providing flexible mechanisms and workflows that reduce the risk of releasing new versions of the applications that they are working with.
- Following the step-by-step tutorials, you gain hands-on experience using Knative Services and different patterns to route traffic to the Conference application. You also gained experience using Argo Rollouts to implement canary releases and blue/green deployments.

Measuring your platforms

This chapter covers

- Learning the importance of measuring platform performance
- Implementing DORA metrics and learning the secret continuous improvement
- Using tools and standards to collect and calculate metrics

In chapter 8, we covered the principles of how to build a platform that helps you deliver software and enables your teams to have the tools they need when needed. This last chapter is all about making sure that the platform is working, not only for application development teams, but for the entire organization. To understand how the platform is performing, we need to be able to measure it. There are different ways of taking measurements on the software we run. Still, in this chapter, we will focus on the DORA (DevOps Research and Assessment) metrics, which provide a good foundation for understanding our organization's software delivery speed and how good we are at recovering from failures when they happen.

This chapter is divided into two main sections:

- What to measure: DORA metrics and high-performant teams
- How to measure our platform initiatives:
  - CloudEvents and CDEvents to the rescue
  - Keptn Lifecycle Toolkit

Let's get started by understanding what we should be measuring, and for that, we will need to look at the DORA metrics.

9.1   *What to measure: DORA metrics and high-performant teams*

After performing thorough research in the industry, the DevOps Research and Assessment (DORA) team has identified five key metrics that highlight the performance of software development teams delivering software. Initially, in 2020, only four keys were defined so that you might find references to the "DORA four keys"' metrics. After surveying hundreds of teams, DORA discovered which indicators and metrics separated high-performant/elite teams from the rest, and the numbers were quite shocking. DORA used the following four keys to rank teams and their practices:

- *Deployment frequency:* How often an organization successfully releases software in front of their customers
- *Lead time for change:* The time that it takes a change produced by an application team to reach live customers
- *Change failure rate:* The number of problems that are created by new changes being introduced to our production environments
- *Time to restore service:* How long it takes to recover from a problem in our production environments

Figure 9.1 shows the DORA metrics by category, where the first two are associated with teams' velocity. The second two, change failure rate and time to restore service, indicate how likely we are as an organization to recover from failure.

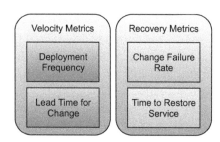

**Figure 9.1
DORA metrics
by category**

In 2022, a fifth key metric focused on reliability was added to cover operational performance. We will only discuss on the four software delivery metrics, because this book focuses on application development teams and not operation teams.

These five key metrics, as shown in the reports, establish a clear correlation between high-performing teams and their velocity expressed by these metrics. If you manage your teams to reduce their deployment frequency (that is, how often they deploy new versions in front of your users) and reduce the time caused by incidents, your software delivery performance will increase.

In this chapter, we will look at how to calculate these metrics for the platforms we are building to ensure that these platforms are improving our continuous delivery practices. To collect data and calculate these metrics, you will need to tap into different systems that your teams are using to deliver software. For example, if you want to calculate *deployment frequency*, you will need access to data from the production environment every time a new release is deployed (see figure 9.2). Another option would be to use data from the environment pipelines performing the releases to our production environment. Figure 9.2 shows how we can observe our CI/CD pipelines and the production environment to calculate a metric like deployment frequency.

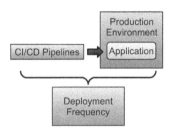

**Figure 9.2
Deployment
frequency data
sources.**

If you want to calculate *lead time for change,* you will need to aggregate data coming from your source code version control system like GitHub/GitLab/BitBucket and have a way to correlate this information with the artifacts that are being deployed into production (figure 9.3).

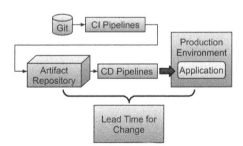

**Figure 9.3
Lead time for
change data
sources**

Suppose you have a straightforward way to correlate commits to artifacts and later to deployments. In that case, you can rely on a few sources, but if you want to have a more detailed understanding of where the bottlenecks are, you might choose to aggregate more data to be able to see where time is being spent.

You might need to tap into incident management and monitoring tools to calculate change failure rate and time to restore service, as in figure 9.4.

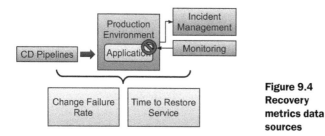

**Figure 9.4
Recovery
metrics data
sources**

For recovery metrics (change failure rate and time to restore service), data collection can be more challenging, because we need to find a way to measure the time when the application performance is degraded or there is downtime. This might involve reports from actual users experiencing problems with our applications.

9.1.1 *The integration problem*

This quickly becomes a system integration challenge. In general terms, we need to observe the systems involved in our software delivery process, capture relevant data, and then have the mechanisms to aggregate this information. Once this information is available, we can use these metrics to optimize our delivery processes and find and solve bottlenecks.

While some projects already provide DORA metrics out of the box, you must evaluate if they are flexible enough to plug your systems into them. The Four Keys project by Google provides an out-of-the-box experience to calculate these metrics based on external outputs. You can read more about it at https://cloud.google.com/blog/products/ devops-sre/using-the-four-keys-to-measure-your-devops-performance.

Unfortunately, the Four Keys project requires you to run on the Google Cloud Platform because it uses BigData and Google Cloud run to do the calculations. Following the principles of this book, we need a solution that works across cloud providers and uses Kubernetes as the baseline. Other tools like LinearB (https://linearb.io/) offer a SaaS solution to track different tools. I also recommend a blog post by Codefresh (https:// codefresh.io/learn/software-deployment/dora-metrics-4-key-metrics-for-improving -devops-performance/) that explains the challenges of calculating these metrics and the data points that you will need to do so.

To have a Kubernetes-native way to calculate these metrics, we need to standardize the way we consume information from different systems, transform this information into a model that we can use to calculate these metrics, and make sure that different organizations can extend this model with their metrics and their very diverse sources of information. In the next section, we will look at two standards that can help us with this mission: CloudEvents (https://cloudevents.io/) and CDEvents (https://cdevents .dev/).

9.2 How to measure our platform: CloudEvents and CDEvents

More and more tools and service providers are adopting CloudEvents (https:// cloudevents.io) as a standard way to wrap event data. In this book, we have covered Tekton (https://tekton.dev) and Dapr PubSub (https://dapr.io), but if you look on the official CloudEvents website (go to https://cloudevents.io and scroll to the Cloud Events Adopters section), you can find all the projects that already support the standard. In that list, you will find Argo Events (https://argoproj.github.io/argo-events/) and Knative Eventing (https://knative.dev/docs/eventing/), projects that we haven't covered but that work very well with the tools described in previous chapters. I find it interesting to see cloud provider services such as GoogleCloud Eventarc (https:// cloud.google.com/eventarc/docs) and Alibaba Cloud EventBridge (https://www .alibabacloud.com/help/en/eventbridge) in the list, which indicates that CloudEvents are here to stay.

While seeing more adoption is an excellent indicator, much work remains when you receive or want to emit a CloudEvent. CloudEvents are simple and thin envelopes for our events data. Figure 9.5 shows the very simple structure of a CloudEvent. The specification defines the CloudEvent required metadata and verifies that the CloudEvent will have a Payload that contains the event data that we want to send to other systems.

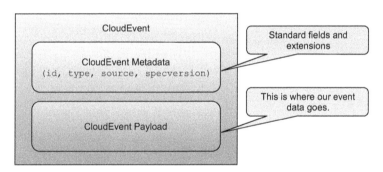

Figure 9.5   CloudEvents, a simple envelope to wrap our events data

Using CloudEvents, developers emit and consume events by relying on the CloudEvents specification to know at least what the events are about. Because the CloudEvents specification is not transport-specific, we can use different transports to move CloudEvents around. The specification includes the definition of bindings for protocols such as AMQP, HTTP, AVRO, KAFKA, NATS, MQQT, JSON, XML, websockets, and webhooks. You can find the full list at https://github.com/cloudevents/spec/tree/ main#cloudevents-documents.

When we used Dapr PubSub in chapter 7, we used the CloudEvents SDK to verify the type of the event and get the CloudEvent payload (https://github.com/salaboy/ platforms-on-k8s/blob/v2.0.0/conference-application/frontend-go/frontend .go#L118). Projects like Tekton, Knative Eventing, and Argo Events already produce and provide CloudEvents sources that we can consume. For example, Knative Eventing provides sources for GitHub, GitLab, the Kubernetes API Server, Kafka, RabbitMQ, etc. (https://knative.dev/docs/eventing/sources/#knative-sources). Argo Events adds to the list Slack and Stripe, but it gives us 20+ out-of-the-box event sources (https://argoproj.github.io/argo-events/concepts/event_source/). While projects like Tekton provide us with internal events for their own managed resources such as pipelines, tasks, pipelineRuns and taskRuns, it would be great to collect events about other tools in a unified way.

If we want to measure how the tools we include in our platform are helping our teams to release more software, we need to tap into these event sources to collect data, aggregate data, and extract meaningful metrics. Figure 9.6 shows different events sources that we can tap into to measure how tools are helping teams to deliver more software, but if we want to calculate metrics, we will need to store these events somewhere for further processing.

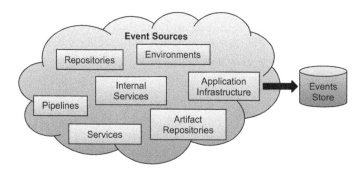

Figure 9.6   Event sources and event store

If we want to use these events to calculate metrics, we will need to open the envelope, read the data, and based on that, aggregate and correlate these events together.

This has proven challenging, as each tool that generates CloudEvents can define its schemas for the CloudEvent payload. We would need to understand how each system is encoding the payload to extract the data we need to calculate our metrics. Wouldn't it be great to have some standard model to quickly filter and consume these events based on what they mean for our software delivery needs? Welcome CDEvents (https://cdevents.dev).

9.2.1   *CloudEvents for continuous delivery: CDEvents*

CDEvents is just CloudEvents but with a more specific purpose. They map to different phases of our continuous delivery practices. CDEvents is an initiative that the Continuous Delivery Foundation (https://cd.foundation) drives, and as its website defines, they focus on enabling interoperability across different tools that are related to continuous delivery: "CDEvents is a common specification for Continuous Delivery events, enabling interoperability in the complete software production ecosystem" (https://cdevents.dev).

To provide interoperability, the CDEvents specification defines four stages (https://github.com/cdevents/spec/blob/v0.3.0/spec.md#vocabulary-stages). These stages are used to group events that are conceptually related to different phases and tools in our software delivery ecosystem:

- *Core:* Events related to the orchestration of tasks usually come from pipeline engines. Here you will find the specification of the events around the subjects "taskRun" and "pipelineRun." Events like "PipelineRun started" or "TaskRun queued" can be found at this stage.
- *Source code version control:* Events related to changes associated with your source code. The specification focuses on covering the subjects: "repository," "branch," and "change." Events like "Change created" or "Change Merged" can be found at this stage.
- *Continuous integration:* Events related to building software, producing artifacts, and running tests. This stage covers the subjects "artifact," "build," "testCase," and "testSuite." Events like "Artifact published" or "Build finished" can be found at this stage.
- *Continuous deployment:* Events related to deploying software in different environments. The subjects covered in this stage are "services" and "environments." Events like "service deployed" or "environment modified" can be found at this stage.
- *Continuous operations:* Events related to the incidents related to our running services.

Figure 9.7 shows these categories and some example events for each.

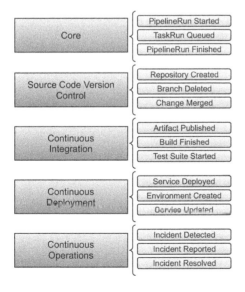

Figure 9.7 The four stages defined by the CDEvents specification

We can easily use CDEvents to calculate our software delivery metrics, because they already cover the subjects that these metrics are interested in. For example, we can use events from the continuous deployment stage to calculate the *deployment frequency* metric. We can combine continuous deployment events and source code version control events to calculate *lead time for change.*

The question then becomes, where do we get CDEvents from? CDEvents is a much newer specification that is currently being incubated at the CDFoundation, and it is my firm belief that as part of the interoperability story, this specification can serve as a hook mechanism for different tools and implementations to map their tools to a standard model that we can use to calculate all these metrics while allowing legacy systems (and tools that are not emitting cloud events) to benefit from them too.

This chapter will use the CDEvents specification to define our standardized data model. We will collect information from various systems using CloudEvents and rely on CDEvents to map the incoming events into the different stages of our software delivery practice. Figure 9.8 shows the most common sources of events that can be related to software delivery.

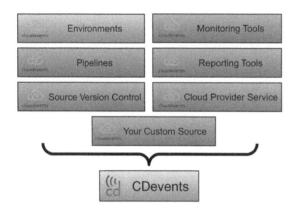

Figure 9.8   CDEvents are more specialized CloudEvents for continuous delivery.

Tools like Tekton are already providing experimental support for CDEvents (https:// www.youtube.com/watch?v=GAm6JzTW4nc), and as we will see in the next section, we can transform CloudEvents into CDEvents using functions. More importantly, the CDEvents Working Group is also focused on providing software development kits (SDKs) in different languages so you can build your applications that consume and emit CDEvents no matter the programming language you are using.

The next section will examine how a Kubernetes-based solution for calculating DORA metrics can be built and extended to support different metrics and event sources. This is important to ensure that different platforms using different tools can use their performance and detect early bottlenecks and improvement points. Notice that this is just an example of how different tools can be wired together in the context of projects related to Kubernetes.

9.2.2   *Building a CloudEvents-based metrics collection pipeline*

To calculate the metrics proposed by the DORA team (deployment frequency, lead time for change, change failure rate, and time to restore service), we need to collect data. Once we have the data coming from different systems, we need to transform the data into a standardized model that we can use to calculate the metrics. Then we need to process the data to calculate the values for each metric. We need to store the results of these calculations, and then we need to make them available to everyone interested, probably using a graphical dashboard that summarizes the data collected and the calculated metrics.

Different tools can be used to build this data collection, transformation, and aggregation pipeline. Still, to build a simple yet extensible solution, we will use some of the tools covered in the previous chapters, such as Knative Serving to build our aggregation and transformation functions, CloudEvents, and CDEvents. We will also use Knative Eventing event sources, but this demo can be easily extended to support any other CloudEvent source, such as Argo Events. This section is divided into three subsections:

- Data collection from event sources
- Data transformation to CDEvents
- Metrics calculations

These sections map one to one with the proposed architecture that, from a high level, looks like figure 9.9.

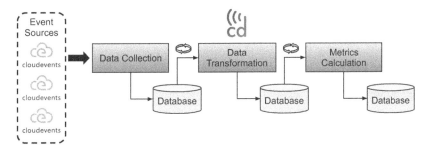

Figure 9.9   Collecting and transforming data to calculate DORA metrics

From a high-level perspective, we need to architect our data collection and transformation pipeline to support any number of event sources, because different companies and implementations will collect data from systems that we cannot anticipate. We are imposing the data to be in the form of CloudEvents before it enters our system. If you have event sources not following the CloudEvents specification, you must adapt their data to follow the specification. This can be easily achieved using the CloudEvents SDKs (https://cloudevents.io/ > SDKs section) to wrap your existing events to follow the specification.

Once the data enters our system, we will store it in persistent storage. In this case, we have used a PostgreSQL database to store all the incoming data and calculations.

Components don't directly call the next stage (data transformation). Instead, each component periodically fetches data from the database and processes all the data that hasn't been processed yet. This stage (data transformation) transforms incoming CloudEvents already stored in the database into CDEvents structures that will be used to calculate the metrics. Once the transformation to the CDEvents structure happens, the result is stored in a separate table in our PostgreSQL database. Finally, the "metrics calculation" stage periodically reads from the database all new CDEvents that haven't been processed and calculates the metrics we have defined.

This simple architecture allows us to plug in new data sources, new transformation logic depending on the data we receive, and finally, new metrics calculation logic for your domain-specific metrics (not only DORA metrics). It is also important to notice that as soon as we guarantee that the incoming data is correctly stored, all the transformations and calculations can be recalculated if the metrics data is lost. Let's look deeper at the stages required to calculate the simplest DORA four key metrics, "deployment frequency."

9.2.3 *Data collection from event sources*

As shown in figure 9.9, we want to consume data from multiple sources, but we have set CloudEvents as the standard input format. While CloudEvents has been widely adopted, many systems still don't support the standard. This section will look into Knative Sources as a mechanism that can declaratively define our event sources and transform non-CloudEvent data into CloudEvents.

The proposed solution then exposes a REST Endpoint to receive incoming CloudEvents. Once we have CloudEvents, we will validate the data and store it in a PostgreSQL table called `cloudevents_raw`. Let's look at Knative Eventing event sources, because we can just install and configure these event sources to produce events for us automatically.

9.2.4 *Knative Eventing event sources*

With Knative Eventing event sources, you can install existing or create new event sources. Figure 9.10 shows some of the event sources provided out of the box and how these events will be routed to the data collection step of our data transformation pipeline.

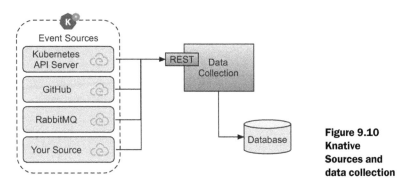

**Figure 9.10
Knative
Sources and
data collection**

Several Knative Eventing event sources are provided out of the box by the Knative community and different software vendors. The following list is not exhaustive, but it covers some of the sources that you might want to use to calculate your metrics:

- APIServerSource
- PingSource
- GitHubSource
- GitLabSource
- RabbitMQSource
- KafkaSource

Check the complete list of third-party sources at https://knative.dev/docs/eventing/sources/#third-party-sources. These sources transform events, for example, from the Kubernetes API Server, GitHub, or RabbitMQ AMQP messages into CloudEvents.

If you want to use one of the available Knative Sources, for example, the `APIServer-Source`, you just need to ensure that the source is installed in your cluster and then configure the source according to your needs(see listing 9.1). For calculating the deployment frequency metric, we will tap into Kubernetes Events related to deployments. You can declaratively configure the source and where the events will be sent by defining an `APIServerSource` resource.

> **Listing 9.1 Knative Source APIServerSource definition**

ApiServerSource is the resource type that we use to configure the Knative ApiServerSource component that reads from the Kubernetes Event stream (https://www.cncf.io/blog/2021/12/21/extracting-value-from-the-kubernetes-events-feed/), transforms these events to CloudEvents, and sends them to a sink (target destination).

```
apiVersion: sources.knative.dev/v1
kind: ApiServerSource
metadata:
 name: main-api-server-source
spec:
 serviceAccountName: api-server-source-sa
 mode: Resource
 resources:
   - apiVersion: v1
     kind: Event
```

As with every Kubernetes resource, we need to define a name for this resource. We can configure as many ApiServerSources as we want.

As defined before, this source is interested in resources of type Event.

Because we are reading events from the Kubernetes API server, we need to have access. Hence, a ServiceAccount needs to exist to enable the ApiServerSource components to read from the internal event stream. You can check the ServiceAccount, Role, and RoleBinding resources that are needed for this ApiServerSource resource to work at https://github.com/salaboy/platforms-on-k8s/blob/main/chapter-9/dora-cloudevents/api-serversource-deployments.yaml.

```
sink:
  ref:
    apiVersion: v1
    kind: Service
    name: cloudevents-raw-service
    namespace: dora-cloudevents
```

In the sink section, we define where we want to send the CloudEvents generated from this source. In this case, we use a service reference to a Kubernetes Service named cloudevents-raw-service, which lives in the four-keys namespace. Knative Sources, when referencing other Kubernetes resources, will check that these resources exist and only be ready when the target service is found. Alternatively, we can point to a URI if the service doesn't live in the Kubernetes API context, but we lose this valuable check that can help us to troubleshoot scenarios where we are sending events to a non-existing endpoint.

As you can imagine, the `ApiServerSource` will generate tons of events, which are sent to `cloudevents-raw-service` and stored in the PostgreSQL database. More complex routing and filtering can be configured only to forward events that interest us, but we can also apply filtering in the next stages, allowing for an approach that can enable us to add more metrics as we evolve our data collection process. With this source, we will receive one or more CloudEvents and store them in the database whenever a new deployment resource is created, modified, or deleted.

If you have a system already producing events but need CloudEvents, you can create your own Custom Knative Eventing event source. Look at the following tutorial for more information on how to do this: https://knative.dev/docs/eventing/custom-event-source/custom-event-source/.

The big advantage of declaring and managing your event sources using Knative Eventing event sources is that you can query your sources as any other Kubernetes resource, monitor and manage their state, and troubleshoot when problems arise using all the tools available in the Kubernetes ecosystem. Once CloudEvents are stored in our database, we can analyze them and map them into CDEvents for further calculations.

9.2.5   *Data transformation to CDEvents*

Now that we have CloudEvents in our PostgreSQL database, we have validated that they are valid CloudEvents. We want to transform some of these very generic Cloud Events into CDEvents, which we will use to calculate our metrics.

As explained in the introduction, these transformations will depend on what kind of metrics you are trying to calculate. For this example, we will look into internal Kubernetes events related to deployment resources to calculate the deployment frequency metric, but completely different approaches can be used. For example, instead of looking into Kubernetes internal events, you can look into ArgoCD events or Tekton Pipeline events to monitor when deployments are triggered but from outside the cluster. Figure 9.11 shows the mapping and transformation process that needs to happen to map CloudEvent to CDEvents.

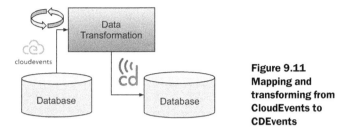

**Figure 9.11
Mapping and
transforming from
CloudEvents to
CDEvents**

We need a way to map a very generic CloudEvent to a concrete CDEvent that indicates that a service deployment has happened or has been updated. This mapping and transformation logic can be written in any programming language as we only deal with CloudEvents and CDEvents. Because of the volume of events we might be receiving, it is essential not to block and process all the events as they arrive. For this reason, a more asynchronous approach has been chosen here. The data transformation logic is scheduled at fixed periods, which can be configured depending on how often we want/can process the incoming events.

For this example, we will map and translate incoming events with `type` equal to `dev.knative.apiserver.resource.add` and `data.InvolvedObject.Kind` equal to `Deployment` to CDEvents of the type `dev.cdevents.service.deployed.0.1.0`. This transformation is particular to our needs because it correlates events from the Knative APIServerSource to those defined in the CDEvents specification, as shown in figure 9.12.

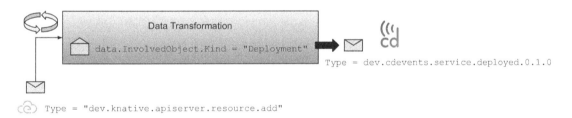

Figure 9.12 Concrete mapping and CDEvent creation for deployments

To calculate different metrics, we will need more of these transformations. One option would be to add all the transformation logic into a single container. This approach would allow us to version all the transformations together as a single unit, but at the same time, it can complicate or limit teams writing new transformations, because they have a single place to change code. An alternative that we can take is to use a function-based approach, we can promote the creation of single-purpose functions to do these transformations. By using functions, only functions that are currently transforming events will be running. All the ones that are not being used can be downscaled. If we have too many events to process, functions can be upscaled on demand based on traffic.

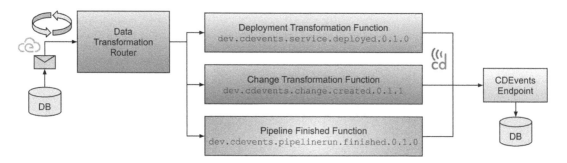

Figure 9.13   Using functions to map CloudEvents to CDEvents

As shown in figure 9.13, a new component is needed to route the CloudEvents being read from the database to concrete functions. Each transformation function can transform the incoming CloudEvent by inspecting its payload, enriching the content with an external data source, or simply wrapping the entire CloudEvent into a CDEvent.

The data transformation router component must be flexible enough to allow new transformation functions to be plugged into the system and multiple functions to process the same event (the same CloudEvent being sent to one or more transformation functions).

Transformation and mapping functions don't need to care about how the CDEvents will be persisted. This allows us to keep these functions simple and focused on transformations only. Once the transformation is done and a new CDEvent is produced, the function will send the event to the CDEvents endpoint component, which stores the CDEvent in our database.

By the end of the transformations, we will have zero or more CDEvents stored in our database. These CDEvents can be used by the metric calculation functions that we will look at in the following section.

9.2.6   *Metrics calculation*

To calculate our metrics (DORA or custom metrics), we will use the same function-based approach we used for the CDEvents transformation and mapping. In this case, we will write functions to calculate different metrics. Because each metric requires aggregating data from different events and maybe systems, each metric calculation function can implement a different logic, see figure 9.14. The mechanisms used to calculate a metric are up to the developers who write the code to perform the calculation.

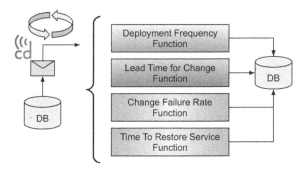

Figure 9.14   Using functions to calculate DORA metrics

To calculate metrics, each function can be configured to fetch very specific CDEvents from the database and with different periods depending on how often we need to get updates for a particular metric. The metric result can be stored in the database or sent to an external system, depending on what you want to do with the calculated data.

If we look at calculating the deployment frequency metric for a more concrete example, we need to implement a couple of custom mechanisms and data structures to keep track of the metric, as in figure 9.15.

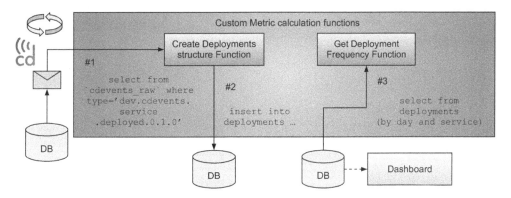

Figure 9.15   Deployment frequency calculation flow

A simplified flow for calculating the deployment frequency metric is shown in figure 9.15 where step #1 is to get CDEvents related to deployments from the `cdevents_raw` table. The `Create Deployments structure function` is in charge of reading CDEvents with type `dev.cdevents.service.deployed.0.1.0`, inspecting the payload and metadata, and creating a new structure that can be later queried. Step #2 is responsible for persisting this new structure in our database. The main reason for this structure is to make our data easier and more performant to query for the metric we are implementing. In this case, a new `deployment` structure (and table) is created to record data we want to use to calculate our deployment frequency metric. For this simple example, the deployment structure contains the service's name, the timestamp, and the deployment's name. In step #3 we can use this data to get our deployment frequency by service and display this information per day, week, or month. These functions need to be idempotent, meaning that we can retrigger the calculation of the metrics again using the same CDEvents as input, and we should obtain the same results.

Optimizations can be added to this flow; for example, a custom mechanism can be created to avoid reprocessing CDEvents that have already been processed. These customizations can be treated as internal mechanisms for each metric, and developers should be able to add integration with other systems and tools as needed. For the sake of the example, the `Get Deployment Frequency Function` can fetch the metrics from the database. Still, in a more realistic scenario, you can have a dashboard directly querying the database where the simplified structures are stored, because many dashboard solutions provide an SQL connector out of the box.

Now that we have covered the flow to calculate the deployment frequency metric let's look at a working example where we will install all the components required for data collection, data transformation, and metrics calculation.

9.2.7   *Working example*

This section will look at a working example, showing how we can combine data collection, data transformation to CDEvents, and metrics calculation for our Kubernetes-based platforms. It covers a very basic example and a step-by-step tutorial on how to install and how to run the components needed to calculate the deployment frequency metric of our deployments (https://github.com/salaboy/platforms-on-k8s/blob/main/chapter-9/dora-cloudevents/README.md).

The architecture implemented in this example puts together the stages defined in the previous sections: data collection, data transformation, and metrics calculation. One of the main aspects covered by this architecture is the extensibility and pluggability of components for data transformation and metrics calculation. This architecture assumes that we will collect data as CloudEvents, so the user is responsible for transforming their event sources to CloudEvents to use this architecture.

Figure 9.16 shows how all the components are tied together to provide the functionality of deciding which events we want to collect and how to transform them into CDEvents so we can calculate DORA metrics with them.

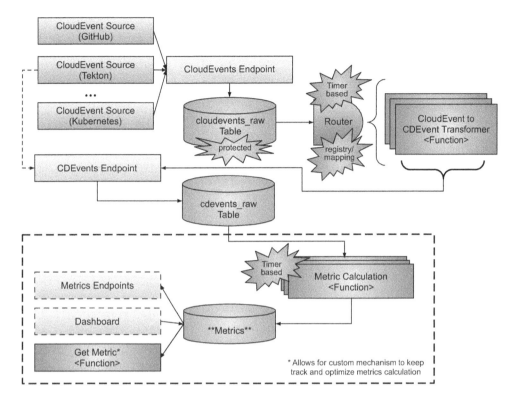

Figure 9.16   Example architecture for capturing and calculating DORA metrics

While the architecture might look complicated initially, it was designed to allow custom extensions and mappings necessary to collect and process events from various sources.

Following the step-by-step tutorial, you will create a new Kubernetes cluster to install all the components needed to collect CloudEvents and calculate the metrics. Still, the architecture is in no way limited by a single cluster. After you create and connect to a cluster, you will install tools such as Knative Serving for our function's runtime and Knative Eventing only for our event sources. Once the cluster is ready, you will create a new `namespace` to host all the components actively processing the data collected and an instance of PostgreSQL to store our events.

STORING EVENTS AND METRICS

Once we have our database to store events and metrics information, we need to create the tables for our components to store and read events. For this example, we will create the following tables: `cloudevents_raw`, `cdevents_raw`, and `deployments`, as shown in figure 9.17.

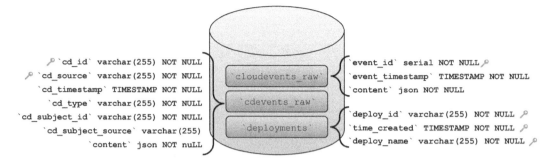

Figure 9.17   Tables, CloudEvents, CDEvents, and metrics calculations

Let's look at what information we are going to be storing in these three tables. The `cloudevents_raw` table stores all the incoming CloudEvents from different sources. The main purpose of this table is data collection:

- The schema of this table is very simple and only has three columns:
  - `event_id`: This value is generated by the database.
  - `event_timestamp`: Stores the timestamp of when the event is received. This can be later used to order events for reprocessing.
  - `content`: Stores the serialized JSON version of the CloudEvent in a JSON column.
- This table is kept as simple as possible because we don't know what kind of cloud events we are getting, and at this point, we don't want to unmarshal and read the payload, because this can be done in the data transformation stage.

The `cdevents_raw` table stores all the CDEvents we are interested in storing after filtering and transforming all the incoming CloudEvents. Because CDEvents are more specific, and we have more metadata about these events, this table has more columns:

- `cd_id`: Stores the CloudEvent ID from the original CloudEvent.
- `cd_timestamp`: Stores the timestamp of when the original CloudEvent was received.
- `cd_source`: Stores the source where the original CloudEvent was generated.
- `cd_type`: Stores and allows us to filter by different CDEvents types. The types of CDEvents stored in this table are defined by the transformation functions running in our setup.
- `cd_subject_id`: Stores the ID of the entity associated with this CDEvent. This information is obtained when our transformation functions analyze the content of the original CloudEvent.
- `cd_subject_source`: Stores the source of the entity associated with this CDEvent.
- `content`: The JSON serialized version of our CDEvent, which includes the original CloudEvent as a payload.

The `deployments` table is custom to calculate the deployment frequency metric. There are no rules to what you store in these custom tables that are used to calculate different metrics. For the sake of simplicity, this table only has three columns:

- `deploy_id`: The id used to identify a service deployment.
- `time_created`: When the deployment was created or updated.
- `deploy_name`: The deployment name used to calculate the metrics.

Once we have the tables ready to store our events and metrics data, we need to have events flowing into our components, and for that, we will need to configure event sources.

CONFIGURING EVENT SOURCES

Finally, before installing the data transformation or metrics calculation functions, we will configure the Kubernetes API Server event source from Knative Eventing to detect when new deployments are being created. See figure 9.18.

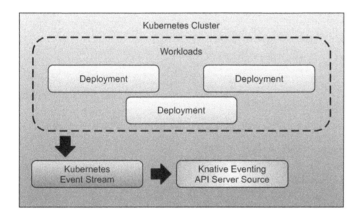

Figure 9.18   Example using the Knative Eventing API server source. We can tap into Kubernetes Event Stream by using the Knative Eventing API Server Source, which transforms internal events into CloudEvents that can be routed to different systems for filtering and processing.

Here, you can use any CloudEvent-enabled data source. The Knative API server source is an example of how easy it is to consume and route events for further processing.

Check projects like Argo Events (https://argoproj.github.io/argo-events/) and other Knative Eventing sources (https://knative.dev/docs/eventing/sources/) to familiarize yourself with what is available out of the box. Also, check the CloudEvents specification adopters list (https://cloudevents.io/), because all these tools are already generating CloudEvents that you can consume and map to calculate metrics.

DEPLOYING DATA TRANSFORMATION AND METRICS CALCULATION COMPONENTS

Now that we have a place to store our events and metrics data, and event sources are configured and ready to emit events when users interact with our cluster, we can deploy the components that will take these events, filter them, and transform them to calculate our deployment frequency metric. The step-by-step tutorial deploys the following components:

- *CloudEvents endpoint:* Exposes an HTTP endpoint to receive CloudEvents and connects to the database to store them.
- *CDEvents endpoint:* Exposes an HTTP endpoint to receive CDEvents and connects to the database to store them.
- *CloudEvents router:* Reads CloudEvents from the database and routes them to the configured transformation functions. This component allows users to plug their transformation functions to transform a CloudEvent into a CDEvent for further processing. The CloudEvents router runs periodically by fetching unprocessed events from the database.
- *(CDEvents) transformation function:* Users can define transformation functions and map CloudEvents to CDEvents. The idea here is to enable users to add as many functions as needed to calculate DORA and other metrics.
- *(Deployment frequency) calculation function:* Metrics calculation functions provide a way to calculate different metrics by reading CDEvents from the database. These functions can store the calculated metrics in custom database tables if needed.
- *(Deployment frequency) metric endpoint:* These metric endpoints can be optionally exposed for applications to consume the calculated metrics. Alternatively, dashboards can query the data directly from the database.

Figure 9.19 shows how CloudEvents flows throughout the different components that we have installed.

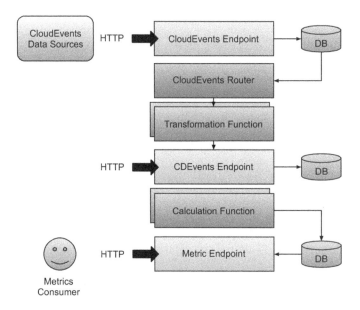

Figure 9.19   Data flows from Data Sources producing CloudEvents to the CloudEvents endpoint whose only mission is to store these events into the Event Store. From there, the CloudEvents Router have the logic to decide where to route events to transformation functions, which allows us to map CloudEvents to CDEvents for further processing. Once we have CDEvents, the Calculation Functions can read these events to aggregate data and produce metrics. Metrics consumers can get the metrics by interacting with the Metric Endpoint, which will fetch the calculated metrics from the metrics database.

As soon as we have our components up and running, we can start using our cluster to generate events filtered and processed by these components to produce the deployment frequency metric.

DEPLOYMENT FREQUENCY METRIC FOR YOUR DEPLOYMENTS

We need to deploy new workloads to our cluster to calculate the deployment frequency metric. The tutorial includes all the transformation and metric calculation functions to monitor events coming from deployment resources.

While development teams can create and update their existing deployments, the platform team can transparently monitor how efficient the platform is to enable teams to perform their work. Figure 9.20 shows the teams involved and how the metrics are calculated for this example.

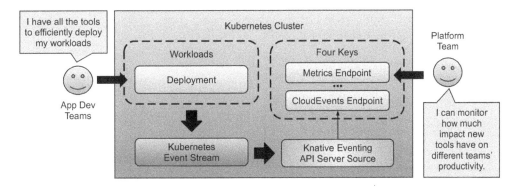

Figure 9.20   Components and data flow to measure performance metrics

Finally, you can `curl` the following endpoint if you are running the example on KinD:

```
> curl http://dora-frequency-endpoint.dora-cloudevents.127.0.0.1.sslip.io/
➥deploy-frequency/day | jq
```

You should see something like the following listing.

Listing 9.2   Getting deployment frequency metrics

```
[
    {
        "DeployName":"nginx-deployment-1",
        "Deployments":3,
        "Time":"2022-11-19T00:00:00Z"
    },
    {
        "DeployName":"nginx-deployment-3",
        "Deployments":1,
        "Time":"2022-11-19T00:00:00Z"
    }
]
```

Transformation and metrics calculation functions are scheduled to run every minute. Hence, these metrics will be only returned after the functions have been executed. Alternatively, you can use a dashboard solution like Grafana to connect to our PostgreSQL database and configure the metrics. Dashboard tools can be focused on the tables that store data about particular metrics. For our deployment frequency example, the `deployments` table is the only one relevant for displaying the metrics.

I strongly recommend you check the example and try to run it locally, follow the step-by-step tutorial, and get in touch if you have questions or want to help improve it. Modifying the example to calculate the metrics differently or adding your custom metrics will give you a good overview of how complex these metrics calculations are but, at the same time, how important it is to have this information available to our application development and operations teams so they can understand how things are going almost in real-time.

In the next section, we will look at the Keptn Lifecycle Toolkit (https://keptn.sh), an open-source and CNCF project that built different mechanisms not only to monitor, observe, and calculate metrics about our cloud-native applications, but also to take actions when things are not going as expected or with integrations with other systems are needed.

9.3   *Keptn Lifecycle Toolkit*

The Keptn Lifecycle Toolkit (KLT) is a cloud-native lifecycle orchestration toolkit. KLT focuses on deployment observability, deployment data access, and deployment check orchestration. Keptn is not only all about monitoring and observing what is going on with our workloads, but it also provides the mechanisms to check and act when things go wrong.

As we saw in the previous section, getting basic metrics such as deployment frequency can be very useful in measuring teams' performance. While deployment frequency is just one metric, we can use that to start measuring our early platform initiatives. In this short section, I wanted to show how KLT can help you with this task by following a different but complementary approach to the one discussed in section 9.2.

Keptn extends the Kubernetes Scheduler component (which decides where our workloads will run on our clusters) to monitor and extract information about our workloads, as in figure 9.21. This mechanism enables teams to set up custom pre/post-deployment tasks by providing Keptn Task Definitions resources. Keptn is planning to use Kubernetes built-in scheduling gates, a feature that, at the time of writing, is being proposed to the Kubernetes community (http://mng.bz/PRW2).

> **NOTE** You can follow a step-by-step tutorial to see Keptn in action by following this link: https://github.com/salaboy/platforms-on-k8s/blob/main/chapter-9/keptn/README.md.

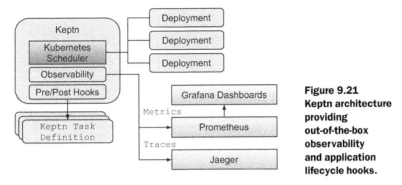

**Figure 9.21
Keptn architecture
providing
out-of-the-box
observability
and application
lifecycle hooks.**

Keptn uses standard Kubernetes annotations to identify which applications are interested in being monitored and managed. I have included the following annotations for the Conference application to make Keptn aware of our services. The Agenda service deployment resource includes the following annotations, as shown in listing 9.3 (https://github.com/salaboy/platforms-on-k8s/blob/main/conference-application/helm/conference-app/templates/agenda-service.yaml#L14).

Listing 9.3   Kubernetes standard application annotations

```
app.kubernetes.io/name: agenda-service
app.kubernetes.io/part-of: agenda-service
app.kubernetes.io/version: v1.0.0
```

Keptn is now aware of the Agenda service and can monitor and execute actions related to this service lifecycle. Notice the `part-of` annotation, which allows us to monitor single services and group a set of services under the same logical application. This grouping allows Keptn to execute pre/post-deployment actions for each service and the logical application (a group of services sharing the same value for the `app.kubernetes.io/part-of` annotation. This example doesn't use that feature because I want to keep things simple and focused on single services.

The step-by-step tutorial installs Keptn, Prometheus, Grafana, and Jaeger so we can understand what Keptn is doing. Once Keptn is installed in your cluster, you need to let Keptn know which namespaces should be monitored, by annotating the namespace resources with a Keptn annotation. You can do that by running the following command to enable Keptn in the default namespace:

```
kubectl annotate ns default keptn.sh/lifecycle-toolkit="enabled"
```

Once Keptn starts monitoring a specific namespace, it will look for annotated deployments to start getting metrics that the Keptn Applications Grafana dashboards can consume, as shown in figure 9.22.

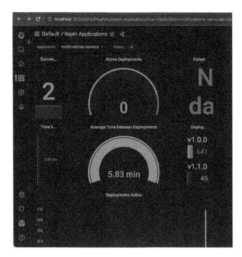

**Figure 9.22
Keptn Application
Grafana
dashboard for
the notifications
service**

This dashboard shows us our deployment frequency for the annotated deployments (all the Conference application's services) running in the default namespace. In the step-by-step tutorial, we make changes to the notification service deployment so Keptn can detect the change and show the new version in the dashboard. As shown in figure 9.22, the average time between deployments is 5.83 minutes. On the side, you can see exactly how long it took to deploy v1.0.0 and v1.10. Having these dashboards available to the teams responsible for each service can help provide visibility on the whole process of releasing new versions. Having this information available from day one can show progress on how teams improve their workflows or find bottlenecks and recurring problems that can be easily fixed.

Besides gaining all this information and out-of-the-box metrics, as mentioned before, KLT goes one step further by providing hook points to execute pre-/post-deployment tasks. We can use these tasks to validate the environment's state before performing a release, send notifications to the teams on call, or just audit the process. After the deployment, we can use post-deployment hooks to run validation tests, send automated notifications to customers about the update, or just congratulate the team for their amazing work.

Keptn introduces the KeptnTaskDefinitions resource, which supports Deno (https://deno.land/), Python3, or any container image reference (https://lifecycle .keptn.sh/docs/yaml-crd-ref/taskdefinition/) to define what the task behavior. The KeptnTaskDefinition resource used by the step-by-step tutorial is quite simple, and it looks like listing 9.4.

Listing 9.4   Keptn TaskDefinition using Deno

```
apiVersion: lifecycle.keptn.sh/v1alpha3
kind: KeptnTaskDefinition
metadata:
  name: stdout-notification
spec:
  function:
    inline:
      code: |
        let context = Deno.env.get("CONTEXT");
        console.log("Keptn Task Executed with context: \n");
        console.log(context);
```

The team will use this resource name to define where this task will be executed. This is a reusable task definition, so this can be called from different services' lifecycle hooks.

We can access the context of the task that is being executed by calling Deno.env.get("CONTEXT"). This provides us with all the details used to create the task, such as which workload requests this task to be executed.

To bind a task definition with one of our services, we use a Keptn-specific annotation in our deployments:

```
keptn.sh/post-deployment-tasks: stdout-notification
```

This annotation will configure Keptn to execute this task after the notification service deployment is changed and the new version is deployed. Keptn will create a new Kubernetes Job to run the KeptnTaskDefinition. This means you can query all the pre-/post-deployment task definition executions by looking at the job executions in the default namespace.

By using annotations and KeptnTaskDefinitions, the platform engineering team can create a library of shared tasks that teams can reuse in their workloads, or even better, they can use mutation webhooks or a policy engine like OPA to automatically mutate the deployment resources to add the Keptn annotation.

If you change the notification service deployment and then tail the logs, you should see the following (listing 9.5).

Listing 9.5   Expected output from the TaskDefinition execution

```
Keptn Task Executed with context:
{
  "workloadName":"notifications-service-notifications-service",
  "appName":"notifications-service",
  "appVersion":"",
  "workloadVersion":"v1.1.0",
  "taskType":"post",
  "objectType":"Workload"
}
```

If you look at Jaeger in figure 9.23, you can see all the steps involved in deploying a new version of our notification service by looking at the Keptn Lifecycle Operator traces.

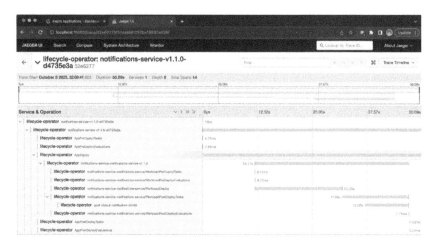

Figure 9.23   Keptn Lifecycle Operator traces for service updates

If you run the step-by-step tutorial on your environment, you can see that the post-deployment hook is being scheduled after the new version of the service is up and running.

In this short section, we have learned the basics of what the Keptn Lifecycle Toolkit can do for us, how we can benefit from having these metrics from day one, and how we can have more control over the lifecycle of our services by adding pre-/post-deployment tasks using a declarative way.

I strongly recommend you check the Keptn website and other more advanced mechanisms that they provide, such as Evaluations (https://lifecycle.keptn.sh/docs-klt-v0.8.1/concepts/evaluations/), which allows us to make decisions and even gate deployments that are not meeting certain requirements, such as increased memory consumption or too much CPU usage.

While Keptn uses a completely different approach from the one described in section 9.2, I strongly believe these approaches are complementary. I hope to see further integrations between Keptn and CloudEvents. If this topic interests you, I encourage you to join the conversation at https://github.com/keptn/lifecycle-toolkit/issues/1841.

9.4   *What's next on the platform engineering journey?*

The examples covered in this chapter highlighted the importance of measuring our technical decisions. In a good or bad way, each decision will affect all the teams involved in delivering software.

These metrics built into our platforms can help us measure improvement and justify investing in tools that facilitate our software delivery practices. If we want to include a new tool in our platform, you can test your assumptions and measure the effect of each tool or adopted methodology. It is quite a common practice to have these metrics accessible and visible for all your teams, so when things go wrong or a tool is not working as expected, you will have hard evidence to back up your claims.

From a platform engineering perspective, I strongly recommend not leaving this topic until the end (as I did with this chapter in the book). Using tools like KLT, you can gain insights with a small investment and use standard monitoring techniques that are well-understood in the industry. Looking into CloudEvents and CDEvents is worth it, not only from a monitoring and metrics calculation perspective, but also for event-driven integrations with other tools and systems. Figure 9.24 shows that by tapping into event sources from the tools that we are using in our golden paths, we can keep our teams informed about their decisions affect the entire software delivery chain.

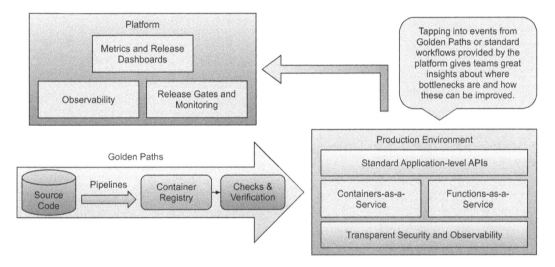

Figure 9.24   Golden paths and workflows provided by our platform are the best source of raw information for calculating the team's performance metrics.

Ensuring that the basic metrics for your platform can be calculated will help your teams to think about end-to-end flows for each release—where the bottlenecks are and where they spend or waste most of their time. If the DORA metrics are too hard for your organization to implement, you can focus on measuring your platform's golden paths or main workflows. For example, based on the examples provided in chapter 6, you can measure how much time it takes to provision a development environment, which capabilities are provided, and how often the team requests new instances, as shown in figure 9.25.

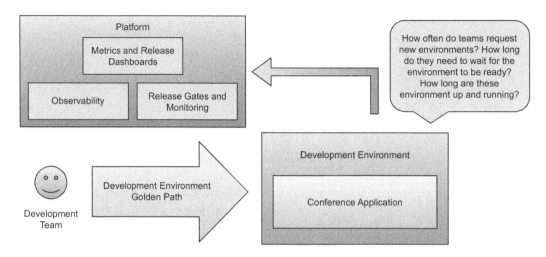

Figure 9.25   Platform and application walking skeleton metrics

By collecting metrics, not only from customer applications but also from platform-specific workflows, like creating development environments, your teams will have full visibility of the tools they are using and how the changes in the tool affect and unlock the velocity of software delivery. Figure 9.26 shows a recap of our platform journey and how important these metrics are for our platform teams. Remember, if you are measuring your platform initiatives, your platforms will get better.

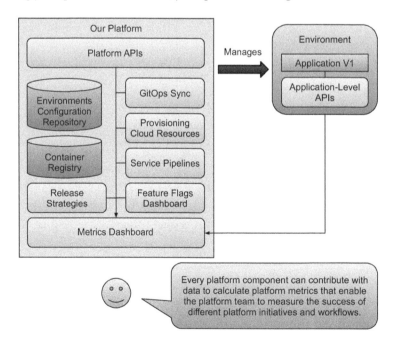

Figure 9.26 Tapping into platform components to collect data and calculate metrics

9.5   *Final thoughts*

I hope that going through the examples of this book has given you enough hands-on experience to tackle real-life challenges. While the examples covered here are not exhaustive or deep in detail, the intention is to show a wide range of topics that platform engineering teams must deal with. The cloud-native space is constantly evolving, and the tools I evaluated when I started writing this book have completely changed in two years, pushing teams worldwide to be very flexible about their decisions. Making mistakes and reviewing decisions is part of the day-to-day work that platform engineers must do for small and large organizations.

Going back to the beginning of this book, platform engineers must encapsulate all these decisions behind platform APIs that they can maintain and evolve, so understanding the capabilities needed by different teams is key to having a successful platform engineering journey. Providing self-service capabilities and focusing on what your teams need should be heavy influencers on the platform engineers' priority lists.

Unfortunately, I don't have an unlimited number of pages or unlimited time to keep adding content to this book, but I did my best to include the topics and challenges I've seen organizations and communities facing while working in the cloud-native space. We have reached a point in the Kubernetes ecosystem where tools are maturing, and more projects are graduating, indicating that more and more companies are reusing tools instead of building their own.

I've intentionally omitted topics such as extending Kubernetes with custom controllers, because balancing what is built in-house for your platforms needs to be carefully defined by platform engineering teams. Creating and maintaining your extensions should be left to very special cases where no tools exist to solve a problem you are trying to solve. For the most common cases, as we have seen in this book, CI/CD, GitOps, infrastructure provisioning in the cloud, developer tools, platform-building tools, and other tools are mature enough for you to use and extend if necessary.

It was quite hard to leave topics such as service meshes, policy engines, observability, incident management, operations tools, and cloud development environments out of this book. There are wonderful projects that would require entire chapters to cover. But as a platform engineer, you must keep researching and keeping an eye on the cloud-native communities to see where new developments and projects can help your organization's teams.

I strongly recommend you engage with your local Kubernetes communities and be active in the open-source ecosystem. This not only gives you a great playground to learn, but it also helps you to make the right informed decisions about which technologies to adopt. Understanding how strong the communities behind these projects are is key to validating that they are solving a problem that first needs a solution and is common enough to be solved in a generic (non-organization) specific way. Tools like OSS Insight (https://ossinsight.io/) provide enormous value for decision-making and ensure that if you invest time and resources in an open-source project, an active community will maintain your changes and improvements.

Finally, keep an eye on my blog (https://salaboy.com), because further articles related to the book will be published to explore other topics that I consider important for platform engineering teams. If you are interested in contributing to open-source, expanding or fixing the examples provided in the book is a great way to get hands-on experience with all the tools most open-source projects use.

Summary

- Using DORA metrics gives you a clear picture of how the organization delivers software in front of your customers. This can be used to understand bottlenecks resulting in improvements on the platforms we are building. Using the team's performance metrics based on our software delivery practices will help you understand how your platform initiatives affect how teams' work and the benefits to the overall organization.

- CloudEvents standardize how we consume and emit events. Over the last couple of years, we have seen a rise in the adoption of CloudEvents by different projects in the CNCF landscape. This adoption allows us to rely on CloudEvents to get information about components and other systems that we can aggregate and collect helpful information that can be used for decision-making.

- CDEvents provides a CloudEvents extension, a set of more specific CloudEvents related to continuous delivery software practices. While I expect the adoption of CDEvents to grow over time, we have seen how to map CloudEvents to CDEvents to calculate the DORA metrics. By using CDEvents as the base model to calculate these metrics, we can map any event source to contribute to the calculations of these metrics.

- If we can measure our platform, we will know what needs improvement and where the organization struggles with its delivery practices. This feedback loop provided by the metrics gives valuable information to platform teams in charge of continuously improving the tools and processes our teams use daily.

- If you followed this chapter's step-by-step tutorials, you gained hands-on experience with setting CloudEvent sources, monitoring deployments, and how CDEvents can help standardize information about our software delivery lifecycle. You also installed Keptn as a different approach to monitor your workloads and execute pre-/post-deployment tasks to validate that newer versions are working as expected.

index